COYOTE WAS GOING THERE

Coyote Was Going There

Indian Literature
of the Oregon Country

Compiled and edited by Jarold Ramsey

University of Washington Press
Seattle & London

Copyright © 1977 by the University of Washington Press

Library of Congress Cataloging-in-Publication Data
Main entry under title:
Coyote was going there.
1. Indians of North America—Oregon—Legends.
I. Ramsey, Jarold, 1937– .
E78.06c68   398.2   76-49158
ISBN 0-295-95731-X (paper)

The paper used in this publication meets the minimum requirements of American National Standard for Information Sciences—Permanence of Paper for Printed Library Materials, ANSI Z39.48-1984.

Title page illustration: Klamath basketry tray. Courtesy of Thomas Burke Memorial Washington State Museum, cat. #3829

Photographs of basketry from the Thomas Burke Memorial Washington State Museum (title page and pp. 3, 41, 87, 123, 177, 225, and 226) taken by Ed Quimby.

To the Indian People of the Oregon Country

those who were
those who are
and those who will be coming soon

Acknowledgments

If the material cause of this book is a Central Oregon childhood spent around Indians and devoted to hunting for the artifacts of their ancestors, the efficient cause is in the works of the late Melville Jacobs. His angry essay on "The Fate of Indian Oral Literature in Oregon" (*Northwest Review*, Summer 1962, pp. 90–99) polarized my own growing awareness, as an Oregonian writer living in New York State, of the imaginative power and historical value of the mythology of the Oregon Indians; and this book first began to take shape around 1968 as a response to Professor Jacobs' challenge to Oregonians to wake up to their native literature—if indeed it wasn't already too late. That it has seemed to me *not* too late is due in large part to Professor Jacobs' own monumental work on Northwest Indian languages and myth. To Mrs. Elizabeth Jacobs, I owe a special debt of gratitude for her encouragement and generosity to me, after her husband's death. A similar debt I happily acknowledge to Professor Isabel Kelly, whose "Northern Paiute Tales" was the first scholarly transcription of myths I read with excitement, suggesting the existence of other readable and accurate texts, which are now the basis of this book.

Many friends, mostly Oregonians, have been so closely and constructively associated with *Coyote Was Going There* that now the whole project—at least in its best parts—seems inconceivable to me without them. Some of the most generous have asked to remain anonymous, and I respect their wishes: but in reading this they will, I hope, recognize themselves, and know how grateful I am for the help they have given. One special friend must be named here: Mrs. Alice Florendo, who took time out one afternoon in August 1970 from managing her busy restaurant near Warm Springs to tell me two fine Wasco stories from her childhood on the Columbia at Wishram. In that initial gift and in all her subsequent help and encouragement, Mrs. Florendo has typified the gaiety, good sense, and vitality of her people; she has greatly fortified my will to finish the work.

Many writers today have begun to hope for an American discovery of Indian literature *as* literature, as part of our fund of imaginative wisdom. With that goal in mind for Oregon at least, I have been heartened from the beginning by the interest, stimulation, and good cheer of poets like William Stafford, W. S. Merwin, Jerome Rothenberg, Gary Snyder, William Matchett, and Ted Hughes—each of them well versed in aspects of Western Indian myth. I confess here that, in fact, one question I generally raised in choosing materials for this anthology was whether poets and writers like these would be excited by such-and-such a story or song.

I have enjoyed unstinting bibliographic aid and indeed comfort from the University of Rochester Library; and also from the University of Oregon Library, the Oregon State Library, Macpherson Library of the University of Victoria, the Library of the American Philosophical Society, and the Umatilla County Library of Pendleton, Oregon, Ms. Jane D. Hamm, Librarian. My students in mythology and regular literature courses at the University of Rochester have puzzled, prodded, and provoked me into what I hope are clarifications, as have my colleagues in the English and Anthropology faculties, notably Professors Howard Horsford, Bruce Johnson, George Ford, Matthew Marino, and the late Gerald Williams. Coyote's blessings on them all.

It was from my grandfather, the late J. R. Mendenhall, my father, the late A. S. Ramsey, and Mr. John Campbell of Madras, Oregon, lifelong *tillicums* of the Indians all three, that I first heard fragments of the kinds of mythic narratives that make up this book—and I have hoped that they would approve. To my own household tribe of "Oregon-grinders"—Dorothy, Kate, Sophia, and John: now, having been patient and listened for so long, it's *your* turn to tell stories!

And to the Indian people of the Oregon country, to whose cultural and educational purposes a portion of this book's income is assigned: *Coyote Was Going There* is mainly for you.

Grateful acknowledgment is made to the following for permission to reprint material copyrighted or controlled by them:

American Folklore Society, for material published in *Journal of American Folklore* and Memoirs of the American Folklore Society: "Coyote and Fox Marry Husbands," "Laptissa'n and the Seven-headed Monster," ed. Herbert Spinden, from *Folk Tales of Salish and Sahaptin Tribes*, ed. Franz Boas (MAFS, 1917); "Cry-Because-He-Had-no-Wife," from Herbert

Spinden, "Myths of the Nez Perce Indians" (*JAF* 21, 1908); "Amhuluk, the Monster of Wapato Lake," from Albert Gatschet, "Oregonian Folklore" (*JAF* 4, 1891); "The Man Who Lived with Thunderer," "Xi'lgo and the Brother and Sister Who Married Each Other," "The Journey across the Ocean" from Franz Boas, "Traditions of the Tillamook Indians" (*JAF* 11, 1898); "The Theft of Fire," from Roland Dixon, ed., "Shasta Myths" (*JAF* 23, 1911); "Genesis," from Leo J. Frachtenberg and Livingston Farrand, eds., "Shasta and Athapascan Myths from Oregon" (*JAF* 28, 1915).

American Philosophical Society Library, for MS materials: "How Fish-Hawk Raided the Sioux," ed. Morris Swadesh, from "Cayuse Interlinear Texts" (1930); "Kalapuya Ceremonial Song"; letter of Archie Phinney to Franz Boas, Nov. 20, 1929.

M. A. R. Barker and the University of California Press, for "The Crater Lake Myth," "The Story of Swa-ya," "Little Porcupine and Coyote," from *Klamath Texts* (University of California Publications in Linguistics, vol. 30, 1963). Originally published by the University of California Press; reprinted by permission of the Regents of the University of California.

Thomas Brundage and Harold Mackay, and *Northwest Folklore*, for "Coyote's Swallowing Match with Grizzly Bear" (*Northwest Folklore*, Winter 1968).

University of California Press for material in University of California Publications in American Archaeology and Ethnology (UCPAAE): "Chiloquin the Hero," from Leslie Spier, *Klamath Ethnography* (UCPAAE 30, 1930); "Tracks of the Creator," "The Thunder Badger," and "The Purging of Malheur Cave," from W. L. Marsden, "The Northern Paiute Language of Oregon" (UCPAAE 20, 1923); "How to Control the Weather" and "A Hunter's First Kill," from Isabel Kelly, "Ethnography of the Surprise Valley Paiutes" (UCPAAE 31, 1932). Originally published by the University of California Press; reprinted by permission of the Regents of the University of California.

University of Chicago Press, for "Coyote and the Frog Women," from Leo J. Frachtenberg, "Myths of the Alsea Indians" (*International Journal of American Linguistics* 1, 1917–20).

Columbia University Press, for "Coyote and the Swallowing Monster," "Cottontail Boy and Snowshoe Rabbit," "Cottontail Boy Steals Thunderer's Wife," "Coyote Becomes a Buffalo,"

"Turtle Outswims White Bull," "Red Willow," "Coyote and the Shadow People," from Archie Phinney, ed., *Nez Perce Texts* (Columbia University Contributions to Anthropology 25, 1934).

Doubleday and Company for lines quoted from Sigmund Freud, *The Future of an Illusion*, trans. W. D. Robson-Scott (Copyright 1961).

Harper and Row, Publishers, Inc., for lines quoted from Mircea Eliade, *Myth and Reality* (Copyright 1963); also for lines quoted from "The Well Rising," in William Stafford, *The Rescued Year* (Copyright 1966).

Holt, Rinehart and Winston, Inc., for lines quoted from "The Gift Outright," from *The Poetry of Robert Frost*, edited by Edward Connery Lathem. Copyright 1942 by Robert Frost. Copyright © 1969 by Holt, Rinehart and Winston, Inc. Copyright © 1970 by Lesley Frost Ballantine. Reprinted by permission of Holt, Rinehart and Winston, Publishers.

Dell Hymes, for the text of "The 'Wife' Who 'Goes Out' like a Man." All rights reserved by the author.

Elizabeth D. Jacobs and the Research Center for the Language Sciences, Indiana University, for "Seal and Her Younger Brother Lived There" and "She Deceived Herself with Milt," in Melville Jacobs, ed., *Clackamas Chinook Texts*, vol. 2 (Copyright 1959).

Elizabeth D. Jacobs and the University of Washington Press for the following texts edited by Melville Jacobs in University of Washington Publications in Anthropology (UWPA): "A Girls' Game," *Texts in Chinook Jargon* (UWPA, 7, no. 1, 1936); "The Kalapuya Way," "The Four Creations," "Ptchiza' and the Seven-headed Snake," "The Indians Hear a Treaty Speech in 1855," *Kalapuya Texts* (UWPA, 11, 1945); "The White Wife of Mouse" (UWPA, 8, no. 2, 1940).

Elizabeth D. Jacobs and *Northwest Review* for "The Fate of Indian Oral Literatures in Oregon," by Melville Jacobs (*Northwest Review*, vol. 5, no. 3, 1962).

Elizabeth D. Jacobs and the Wenner-Gren Foundation for Anthropological Research for "Coyote and Badger Were Neighbors," in Melville Jacobs, *The Content and Style of an Oral Literature* (Copyright 1959 by the Wenner-Gren Foundation for Anthropological Research, Inc., New York).

Elizabeth D. Jacobs and University of Oregon Books, for "South Wind Marries Ocean's Daughter," "The Exploits of

South Wind," "Wild Woman Ate Children," in *Nehalem Tillamook Tales*, ed. Elizabeth Jacobs. Copyright © 1959 by the University of Oregon.

Verne Ray and the University of Washington Press for "Modoc Prayers," in *Primitive Pragmatists: The Modoc Indians of Northern California* (Copyright 1963); and for "Wren Kills Elk," in *Lower Columbia Ethnographic Notes* (University of Washington Publications in Anthropology, 7, no. 2, 1938).

Smithsonian Institution Press, for material in United States Bureau of American Ethnology Bulletins (USBAEB): "How the Coos People Discovered Fire," ed. Leo J. Frachtenberg in *Handbook of American Indian Languages*, ed. Franz Boas (USBAEB, 40, 1922); "Thunderstorm Exorcism" and "The Magic Hazel Twig" in *Alsea Texts and Myths*, ed. Leo J. Frachtenberg (USBAEB, 67, 1920).

University of Washington Press, for "Wishram Naming Ceremony," in Leslie Spier and Edward Sapir, *Wishram Ethnography* (University of Washington Publications in Anthropology, 3, 1930).

University of Oregon Books for permission to reprint petroglyphs from Luther Cressman, *Petroglyphs of Oregon* (University of Oregon Monographs, Studies in Anthropology, no. 2, 1937). Reprinted by permission, University of Oregon, 1937.

Western Folklore and Jarold Ramsey, for "Three Wasco–Warm Springs Stories" (*Western Folklore* 31, April 1972).

Estate of C. E. S. Wood and Vanguard Press, for "How the Cayuse Got Fire" and "Coyote in Love with a Star," in *A Book of Indian Tales* (Copyright 1929).

J. W. R.
Rochester/Madras
October 1976

Contents

Introduction

Begin with the right setting. It is deep winter night along the Columbia River on the Oregon shore. Outside the lodge, the wind blows full of snow; snow covers the canoes, the fishing platforms, the drying racks, the trails east and west along the river and inland to the south. Inside, acrid smoke from the big fire drifts this way and that: and more faintly, there comes the smell of food long since safely gathered, dried, smoked, stored in corners and hung up along the ridgepole. It is winter here, and there is little for the People to do but stay indoors and try to keep warm. It is the season of *stories*, the time when Coyote and Raccoon and Tsagigla'lal come back as they were in the Old Time. Only in winter can they come with their stories: to bring them back in summer, when the People should be out working, would be to risk a rattlesnake bite or a twisted mouth. But now it is the right time, and with the rest of the People you wait.

Pretty soon an old woman, Grandmother, comes in and hunkers down close to the fire. She spits, peers wrinkling around the lodge, and spits again. Then she asks, "If I tell the stories, what are your favors for me?"

Someone says," Acorns."

Grandmother spits and says, "No-o-o."

Someone else offers, "Kinnikinnick, ready to smoke."

A negative grunt.

Someone else—your uncle—says, hopefully, "Jerky—with huckleberries!"

"Ahhh. Pretty good." Eyes fixed on the fire, voice faint above the wind, she begins. "Coyote was going there, and when he came to the mouth of the river . . ."

Three, even two generations ago, you might have heard some of the stories in this book told in such a setting. Now, most of the stories and much of the complex arts of reciting them and listening to them are lost like smoke through a smokehole. When the first settlers reached Oregon in the 1840s and the occupation of the land began, there were at least forty independent tribes on that land, speaking an estimated twenty-five distinct languages.[1] A rich matrix for the flourishing of oral literatures—

made richer by Oregon's strategic location, with outland tribes bringing trade goods and (presumably) stories from California and the Great Basin to the south, from the Rocky Mountain countries to the east, and from Walla Walla and Puget Sound lands to the north. I have considered something like five hundred story-texts for this book—but the sad certainty is that this number represents only a tiny fraction of the once-available total repertory; whole tribes and their languages have vanished without leaving a trace of their mythological heritage behind. No wonder, then, that the dean of Northwest anthropologists, the late Melville Jacobs, could ask grimly in 1962: "Are the state's Indian literatures so shabbily represented, in such deteriorated versions, or so bleakly unaccompanied by back-grounds of the socio-cultural systems which had maintained them, that annotative commentary on their features of expressive content and style is not possible?" [2]

How we happen to possess even those five hundred stories today is itself a story of heroic proportions—written largely by a few dedicated anthropologists and linguists from outside Oregon like Jacobs and before him Edward Sapir, Franz Boas, and Albert Gatschet who, recognizing that Oregon's native literatures were rapidly vanishing, sought with a kind of frenzy against time to learn the languages and accurately transcribe the myths before the old tellers died and their younger listeners perhaps forgot forever. What the transcribers accomplished—without the aid of tape recorders!—is prodigious; the trouble, however, is that the fruits of their labors went into academic journals and monographs and became generally inaccessible to the public. The Northwestener interested in Indian arts, or (to put it more crucially) the young Oregon Indian trying to repossess his cultural heritage, may very well not know that impressive remnants of what he's looking for have been pre-served but are scattered through the university libraries. With the exception of Ella Clark's excellent but topically limited collection, *Indian Legends of the Pacific Northwest*, he has had nothing but a variety of garbled, romanticized, usually bowdlerized texts and "popular versions" to work with—the innumerable florid redactions of "The Bridge of the Gods" story, for example.

Hence this anthology. Its chief claim to originality, I think, lies in the intention to make a representative selection of ac-curately rendered Oregon Indian myths accessible to the general public as literature. In reclaiming stories from anthropological and linguistic journals and monograph series, I have endeavored to include only those texts that can be called *scholarly*, in the sense of a knowledgeable attempt to be faithful to the original Indian wordings in performance. There is no use denying Professor Jacobs' view of these texts as a sorry vestige in proportion to the rich mythology we might have possessed—but what we *do* have is not "sorry," surely, when taken on its own terms.

In editing the stories, I have tried to keep emendations, rewordings, reorderings, and elisions to a minimum, in the conviction that as between two extremes, an accurate literalism is preferable to guesswork, even if sometimes felicitous, on my part. Between the stylistic elegance (and, often, the verbal prudishness) of the earlier collectors and the simpler, more colloquial styles of translators like Jacobs, there is, admittedly, a great diversity in the language of these translations, and in the degree of literary awareness in them. Better to accept *that*, however, than to impose a single style on all of these stories, one that runs the risk of misrepresenting and distorting them. With the exception of a few rewritten "literal" translations, the texts presented here are essentially unchanged from their original printed forms; occasional departures from this principle are described in the Editor's Note (p. xxxv) and identified in individual notes. The reader is urged to delve into the original texts, as listed in the Notes and the Bibliography. By doing so, he may gain insight into the difficulties faced by the translators and editors of Indian myth-literature, and see for himself the richness of what has come through to us despite these difficulties.

It may well be that most of the scholarly transcribers of the stories included here never thought that their transcriptions would appear in a popular collection of this sort: some might object strenuously on ethnological grounds that the stories are unintelligible without full annotations, or at least woefully subject to the distortions of ignorance. Against such objections from the collectors and transcribers, to whom every credit is due, I can only argue from teaching and reciting the stories that they seem to make very good sense to general audiences with a minimum of footnoting; and express the hope that the reader will discover for himself how richly imaginative and expressive they are, and how deserving of his full attention.

How expressive, *why* deserving? Well, for anyone who cares about the mountains, lakes, rivers, forests, deserts, seashores, weathers, and climates of the Oregon country, these stories will strike a deep chord, filled as they are with a vivid sense of place. As a settled region Oregon is still too new for white men's legends to have taken deep root—no sooner does a promising story get told about Dirty Pat McGinty's escapades on the Upper MacKenzie, than someone denies it all on historical grounds—"Naw, it wasn't that way at all!" One remembers Robert Frost's description of the American land "vaguely realizing westward, /But still unstoried, artless, unenhanced . . ." [3] But in these stories from the Coos, the Wascos, the Paiutes, the very terrain they lived on is storied and enhanced, is lifted imaginatively into indisputable myth; the natural features that still delight and haunt us are given supernatural dimensions they otherwise lack, are given a truly native "local habitation and a name."

It is no exaggeration, I think, to claim that you can't really "possess" the countries of the Columbia and the Klamath until you have experienced the sense of those places evoked in the Indian stories set in them. A typical Wasco story about Coyote is wholly lacking in "local color" in the self-conscious literary sense, but from first to last it eloquently implies a climate, a landscape, a set of ecological conditions that the Indians had been coming to terms of existence with since the beginning.

Geologically and ecologically, Oregon is a very diverse state, and yet within its present official geopolitical unity, and corresponding to it, there is a certain natural wholeness of parts that the Indian groups which lived from the Columbia to the Klamath country and from the Pacific to the Snake River seem to have recognized, in their sense of "home" and their awareness of each other's territorial claims. At any rate, so far as the stories are concerned, I have tried to regard "Oregon" not just as a limiting geopolitical fact, but also as a viable and I hope not merely arbitrary concept of selection and organization, as an ecological idea. Thus besides strictly "domestic" materials I have included Paiute stories that were in fact recorded across the California line in Fort Bidwell, and Nez Perce stories that were probably as current among Idaho and Washington bands as they were among the "Oregon" Nez Perce. To refrain from doing so would surely be perverse.

Bearing in mind, then, the diverse terrains and climates that constituted "Oregon" to its first peoples as they still do to us, I have tried to select and arrange the myths by ecological regions, so as to suggest how deeply and variously the literature of the state's native inhabitants reflects their responses to the special natural environments they knew as home, and of which we are the unlikely inheritors.

(Just how unlikely can be seen, metaphorically, by considering that the names of four of Oregon's biggest cities are *Portland*, *Eugene*, *Salem*, and *Medford*. Their equivalents in Washington state are *Seattle*, *Tacoma*, *Spokane*, and *Yakima*. Why did the empire-builders north of the Columbia accept native place-names, while those to the south ignored or avoided them? In fact, not one major Oregon city bears an Indian name—unless one counts *Klamath* Falls or *Coos* Bay. And, moving from nomenclature back to the question of native literature, it is a scandalous fact that to date just one scholarly book or monograph on the mythology of Oregon Indians has been published in the state, Elizabeth Jacobs' *Nehalem Tillamook Tales* [University of Oregon Books, 1959]. Except for university presses in California, Washington, Indiana, New York, and elsewhere, there would now simply not be a transcribed native Oregon literature to consider!)

For the modern reader—Oregonian or not—stories like the ones in this book possess an extraordinary strength and simplicity of imagination, against which category-words like "primitive" seem to lose their usefulness. It is an imagination that celebrates a profound sense of harmony with the natural order. For the Indian who lived *on* the land, nothing could be taken for granted about man's place in that generous, unforgiving order. To slacken even momentarily his animistic piety, his alertness to the great inexorable orbit of Nature was to risk expulsion from that orbit—"death from natural causes," a she-bear, a rattlesnake, winter starvation. In mythic terms, in the Wasco story "The Elk, the Hunter, and the Greedy Father," the hunter, by yielding to his father's demands for bigger, more wasteful kills, offends and is abandoned by his spirit guardian, and subsequently dies.

The distinguished Oregon poet William Stafford, a keen student of Western Indian culture, often summons in his poems the positive aspect of this mentality and the imagination that sustains it; one poem in particular, "The Well Rising," though not given an Indian setting, unforgettably expresses the Indian's reverential view of his world, concluding, "I place my feet with care in such a world." [4] *Feet placed with care, nothing taken for granted:* how different from our presumptions today, living off, under, above, across, but never truly *on* or *with* the Indians' land! What is the natural order? That's Nature's business, we've been saying: we humans have our own. But what is Nature? Something generally pleasant we can drive to, something we can take for granted as there when needed, something we can treat as a sort of moral gymnasium or as an open-pit mine, depending on our instincts. And now that our presumptuousness (our fatal lack of imagination) has begun to haunt us with images of perpetual smog over the Willamette Valley and detergent-filthy rivers and coyotes preserved only in zoos and trees full of barren nests, these stories of how men and women once found and kept their place in Nature seem downright indispensable. To feel this is not, I insist, to sentimentalize them.

How to understand, how to "take" them? Although the bulk of the texts considered for this collection have been in print for at least thirty years, we are only just beginning to recognize them as *literature* at all; and the analytical and interpretive study through which any literature unfolds and in an important sense fulfills itself is to date nonexistent, except for fine pioneering efforts by Melville Jacobs and Dell Hymes.[5] For the present (and with hopes for the future), my basic assumption is that these stories are imaginatively so strong, and so rooted in the Oregon earth we still know, that we can begin to take them to heart without volumes of ethnological commentary on their undeniable obscurities. This is a necessary generalization: for these stories, even to the critic and the ethnologist, are like pictures that lack frames to limit and orient their meanings. Even the most enigmatic picture by Klee or story by Kafka is limited and clarified by the cultural "frame" around it—that is, the context of cultural assumptions and conventions we share with the artist. But what assumptions and conventions circumscribe these Indian stories? They first strike the modern mind very much as the Indian pictographs on our native cliffs do: vividly *there*, but unlocated, unlimited in their implications. So much seems to be implied, taken for granted, left operating beneath the surface of the narrative: as an old Papago woman, Maria Chona, once explained to her transcriber—"The song is very short because we understand so much." [6]

Much of what we do know about the stories comes by a circular process from the repertories themselves. Which is only to say that the texts tend to illuminate one another, like all literary works: the more tales about Coyote's exploits you know, the better, probably, you will understand a particular adventure. Most of the commentary which follows is based on information of this sort—would that we knew more, but what we do know is helpful and worth considering.

First of all, in their thrust of imagination these are in most cases truly *mythic* stories: assuming a fixed present reality, they carry us back to beginnings, to a time before time when the natural and human world we know was being irrevocably established, feature by feature, through the decisions and actions of the first beings. Supernatural in their power to set precedents for all life to come, these beings, like their equivalents in all mythologies, are often all too human in their careless exercise of that power. In the Wasco story, "Coyote and Eagle Visit the Island of the Dead," for example, death becomes a fixture of human life because impatient Coyote does *not* "place his feet with care" in the unfinished world; he loves his wife too much to be patient or careful. But even in such unhappy myths, there is felt, as Mircea Eliade has suggested, a sense of human knowledge and power in being imaginatively "in on the beginnings" of things. In experiencing mythically *how* the world first became what it is, one perceives *why*, and thus shares in the logic of creation, according to one's own culture. To know how Coyote first caught and prepared salmon is to know how these crucial acts are to be performed, and why they must be done "just so" as rituals— "as it was in the beginning." As Eliade explains it in *Myth and Reality*, myth is always related to a creation, to how things came to be, or to "how a pattern of behavior, an institution, a manner of working was established; this is why myths constitute the paradigms for all significant human acts. . . . By knowing the myths one knows the 'origin' of things and hence can control and manipulate them at will. . . ." More generally, Eliade declares that

the man of the societies in which myth is a living thing lives in a World that, though "in cipher" and mysterious, is "open." The World "speaks" to man, and to understand its language he needs only to know the myths and decipher the symbols. Through the myths and symbols of the Moon man grasps the mysterious solidarity among temporality, birth, death, and resurrection, sexuality, fertility, rain, vegetation, and so on. The World is no longer an opaque mass of objects arbitrarily thrown together, it is a living Cosmos, articulated and meaningful. *In the last analysis, the World reveals itself in language.*

It speaks to man through its own mode of being, through its structures and its rhythms.[7]

So, in the Northern Paiute text that concludes this anthology, Doctor Sam Wata tells his version of the Paiute creation, and then explains how it is that the whites have violated the mythic order of the Paiute "way": "Maybe white people don't know about the beginning of this earth."

Now it is frequently difficult in reading the stories to know "what time it is," mythologically speaking. Oregon's Indians apparently did not worry very much about epochs, or follow the Greeks in dividing the history of their world into ages of Gold, Silver, Iron, and so on. But most of their narratives do seem to be set in one or another of three loosely defined and overlapping periods—the Myth Age, the Age of Transformation, and the Historical Age.[8] In the earliest of these, the Myth Age, the great primal beginnings took place; there were no human beings yet; the world was peopled with animal-spirits in more or less human form; monsters, freaks, and confusions of nature were abroad, threatening general disorder. The Myth Age flows into the Age of Transformation, when Coyote or some other transformer went about ordering the world (not necessarily "perfecting"— is it perfect now?), turning animal-people into animals *per se* and certain beings into natural landmarks—usually with the unsettling prophecy that "the People" (i.e., the real Indians, like those listening to the story) "are almost here now." The arrival of the People does not seem to mark the end of this crucial period: the stories about Coyote's metamorphosis of the woman-chief Tsagigla'lal into a petroglyph and his oral surgery on the Mouthless People seem in their logic to be set in an age of transformations—unless one assumes that these beings are *not* "the People."

The third age is "historical" only in the sense that its events are not cataclysmic or precedent-setting; transformations still occur but not as a matter of course; the world with its human and animal inhabitants has settled down and pretty much taken on its present reality. Narratives set in this age are really more stories or tales than myths: the realistic main events of "A Wasco Woman Deceives Her Husband" will illustrate the distinction. (I have ventured to include some texts of a fourth, truly "historical" kind: prophecies, stories, and personal memoirs dealing with the advent of the white men in the nineteenth century, and expressive of the Indians' response to the onset of this ultimate and shattering "age of Transformations.")

Reading these stories off the printed page, we are inclined to forget that they have been utterly transformed for us—taken down from a wholly oral/traditional mode of existence in an unthought-of mode, print, and translated out of the original languages into an alien language, English. More seriously, seeing them unfold in orderly rows of type across uniform pages we may fall into the habit of reading them simply as stories in our terms, as prose narratives. To experience them in this way is to lose imaginative contact with the artistic and social conditions that govern them. When Archie Phinney, a Nez Perce trained by Franz Boas, returned to his tribe and began transcribing their myths, he became so distressed by what he was losing in the process that he wrote to Boas: "A sad thing in recording these animal stories is the loss of spirit—the fascination furnished by the peculiar Indian vocal tradition for humor. Indians are better story-tellers than whites. When I read my story mechanically I find only the cold corpse." [9] What Phinney implies about Indian stories, Melville Jacobs and others have demonstrated: they are essentially *dramatic* in conception, monodramas in which one highly skilled actor-narrator played all the parts before an enthralled audience which knew the stories backwards and forwards and thrilled to the vividness of the impersonations, and to the narrator's skill in weaving familiar episodes into new cycles.[10]

Reconsider the probable setting with which we began. After the Grandmother had well begun her acting-out (with elaborate gestures, grimaces, vocal mimicry) of the roles of Coyote and his neighbors, she would, according to Wasco Indian sources, suddenly break off with an interrogatory grunt, "Unnhhh?"—i.e., *Are you following?* And the audience, so long as it wanted more, would respond emphatically, "Nunnnhhh"—*Yes, keep going!* This periodic deliberate breaking of the dramatic illusion may very well have served to *intensify* that illusion, bringing the audience back to itself so as to send it off again with a renewed sense of participation in the illusion of the play.

At the heart of these dramatic forms lies, I think, a rich convergence of myth and ritual. The chief religious ceremonies *per se* of the Oregon tribes were (for that matter still are) the solitary quest for a personal guardian spirit, the communal exercises of *naming*, and singing and dancing in winter for spirit power. Yet surely the public acting-out of the myths of the tribe must be reckoned as one of the tribe's primary rituals, too. The rituals of story-telling seem to have been less infused with sacred purpose and more concerned with moral and existential education, to be sure (literature is not liturgy); but they dramatically set forth, one by one, the mythic origins and rationales of particular tribal rites (as for mourning, "first fruits," and so on), and conveyed directly a sense of the power informing all ceremonies based on mythic beginnings. That refrain of Transforming myths, "The People are almost here," must have evoked in Indian listeners at once a sense of tribal identity and purpose (they *were* "the People") and a sense of wonder at a time before them, when they had no being, but were being anticipated.

To deny ritual significance to the dramatic recitation of myths, to desacralize them to the status of pedagogical entertainments, is to ignore, among other things, how intimately drama has been linked with ritual and ceremony in other cultures, including classical Greek and medieval European, and how an intensely dramatic acting-out in heightened language of inherited stories would inevitably partake of the power of the tribe's formal acting-out of private and (especially) public ceremonies. No denying that on one end of a scale of "ritual gravity" the stories might be told or referred to very casually: but I am arguing that on the upper end of such a sliding scale (we have no modern counterpart to it), the same stories would in their full winter-night's recitation be ritually dramatic, intensely so, and best understood as such.[11]

At issue here is what Oregon's natives would come to "know" through their ceremonies and through their story-recitations. I submit: essentially *one* kind of knowledge about the human order, relative to the rest of the world, natural and supernatural; not two kinds of knowing, "ritual" as distinct from "mythic," and not an abstract knowledge either, but (as Eliade observes) "a knowledge that one experiences ritually, either by ceremonially recounting the myth or by performing the ritual for which it is the justification. . . . In one way or another one 'lives' the myth, in the sense that one is seized by the sacred, exalting power of the events recollected or enacted."[12]

Nowhere is this fundamental relationship between ritual and myth in the Indian storytelling more clearly revealed than in an ending formula used by Clackamas Chinook recitalists at the conclusion of extended performances, according to Melville Jacobs. At the end of the telling *per se*, the various beings the teller had been impersonating would say, through him, "Now let us . . . separate and go our ways to the rivers, the mountains, or into the air. . . ." [13] The lodge had been full of the presence of these spirits from the old time and full of their power, invoked by the art of the storyteller, embodied in him, and communicated by him to his audience. Now he had to release them ceremoniously to return to their mythic elements, like Shakespeare's wizard Prospero releasing his "elves of hills, brooks, standing lakes and groves" from the summons of his "so potent art."

The prominence of conventional elements and repeated motifs is striking in these myths, but hardly surprising, given their oral-dramatic basis and the storyteller's natural dependence on repeatable formulae to organize and draw out his story-material. Some of these formulae are clearly *ritualistic:* it seems, for example, that everything of importance must happen or be attempted a magical five times, with the fifth time being "the charm." Coyote disguised as Frog in the House of the Dead must take five leaps to the moon; he accosts five sisters along the Columbia and comes to grief with the fifth (as in European stories, the youngest sibling is always the smartest or at least the most successful). Most accounts suggest that an Indian recitalist would not have been likely to abridge these sequences of five for the sake of brevity, nor would a formal audience have expected it: that would be an impatient white man's trick! Frequently too, the action involves rituals of divination, as when Coyote, in a quandary, defecates and consults his excrementa about what to do next—a detail linking the mind and the bowels that should have caught Freud's eye. Further, every tribe seems to have had some formulaic way of ending its cycles of stories, ranging from the dramatically elaborate Chinook dismissal of spirit actors described above, to the charmingly casual ending of the Coos narrators: "Story story."

Periodically, in the grip of strong feeling, actors in the myths break into brief *songs*, which in their lyric repetition seem very ritualistic. Again, a leap of the imagination is required to hear them properly as dramatic songs; in some transcriptions the music was actually taken down, and I have provided a few examples. Did the songs represent a formal shift in the story from "prose" to "verse"— or should we think of each myth-drama as essentially poetic, rising to formal lyricism in the songs? [14]

Could there have been a place for *dance* in formal recitals, either by the recitalist himself or by a "chorus"? Were the stories invariably recited with word-for-word fidelity to traditional versions, in keeping with the general Indian respect for the accuracy and power of words; or did the performer sometimes break into innovations, creating as well as performing? Were some stories considered more open to such innovations than others; were some tribes more likely to innovate than others?[15]

These questions about possible interactions between the Indians performing arts are as fascinating as most of them are presently unanswerable. The same must be said about another possible interrelation: between the stories and Oregon's plentiful pictographs and petroglyphs. In only two recorded stories (both in this book: "Tsagigla'lal" and "A Wasco Woman Deceives Her Husband") is there any reference to rock-paintings and carvings—otherwise, the two art forms (unlike their counterparts in Australia and Africa) simply do not illustrate each other. Are the crudely vigorous human and animal figures on eastern Oregon cliffs actually portraits of Coyote, Bear, and so on; or were these rock-figures either too insignificant to mention in the stories, or too sacred?

Although the fact is necessarily somewhat obscured in a selection of this kind, certain narrative motifs and stock situations reappear from story to story and indeed from tribe to tribe; and to facilitate comparative study the note for each text lists the standard motif-index system used by folklorists.[16] The Ascent to the Land of the Sky People (usually by means of a chain of arrows), the Descent to and Return from the Land of the Dead, the Marriage of the Living Bride and the Dead Groom, the astonishing story of the Vagina Dentata and how this terrible predicament was resolved, the Discovery of Fire, the Rolling Head or Skull, the Eye-Juggling Contest, and of course Coyote's metamorphoses and embarrassments (especially the loss and recovery of his penis): versions of these motifs and others are found in Indian mythology all over Western America, suggesting, if not a common origin, then a continual process of cultural interaction between the tribes—through marriage, slave-trading, bartering expeditions, and the like. Our efforts to grasp the ritualistic seriousness of many of the myths should not keep us from recognizing that the Indians simply loved to hear a good story told well, and, when they liked an outlander's tale, would add it to their own repertory.

Witness the "Ptchiza'" stories of several Willamette Valley tribes, to take an extreme example. When French-Canadian trappers of the Hudson's Bay Company retired to Valley farms in the 1830s and 1840s (many took Indian wives), they evidently spent much time entertaining their Indian neighbors with French tales, especially those dealing with the Provençal folk hero "Le Petit Jean." The Indians must have been charmed, for "Ptchiza'" becomes a native hero as well, in a cycle of stories at once European in content, and Indian in narrative method and detail! (Other tribes—the Nez Perce, for example—picked up "Petit Jean" stories, too, presumably from French-Canadian trappers and guides who passed through. The Nez Perce called him "Laptissa'n.")[17]

It seems likely that the Indians of the Oregon country took Le Petit Jean to heart not because he was an exotic figure, but because he embodied a kind of wily, resourceful, questing heroism that they were prepared to enjoy. And, to conclude these introductory notes, we should move from mythic and literary questions about the stories to ask: what was their relation to the Indian cultures that sustained them? Beyond education and exaltation through myth, what cultural purposes did they serve? Again, such ethnocultural knowledge as we can bring to the stories is largely derived *from* the stories—but at least a few values can be established without danger of interpretive circularity.

The mythological literature of each tribe seems to have served, along with the winter "power" ceremonies, as a chief source of the continuity of its culture. For the stories are, on one level, thoroughly *didactic:* they are designed to convey social and moral instruction as well as delight—indeed, the two purposes, generally at odds in our literature, strike a remarkable imaginative balance in them. Every myth in this anthology offers dramatic affirmations of what must have been central cultural values to its audience—unstinted hospitality, respect for elders, unceasing caution and alertness in all dealings with people and animals, the subordination (at least officially) of women to men, the superiority of one's own tribe or clan to all others, the adjustment of individual personality to the "identity" of the tribe, the importance and dignity of work, and so on. By the same token, most of these stories dramatize the dire consequences of rejecting or neglecting these values: death to the unwary, the taker-for-granted; "social death"—exposure, shame, ostracism—to the flaunter of mores, the self-seeking, the disrespectful.

To take just one example, "Raccoon and His Grandmother" in Part Two: a Wasco–Warm Springs listener would have understood that "justice prevails" in this seriocomic Myth Age story more or less as follows. Raccoon's grandmother deserves some of her grandson's insolence by spoiling him unduly; he should have been gathering food like everybody else. After he steals the acorns and tries to replace them with his dung, Raccoon learns to his shame that news of one's bad deeds always travels quickly. The painful metamorphosis of the grandmother into a scolding bluejay is a direct consequence of his mischievous delays in helping her—childlike, he only obeys the "letter" of her request for water, not the "spirit", and this disrespect results in calamity for them both.

I am not suggesting that recitals of such stories were followed, Aesop-like, with a set of moral truisms like these: the story carried its own meaning; its action dramatically confirmed, without direct moralistic commentary, the values of the audience. But it is a fact that Indian parents did frequently invoke such stories to their children, as occasion—and misbehavior!—suggested them. One of my own informants, a member of the Confederated Warm Springs Tribes, remembers being told as a child to wait on her own grandmother with deference and dispatch—"If you're poky, she'll turn into a bluejay too!" And she still tells her own son not to be so picky with his food, lest he, like the spoiled Raccoon, get into trouble.

In the stories featuring Coyote, the cultural meanings of these myths can be seen most clearly, perhaps, and in something like their full complexity. In their way, Coyote's adventures must have served a didactic purpose, too, but in no simple fashion. If he was a sort of culture hero to tribes as diverse as the desert Paiutes and the seacoast Coos, his "heroism" was of a very ambiguous kind; his doings, taken together, seem patterned to satisfy a wide and sometimes contradictory variety of felt needs in Indian life. In his appearances as Transformer, of course, he is a straight-forward mythic hero—the conqueror of At'at'a'hlia, the engineer of the Columbia River, the inventor of salmon fishing and its rites. But in other stories, "Eye-Juggler" and "Coyote's Carelessness," for example, he has become secularized; as the hero of these stories he is by turns Delightful Rogue and Horrible Example, and his once-Promethean deeds give way to self-seeking schemes and deceptions that often backfire uproariously. Assuming that Coyote *is* a single personage ("*that* Coyote"), how can he still be understood as a "hero"?

In this way, I think. The social fabric of the Oregon Indian tribes from which these stories come must have been in some respects quite rigid and repressive. They were "shame societies," maintaining order through a tradition of community approval and disapproval that must have been in its way tyrannical. Instead of fearing a guilty conscience, a potential wrong-doer in an Indian community feared public exposure and shame above all. A bad conscience can be eased, even put aside, but a morality based on fear of social castigation is unrelenting; its pressures cannot be ignored. Now in such a shame society, Coyote's outrageous sexual antics, his thorough selfishness, his general irresponsibility in the stories allowed the "good citizens" of the tribe to affirm the system of norms and punishments that Coyote is forever comically running afoul of—at the same time that they could vicariously delight and find release in his irresponsible freedom. My point is that through the mediation of Coyote the Trickster, the people could have their morality both ways: they knew that his scheming but always reckless pursuit of women, wealth, and pleasure would come to no good end, according to tribal values —but before that end arrived, they could richly enjoy themselves, as if on holiday! [18]

Perhaps it is not too far-fetched to recall Freud's observations about the culture-preserving functions of art: "Art serves as nothing else can to reconcile men to the personal sacrifices they must make to maintain their civilization." [19] Coyote is not one to make such sacrifices; my point is that both his self-indulgences and his embarrassments may have made his Indian audiences feel better about *their* personal renunciations on behalf of tribal order. Coyote is often, in Claude Lévi-Strauss's engaging word, a *bricoleur*,[20] a sort of roving "handyman" in the midst of mythic creation, working with "the available material," with humanly mixed motives and with mixed success. Like Loki in Scandinavian myth, like Anansi the Spider in African tradition, like Crow in Indian stories of other regions, Coyote keeps mediating, now creatively, now mischievously, between the Way of the Tribe, and the Way of the unrestricted Ego.

I have said nothing but I hope I have suggested something about the rich humor in these stories. Nothing in them is more expressive of the Indians' freedom of imagination—or more perplexing. Anthropologists have largely ignored the subject, anthologists heretofore have uniformly followed mid-Victorian standards in excluding all the vivid sexual and scatalogical comedy from their collections: surely it is time, surely we are ready for that comedy, and for the recognition that the Indians may have been as bawdy-minded as we are. Only much more open about it. The humor in this selection is, I think, fairly representative: it is broad, often outrageously physical, even manic. Rabelaisian in form, in significance it is pre-eminently social and satiric, perhaps cathartic. It ought to warn us against the temptations to prettify the Indians' literature *à la Hiawatha*. The stories seem to invite laughter *at* characters like Coyote who are stupid, or unsophisticated, or recklessly bent on deception. Presumably, solid citizens like Eagle or Salmon would never get into such predicaments and become public butts. Among modern Indians, this sense of humor survives, in part as a defense against white society: they can be really devastating satirists, using broadly comic techniques to expose what appear to the outsider to be quite subtle violations of decorum.

Today's Northwest Indians themselves do more than survive, certainly; they begin to flourish, and the wonder of it is that they have brought so much of a viable Indianness with them through their ordeals. Inescapably, I have used the past tense here in trying to introduce their myths to general readers: but in dwelling so much on matters of tradition and pre- or mythic history, I do not want to imply that the continuities of Indian life, culture, and art have been broken. Much *has* been lost or at least attenuated—the opportunity to hear formal recitals of stories in Indian languages, for example, and the deep ties to specific homelands—but more goes forward in the Indian Way than is commonly recognized by whites. Anyone who hopes to engage and cherish these stories should understand, if he is not Indian, that without taking pains to acknowledge the continuity of Indian life, its *futurity* as well as its history, he is in danger of merely sentimentalizing a rich native literature. Such sentimentality—"Lo! the poor Indian, exotic, pathetic, bound to a classical past, and safely in hand"—is ultimately vicious. It is a way of keeping a wise and gifted people in the place we have made for them, a way of continuing to ignore what they and their traditional literature might give us now.

What I cherish in these stories, beyond their Northwestern settings, is their wide, healthy emotional range, the openness and strength of the imaginative energy working in them, the sense of celebration of life's natural simplicities they convey. Are they not powerful accommodations to living? But re-reading them, trying to *hear* them, I am haunted by the way their art (to misquote Freud) serves to call into question so many of the personal and collective sacrifices we feel we must make to maintain our progress-ridden civilization. It is the earth itself we have sacrificed, these stories seem to tell us: the mythic earth which might seize our imaginations still, as an avid intelligible World, ours because we know we belong to it, like the other creatures.

What if you and I had been named by our family and friends according to the Wishram ceremony: given the name of some long-dead illustrious tribesman and identified as human beings in the presence of all the communities of our lives on this earth, natural, supernatural, and human? A ritual leader speaks to the group, and it responds in unison:

This person will be *Spedis*.
A-xi.
This name used to belong to *Spedis*, who died a long time ago.
A-xi.
We want the mountains, creeks, rivers, bluffs, timber to know that this person is now named *Spedis*.
A-xi.
We want to let the fishes, birds, winds, snow, rain, sun, moon, stars to know that *Spedis* has the same as become alive again. His name will be heard again when this person is called.
A-xi.[21]

Editor's Note

Except where indicated otherwise in the Notes, bracketed passages are mine, added for the sake of clarity. When there is an ambiguity of pronoun reference (a common difficulty in myth texts that would resolve itself in performance), I have generally added the name of the actor being specified; in other instances I have brought in clarifying material drawn from the footnoted annotations and explanations provided by the original transcribers. Where the transcribers have already inserted clarifying phrases, words implied in performance but not actually recorded in transcription, and so on, into their texts, I have retained these interpolations in the present text. In those few stories containing both the transcribers' bracketed interpolations, and mine, I changed the former to parentheses to avoid confusion (for example, see the Klamath stories transcribed by M. A. R. Barker in Part Five). In a few cases of nonfunctional repetition, digression, and loss of intelligibility, I have excised phrases in the original texts; such excisions are indicated here with ellipses.

In all questions concerning editorial method, the reader is urged to consult the individual notes and, when possible, the original texts themselves.

A Note on the Indian Language of the Oregon Country

The texts included in this collection are drawn from the literatures of about twenty Indian languages, each one more or less unintelligible to the others. Small wonder that Northwest Indians developed Chinook Jargon and forms of sign language for trade and diplomatic use.

Work on the classification of the two-hundred-odd languages known to have been spoken north of Mexico has continued since the days of John Wesley Powell without much sign of producing a final definitive system. But the following arrangement of the major Oregon Indian languages corresponds to current knowledge, and reflects the geographical ties between related languages, where they exist:

Utaztecan (related to Comanche, Hopi, Papago)
Northern Paiute, Bannock
Penutian (related to Maidu, Miwok, Wintun, Yokuts, Cos-
tonoan, of California; and Tsimshian of Canada and
Alaska)
Chinookan: Clackamas Chinook, Wasco, Wishram
Coos-Takelma: Alsea, Siuslaw, Coos
Kalapuya, Takelma
"Lutuamian"—Klamath, Modoc
Sahaptian: Nez Perce, Umatilla, Yakima, Klikitat, Warm
Springs (Tygh, Tenino); perhaps Cayuse; perhaps Mo-
lale
Salishan (related to Interior Salish—Flathead, Colville, Oka-
nogan, etc., and Coastal Salish—Chehalis, Snohomish,
etc.)
Tillamook
Athapaskan (related to Apache, Navaho; Hupa, Tolowa,
Chasta Costa, Mattole, in California)
Joshua-Tututni, Upper Umpqua

Beyond their differences in syntax, diction, and inflections,
the Indian languages in Oregon differ markedly in *pronuncia-
tion* among themselves, just as they all make use of sounds for
which there are no real equivalents in English; hence any
overall guide to the voicing of Indian words is bound to be an
oversimplification. But for the native proper names, place
names, and terms used in this book (the various orthographies
of which I have tried to regularize, using as few diacriticals
and special symbols as possible), the following table will be of
some help. It seems to me to be important that we now try
to confront such names and words and learn to voice them
correctly in their stories, instead of accepting the denatured
English substitutes—*at'at'a'hlia* in place of "Owl Woman";
Diabᵻxwa'sxwas in place of "Chief Big Foot."

Vowels

a a*w*e
ä *a*dd
e l*a*te
ɛ *e*nd
i mach*i*ne
ɩ s*i*t
o *o*ld
ö German "sch*ö*n"
u p*oo*l
ü German "gr*ü*n"
ə d*u*n (obscure vowel)
ai b*i*te
au ab*ou*t

Consonants

As in English, except for:

g hard, as in "*g*irl"
h *h*at
hl so-called voiceless L, as in Welsh "Lloyd": with tongue
pressed against roof of mouth, let breath escape along
the sides
q velar (back-throat) "k"
kw *qu*ick
ñ as in Spanish "se*ñ*or"
tl roughly "t" plus "hl" (see above)
ts bi*ts*
x Berman "ch," as in "Ba*ch*"
ch *ch*air (simplified from č)
sh *sh*ine (simplified from š)

– lengthening of preceding vowel
ʼ glottal stop or catch, as in "oh-oh" ("oʼo")
ʹ syllabic accent mark

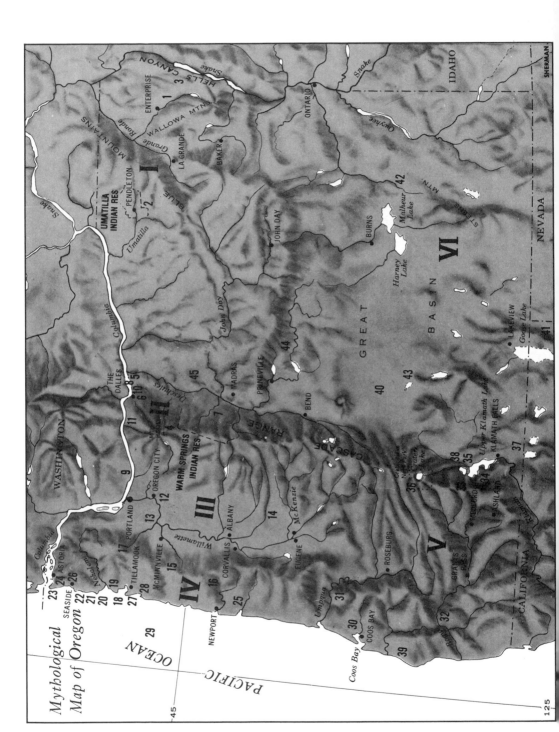

Mythological Map of Oregon

COYOTE WAS GOING THERE

Part One

NORTHEASTERN OREGON

Nez Perce

Cayuse

Umatilla

Bannock

Wanapum

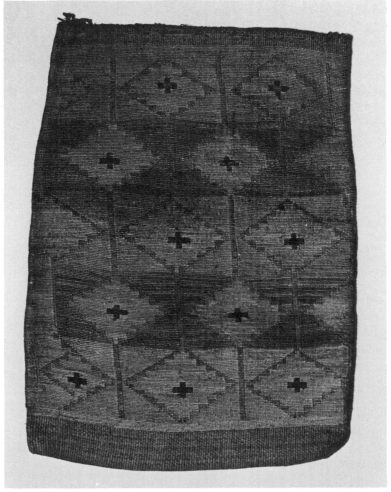

Nez Perce carrying bag *Courtesy of Thomas Burke Memorial Washington State Museum, cat. #2-4140*

"Raven Blanket—Nez Perce"

"Holiday Trappings—Cayuse"

Photographs by E. S. Curtis
Courtesy of Photography Collection, Suzzallo Library, University of Washington

THE INDIANS who occupied northeastern Oregon before the whites came mingled freely with their fellow Sahaptians along the Columbia, but "at home" they lived a very different sort of life. For home was not centered on a great river, with its bounty of food and traffic east and west, but rather spread out over the great steppes of the Umatilla country, the pine forests of the Blue Mountains, the Alpine crags and high lakes of the Wallowas, and on east into Idaho. Without a river to flow for them, these Indians kept on the move themselves, and their myths and stories reflect the ecology of a nomadic but by no means impoverished life: an awareness of a diversity of landscapes to be traveled through in different seasons, emphasis on hunting and on the big game of the endless hunt—deer, elk, even buffalo.

Chief in fame and power among them were the Nez Perce, expert hunters and expeditioners who ranged over Eastern Oregon and Washington, Northern Idaho, and Montana, but claimed the magnificent Wallowa Valley as their spiritual home. Every nineteenth-century explorer who ventured into Nez Perce country testified to their decency and nobility, beginning with Lewis and Clark, who recuperated among them in September 1805 when westward-bound, and trusted their "Chopunnish" hosts so far as to leave thirty-eight horses and gear with them for safekeeping. In May 1806 the explorers returned from the mouth of the Columbia to reclaim what they had left, and were so well treated during another long visit that Clark was moved to write: "These people have shown much greater acts of hospitality than we have witnessed from any nation or tribe since we have passed the Rocky Mountains. In short be it spoken to their immortal honor, it is the only act which deserves the appellation of hospitality which we have witnessed in this quarter." [1]

Both the grateful explorers and their generous hosts would have been dismayed to see, seventy years later, how the course of events had run: now the erstwhile "guests" were demanding that the Nez Perce give up even their sacred Wallowa Valley for white settlement, and move onto reservations. The story of their refusal and subsequent brilliantly executed flight en masse toward Canada under the leadership of Chief Joseph and the gallant Looking Glass has been told and retold, as tragic stories should be. [2] *Within a decade after Joseph declared to General Miles in 1877 that "from where the sun now stands, I will fight no more forever," about one-half of his Nez Perce "army"— women, children, old people as well as braves—were dead of*

*sickness and privation, having become displaced persons in Okla-
homa Territory as a matter of government policy.*

*The other tribes and bands ranging in Oregon's northeast quar-
ter were closely related to the Nez Perçe, either as mortal enemies, such as the Shoshones and the Bannocks of the Snake River
country, or as less powerful allies, such as the Umatillas and the
Cayuse. The Cayuse, who struck early explorers as being as
mean and surly as the Nez Perce were gracious, gained more
than their share of infamy in 1847 when a band of them per-
petrated the Whitman Massacre, at the mission of Marcus Whitman and Henry Spaulding near Walla Walla. The Cayuse were
able horse-breeders, and today a "cayuse" is a small tough horse
of the sort they prized and bred.*

Umatilla man. Photograph by Frank LaRoche *Courtesy of Photography
Collection, Suzzallo Library, University of Washington*

Left: Wa-nik-noote, Nez Perce.
Photograph by Frank LaRoche
Courtesy of Photography Collection, Suzzallo Library, University of Washington

Bottom left: Falling-on-the-Land.
Photograph by E. S. Curtis
Courtesy of Photography Collection, Suzzallo Library, University of Washington

Bottom right: Fish-Hawk. Photograph by Lee Morehouse

The Umatillas are famous nowadays for their colorful annual participation in the Pendleton Roundup; they live, along with some Cayuse, Walla Walla, and Nez Perce, on the Umatilla Reservation northeast of Pendleton. A larger group of Nez Perce lives on the Colville Reservation near Grand Coulee Dam in northeastern Washington, where the survivors of the 1877 uprising were finally re-located, and where Chief Joseph is buried.

Compared to that of the Columbia River tribes, the nomadic pre-white culture of this region is rather sparsely represented to us: very few rock carvings and pictographs, little basketry, a poverty of myths and stories collected from groups other than the Nez Perce. But the Nez Perce, at least, have left a rich, diverse mythic heritage—and it is at once pleasant and historically sobering to imagine Captains Meriwether Lewis and William Clark in some Nez Perce lodge, laughing as the droll tale of Cottontail Boy and Snowshoe Rabbit was translated for them, and then reflecting on the infinitely sad Orpheus story of Coyote in the land of the Shadow People.

Umatilla girl. Photograph by E. S. Curtis *Courtesy of Photography Collection, Suzzallo Library, University of Washington*

Coyote and the Swallowing Monster

NEZ PERCE

COYOTE WAS building a fish-ladder, by tearing down the waterfall at Celilo, so that salmon could go upstream for the people to catch. He was busily engaged at this when someone shouted to him. "Why are you bothering with that? All the people are gone; the monster has done for them." —"Well," said Coyote to himself, "then I'll stop doing this, because I was doing it for the people, and now I'll go along too."

From there he went along upstream, by the way of the Salmon River country. Going along he stepped on the leg of a meadow-lark and broke it. The meadow-lark in a temper shouted, "*lıma', lıma' lıma'*, what a chance of finding people you have, going along!" Coyote then asked, "My aunt! Please inform me, afterwards I will make you a leg of brush-wood." So the meadow-lark told him, "Already all the people have been swallowed by the monster." Coyote then replied, "Yes, that is where I, too, am going."

From there he traveled on. Along the way he took a good bath, saying to himself, "Lest I make myself repulsive to his taste," and then he dressed himself all up, "Lest he will vomit me up or spit me out." There he tied himself with rope to three mountains. From there he came along up and over ridges. Suddenly, behold, he saw a great head. He quickly hid himself in the grass and gazed at it. Never before in his life had he seen anything like it; never such a large thing—away off somewhere melting into the horizon was its gigantic body.

Now then that Coyote shouted to him, "Oh Monster, we are going to inhale each other!" The big eyes of the monster roved around looking all over for Coyote but did not find him, because Coyote's body was painted with clay to achieve a perfect protective coloring in the grass. Coyote had on his back a pack consisting of five stone knives, some pure pitch, and a flint fire-making set.

Presently Coyote shook the grass to and fro and shouted again, "Monster! We are going to inhale each other!" Suddenly the monster saw the swaying grass and replied, "Oh you Coyote, you swallow me first, then; you inhale first." Now Coyote tried. Powerfully and noisily he drew in his breath and the great monster just swayed and quivered. Then Coyote said, "Now you inhale me, for already you have swallowed all the people, so swallow me too lest I become lonely."

Now the Monster inhaled like a mighty wind. He carried Coyote along just like that, but as Coyote went he left along the way great camas roots and great service berries, saying, "Here the people will find them and will be glad, for only a short time away is the coming of the human race." There he almost got caught on one of the ropes, but he quickly cut it with his knife. Thus he dashed right into the monster's mouth.

From there he walked along down the throat of the Monster. Along the way he saw bones scattered about and he thought to himself, "It is to be seen that many people have been dying." As he went along he saw some boys and he said to them, "Where is his heart? Come along and show me!" Then, as they were all going along, the bear rushed out furiously at him. "So!" Coyote said to him, "You make yourself ferocious only to me," and he kicked the bear on the nose. As they were going along the rattlesnake bristled at him in fury. "So! only towards me you are vicious—we are nothing but dung [?]" Then he kicked the rattlesnake on the head and flattened it out for him. Going on he met the brown bear, who greeted him, "I see he [the Monster] selected you for the last." —"So! I'd like to see you save your people. . . ."

Thus all along the people hailed him and stopped him. He told the boys, "Pick up some wood." Here his . . . friend fox hailed him from the side, "He's such a dangerous fellow, the Monster, what are you going to do to him?" —"So!" replied Coyote. "You too hurry along and look for wood."

Presently Coyote arrived at the heart, and he cut slabs of fat and threw them to the people. "Imagine you being hungry under such conditions—grease your mouths with this." And now Coyote started a fire with his flint, and shortly smoke drifted up through the Monster's nose, ears, eyes, and anus. Now the Monster said, "Oh you Coyote, that's why I was afraid of you. Oh you Coyote, let me cast you out."

And Coyote replied, "Yes, and later let it be said, 'He who was cast out is officiating in the distribution of salmon.'" —"Well, then, go out through the nose." Coyote replied, "And will not they say the same?" And the Monster said, "Well then, go out through the ears," to which Coyote replied, "And let it be said,

'Here is ear-wax officiating in the distribution of food.' " —"*Hn, hn, hn*, oh you Coyote! This is why I feared you; then go out through the anus," and Coyote replied, "And let people say, 'Feces are officiating in the distribution of food.' "

There was his fire still bearing near the heart and now the Monster began to writhe in pain and Coyote began cutting away on the heart, whereupon very shortly he broke the stone knife. Immediately he took another and in a short time this one broke also, and Coyote said to all the people, "Gather up all the bones and carry them to the eyes, ears, mouth, and anus; pile them up and when he falls dead kick all the bones outside." Then again with another knife he began cutting away at the heart. The third knife he broke and the fourth, leaving only one more. He told the people, "All right, get yourselves ready because as soon as he falls dead each one will go out of the opening most convenient. Take the old women and old men close to the openings so that they may get out easily."

Now the heart hung by only a very small piece of muscle and Coyote was cutting away on it with his last stone knife. The Monster's heart was still barely hanging when his last knife broke, whereupon Coyote threw himself on the heart and hung on, just barely tearing it loose with his hands. In his death convulsions the Monster opened all the openings of his body and now the people kicked the bones outside and went on out. Coyote, too, went on out. Here now the Monster fell dead and now the anus began to close. But there was the muskrat still inside. Just as the anus closed he squeezed out, barely getting his body through, but alas! his tail was caught; he pulled, and it was bare when he pulled it out; all the tail-hair peeled right off. Coyote scolded him, "Now what were you doing; you had to think up something to do at the last moment. You're always behind in everything." Then he told the people, "Gather up all the bones and arrange them well." They did this, whereupon Coyote added, "Now we are going to carve the Monster."

Coyote then smeared blood on his hands, sprinkled this blood on the bones, and suddenly there came to life again all those who had died while inside the Monster. They carved the great Monster and now Coyote began dealing out portions of the body to various parts of the country all over the land; toward the sunrise, toward the sunset, toward the warmth, toward the cold, and by that act destining and forenaming the various peoples; Coeur d'Alene, Cayuse, Pend Oreilles, Flathead, Blackfeet, Crow, Sioux, et al. He consumed the entire body of the Monster in this distribution to various lands far and wide.

And now Fox came up and said to Coyote, "What is the meaning of this, Coyote? You have distributed all of the body to faraway lands but have given yourself nothing for this immediate territory." —"Well," snorted Coyote, "and did you tell me that before? Why didn't you tell me that awhile ago before it was too late? I was engrossed to the exclusion of thinking. You should have told me that in the first place."

And he turned to the people and said, "Bring me water with which to wash my hands." They brought him water and he washed his hands and now with the bloody washwater he sprinkled the local regions, saying, "You [Nez Perce] may be little people but you will be powerful. Even though you will be little people because I have deprived you, nevertheless you will be very, very manly. Only a short time away is the coming of the human race."

Smohalla's Ghost-Dance Cosmogony

WANAPUM

"ONCE THE WORLD was all water and God lived alone. He was lonesome, he had no place to put his foot, so he scratched the sand up from the bottom and made the land, and he made the rocks, and he made the trees, and he made a man; and the man had wings and could go anywhere. The man was lonesome, and God made a woman. They ate fish from the water, and God made the deer and other animals, and he sent the man to hunt and told the woman to cook the meat and to dress the skins.

"Many more men and women grew up, and they lived on the banks of the great river whose waters were full of salmon. The mountains contained much game and there were buffalo on the plains. There were so many people that the stronger ones sometimes oppressed the weak and drove them from the best fisheries, which they claimed as their own. They fought and nearly all were killed, and their bones are to be seen in the hills yet. God was very angry at this and he took away their wings and commanded that the lands and fisheries should be common to all who lived upon them; that they were never to be marked off or divided, but that the people should enjoy the fruits that God planted in the land, and the animals that lived upon it, and the fishes in the water. God said he was the father and the earth was the mother of mankind; that nature was the law; that the animals, and fish, and plants obeyed nature, and that only man was sinful. This is the old law.

"I [Smohalla] know all kinds of men. First there were my people (the Indians); God made them first. Then he made a Frenchman, and then he made a priest. A long time after that came Boston men, and then King George men. Later came black men, and last God made a Chinaman with a tail. He is of no account and has to work all the time like a woman. All these are new people. Only the Indians are of the old stock. After awhile, when God is ready, he will drive away all the people except those who have obeyed his laws.

"Those who cut up the lands or sign papers for lands will be defrauded of their rights and will be punished by God's anger. Moses [chief of the Sinkiuse] was bad. God did not love him. He sold his people's houses and the graves of their dead. It is a bad word that comes from Washington. It is not a good law that would take my people away from me to make them sin against the laws of God.

"You ask me to plow the ground! Shall I take a knife and tear my mother's bosom? Then when I die she will not take me to her bosom to rest.

"You ask me to dig for stone! Shall I dig under her skin for her bones? Then when I die I cannot enter her body to be born again.

"You ask me to cut grass and make hay and sell it, and be rich like white men! But how dare I cut off my mother's hair?

"It is a bad law, and my people cannot obey it. I want my people to stay with me here. All the dead will come to life again. Their spirits will come to their bodies again. We must wait here in the homes of our fathers and be ready to meet them in the bosom of our mother.

". . . My young men shall never work. Men who work cannot dream, and wisdom comes to us in dreams."

Dream Prophecy Song

NEZ PERCE

How the Cayuse Got Fire

CAYUSE

THE CAYUSE call themselves Te-taw-ken (we, the people), and they say at one time all the fire in the world was inside of Mt. Hood. From the top of the mountain fire and smoke used to come as if from a chimney, and all inside of the mountain was a great lake of fire. Hon-ea-woat (the Creator) had given this fire into the care of an old demon, and he had under him many demons—more than can be counted or even thought of. He and his devil army kept the fire from every one; from all animals and from all men. The animals and birds did not need fire, and the [people] did not need fire while they were animals; and they did not need fire while they could change from animals to men and back to animals.

But one time in the autumn the people had a great feast, and they put off all their skins as animals and came away to dance naked as men, leaving their warm animal hides folded up on the prairie. While they danced as men and women, Hone-ea-woat sent a great eagle to carry away the skins which the people had put off. He blackened the sky with his wings and made the air to shake. The people were afraid and ran for their skins, as a gopher runs for his hole; but when the sky cleared they found themselves naked men and women forever, and they were very cold. It was then that they first began to kill their brethren and take their hides to keep themselves warm; but nevertheless they were cold, and they sickened of raw food.

Takhstspul was the most knowing of all the tribe, and he was *homonick* (a brave). Ipskayt was the most cunning; he could steal the hair from your head. These two decided to steal fire for the people from the demon of the fire mountain. At that time all the country was bare of trees, covered only with grass, as the Snake River country is now. Takhstspul and Ipskayt journeyed together toward the mountain top. Takhstspul wished to travel right along, but Ipskayt would travel only in the night-time; so in the day they lay in a ditch or on the prairie like two stones.

When they had finally reached the top of the fire mountain, Ipskayt said to Takhstspul: "You wait here, and I will creep in and steal the fire; then you must carry it away." Ipskayt disappeared just as the fog does in the morning: it is just gone, you

15

know not how. He crept into a crevice in the mountain; and, making himself flat, he slipped in little by little. It was a long time; sometimes he would move only an inch; sometimes he would not move for two hundred heartbeats.

At last he came to where the fire was, and the great Demon was walking about watching it. There was a pile of wood from which other devils fed the fire. Ipskayt crept behind this wood and covered himself all over with the gray bark and moss. When he was all covered he rolled himself toward the fire—Oh, ever so little at a time, watching when the demons' backs were turned. Just as he was getting near to the fire, so that he could almost take some, one of the fire devils said, "Here is a log for the fire!" But as he took hold of it, Ipskayt jumped up, leaving the bark in the claws of the fire devil; and, snatching a piece of the fire, he flew down the dark crevice out to the light.

The Fire Demon followed him, calling all his servants to come, and they crowded into this crevice so it was like a swollen stream under drift logs; no more could come until the first had gone through. Ipskayt burst into the light and gave the fire to Takhstspul, who fled down the mountainside. After him followed the Fire Demon, still calling his devils; and they flocked from everywhere, thicker than blackbirds. They darkened the sun!

Takhstspul fled so fast he melted the snow as he ran. The John Day River marks his path. But very fast also came the Fire Demon. Takhstspul was out of breath; he turned and shot his arrows at the Demon, but they only made him stop for a very little while, until he could cure himself. Then the arrows were all gone, and Takhstspul stood on the banks of the Columbia. The river his footsteps had made was flowing into it. He lifted up his hands to Hon-ea-woat and asked for help; then he jumped into the water.

The Great Spirit changed all the demons instantly into pine trees, and that is why the trees are so thick high up on the mountain; those which scatter out toward the river are the demons that were ahead of the others. The Great Spirit was willing his children should have the fire they had stolen; so he changed Takhstspul into a beaver, as he is to this day, the most knowing of animals. The beaver swam across the Columbia and spat the fire into a willow log lying on the bank; that is why the willow is chosen as one of the woods from which to rub fire.

Ipskayt was changed by Hon-ea-woat into the little gray woodpecker; and today he hugs the tree, so much like the bark that if he is quiet you cannot see him. He goes creeping up and down, and stealing around the tree, tapping with his bill to show that fire is in the wood.

Cottontail Boy and Snowshoe Rabbit

NEZ PERCE

THERE WERE Cottontail Boy and his friend Snowshoe Rabbit. It was cold, very cold. Cottontail Boy lived by the river in its warmth, and there he would say, "I wonder what my friend Snowshoe Rabbit could be doing there far yonder where the gray coldness looms?" But there Snowshoe Rabbit was saying the same, "I wonder what my friend Cottontail Rabbit could be doing there where the blue haze of warmth looms?"

One day they met. "So, my friend, we meet. Is it that you are in good health?" —"Eh! I should be asked when you are the one! I used to think about you, 'What things can my friend be doing there where the blue haze of warmth looms?'" —"Is that it? Well, I am just living very, very comfortably," Cottontail Boy said to him. There I have such a good, warm lodge under a beautiful overhanging cliff. There I kick up a hackberry bush by the roots and I bring this food home to burn. [It] burns so well, and then I take some root food over which I pour some water and the water is absorbed instantly. I recline comfortably there now and eat very heartily, so heartily. But I thought of you often and I would say to myself, 'What can my friend be doing there where the gray coldness looms?'"

"Oh, I, too, live just comfortably from day to day," Snowshoe Rabbit told him. "I have a very comfortable living place. There is a big growth on a pine tree and my home is there at the root. There I may just kick apart fallen chunks of wood to burn. Oh, how this now burns to coals and ashes! Then I take fatty dried meat and toast it somewhat, just to a red crispness. There I lean back and eat so heartily; eat until I feel a complete and happy . . . contentment."

"Yes, it seems that both of us are living very well." Then they said to each other, "Farewell, we will meet again sometime."

Cottontail Boy Steals Thunder's Wife

NEZ PERCE

Cottontail boy and his grandmother dwelt there. The boy said to her, "I am going now, to take away from Thunderer that wife which is his most beloved. She will prepare our food for us and do various other little tasks." —"Yes, boy, but not so! Thunderer is to be feared. He will hurt you badly." —"To be feared! You are not even afraid of me! I, also, am fearsome." And he went.

He saw many people there. They were women digging roots; very many people digging roots. He came up to them. "Where are Thunderer's wives?" —"There they are," they told him, and now they said to one another, "Why does the boy inquire about Thunderer's wives?" But now Cottontail Boy went over to the designated women. There he found five women, digging camas roots. He said to them, "You are Thunderer's wives?" —"Yes," they told him. Now he said to them, "Which one of you is Thunderer's most beloved?" —"Oh," they exclaimed to one another, "Wherefore is this the boy says, 'Which one is Thunderer's most beloved?' The hateful thing! But then let us tell him!" Now they replied, "*There* is Thunderer's most beloved wife."

Here Cottontail Boy went over to that one and told her, "Put your digging stick aside." —"Oh!" the woman exclaimed, addressing the others, "the boy says, 'Put your digging stick aside.' In what manner has he gone crazy?" —"Lay aside your digging stick and let us see what he will do," her companions told her. She threw away her digging stick. Thereupon he said to her, "Lay aside your bag." —"He says, 'Put away your bag.' Some craziness has possessed the boy," the woman exclaimed. "Then do it," the others said, "let us see what he wants to do." So now she laid aside her bag. Cottontail Boy then said to her, "Now come. Follow me." —"He says, 'Follow me!' But I will not follow him." She turned to the boy and said, "Boy, you speak very foolishly. Why should I go with you!" But the boy seized her by the arm and began to drag her along. Even though she tried to brace herself with her feet, nothing availed. He pulled her along.

The other women ran to help her but the boy pulled them along, too. Now the women ran to tell their husband, Thunderer. They told him, "Cottontail Boy has taken your wife. He is taking her away with him." There Thunderer became very angry and spoke his thunderous wrath. The boy's grandmother far away there worried deeply, and she wept. "Grandson! I told him already, 'A fearsome one's wife you are dealing with!' I tried to dissuade him, 'Do not do this!' "

Here Cottontail Boy was bringing the woman along; but Thunderer, meanwhile, had started in pursuit. The clouds thundered and the lightning flashed. Now Thunderer spied the boy. Cottontail Boy placed the woman under his body, and he began to stare at the lightning. Thunderbolts struck first to one side of him and then to the other side of him, but he did not blink his eyes. He stared hard and straight at the thunder. From time to time he would thrust out his hand and with one sweep dispel the clouds. He would shout, "Only yourself overwhelm!" and the sky would be clear for a moment. He knew, "If I do not stare with utmost steadiness, if I even blink my eyes, Thunderer will be able to hit me."

At first Thunderer had been careful in his attack lest he should hurt the woman; he had not aimed directly at Cottontail Boy. The boy continued to look at him squarely and with unblinking eyes, in realization that, "If I blink my eyes he will strike both of us." Thunderbolts struck first on the one side and then on the other. Now Thunderer made his last and fiercest attack. It was a tremendous and desperate effort, but Cottontail Boy only exclaimed "Oh, bother!" and with a sweep of his hands, dispelled the thunderclouds. Suddenly there slid to earth a man— Thunderer.

He said to him, "Boy, you have vanquished me. I have always thought myself very fearsome, but truly you are more to be feared than I. You have taken my wife away from me. She was my most beloved wife but now you have taken her. Only a short time away the human race will come, and they, too, will do this thing. People will take wives away from one another. Even though a wife will be devotedly loved by her husband she will be carried away by another man, as you have taken mine away from me." Thus he ordered that practice. "Not I, alone, am indignant. Many will be indignant."

Now Thunderer went home. He was a very wealthy man because he ruled over many people. Cottontail Boy now said to the woman, "We are going home." And he took her home, to whatever kind of lowly home he had, because they were not wealthy. They arrived and there outside close by he left her while he went inside to his grandmother. "I have brought a wife," Cottontail

Boy told her. His grandmother heard him with fear and remorse. "But it is the wife of the fearsome one!" Nevertheless she went out presently and saw the woman sitting there. She said to her, "Come, let us go into the lodge." And they went into the lodge. The young woman became Cottontail Boy's wife, and they dwelt there.

Coyote Becomes a Buffalo

NEZ PERCE

COYOTE WAS going along upstream, hungry as usual. He came upon a big fat buffalo bull. Coyote said to him, "Friend, I am hungry. Is it so impossible that you change me into a bull just like you, so that I, too, could become fat and sleek?" Bull heeded him not in the least. He only wandered away, grazing, and not a word would he reply to Coyote. Coyote was insistent. He said again and again, "I wish that I, too, were a bull so that I could get fat." Finally Bull got tired of hearing this and said to him, "Coyote! You are inveterately foolhardy in the things you do; you could never do what I might ask of you. You are becoming a big bother." Coyote replied, "No, friend, I will do exactly what you tell me to do. Here I see you fat and sleek. Here is much grass and you live well, while, you see, I am painfully hungry. I will do just anything you tell me to do."

Bull then said to him, "Then go over there and lie down." Coyote accordingly went and lay down. "Now," said the bull, "do not flee or even move when I dash at you. You must absolutely remain still, and I will heave you upwards with my horns." —"Yes, friend," said Coyote, as he lay down, "why should I flee?" Bull went off to the one side, and there he incited himself to terrific anger. He tore up the turf, he threw dirt upwards; he bellowed and breathed clouds of vapor from his nostrils. He became terribly angry and then he dashed upon Coyote. But Coyote had been glancing at Bull, and had seen him become so terrible. He saw Bull come at him and he jumped quickly aside.

"Now that is just what I spoke of—that you would run away," Bull said to him. "Let me try again, just once more," Coyote said.

"I will not move next time." But Bull just went away, even though Coyote begged him. Coyote followed, tearfully entreating him, "Once more, just once more: I will not run away again!" Bull said to him, at last, "You are most bothersome to me. Now I will try you once more, and if you move, do not beg me any more, for I will never heed you again. We are trying for the last time."

Coyote placed himself on the designated spot again, and Bull went aside, as before, to become terribly angry. Now he dashed at Coyote. This time Coyote steeled himself and Bull threw him high into the air with his horns. Coyote fell and suddenly became a buffalo bull. He walked away, and went along grazing. He saw all kinds of new things, and ate them. Then finally he parted with the other bull, which wandered off somewhere, feeding.

Here now another coyote came along and recognized him as once Coyote. "Oh friend, how is it, friend, that you have become like that? I am terribly hungry; I wish that you would make me into a bull, too!" Coyote-Bull only looked at him sullenly, and walked away to feed, unmindful of what the other said. The [second] coyote insisted, "Friend, make a bull of me, too. Look, I fare piteously, and you are very fat." Coyote-Bull then spoke to him, "You are very bothersome. You would never do those things which I would ask you." —"Yes, friend, I will follow out absolutely every word you say. Try me!" —"You have been a nuisance to me," Coyote-Bull said to him, "but place yourself there and I will dash upon you angrily and toss you into the air with my horns. You are absolutely not to move. If you run away, do not beg me for another chance."

The second coyote now placed himself there, while Coyote-Bull made himself angry. He bellowed and pawed the ground. He imitated in every way those things he had seen the real bull do. Now Coyote-Bull dashed upon him, and oh! he picked that coyote up and hurled him into the air with his horns. The second coyote fell—*thud!* To the ground he fell, still a coyote. At the very same moment Coyote-Bull, too, changed back into a coyote. Here they were suddenly standing there, both coyotes. They stormed and they scolded each other: "You! You have caused me to change back into a coyote! There I was a bull, living happily, and you have caused me to change back into a coyote!" —"Ha, you imitator! You thought you could make me into a bull, too, as the other did to you!"

Now one chased the other up the valley. Then the first coyote lost interest and forgot [about it]. "Thus I was acting silly—had become a bull!" He went along up the valley away from there, unmindful of all that had happened.

Turtle Outswims White Bull

NEZ PERCE

WHITE [BUFFALO] Bull was greatly to be feared as a racer. He would outdistance even the touted ones. Turtle deliberated, and decided, "Now I shall race him." Whereupon he went to White Bull and said, "I challenge you. We will race." Bull replied, "Very well, we will do so." Turtle said next, "I will just go along in the water because on shore I could not run at all; only under water." Bull did not think well of this at all, but nevertheless he said, "Yes, we will vie. . . ."

"Yes," Turtle replied, "but you seem to be uneasy and skeptical because I will be going along in the water, so, let it be that you will see me three times. When we start I will go out of sight, to appear somewhere about midway, and I will say to you, 'Here I am, going along.' Then I will go out of sight once more to appear again. Then I will appear at the finish again, and that will be for us to see which one is ahead. We will wager nothing; only ourselves to be the stake." —"All right," said Bull.

Turtle now went to his friends. He said to them, "I have challenged Bull. For the killing of one or the other we are to race. We will kill Bull and from him have a great taking of meat. . . ."

The day of the race came, and the people assembled to watch. They said to each other, "It will be so one-sided, what Bull will do to poor Turtle. Why, Bull wins over even those who are to be feared!" Many people had assembled, and now Turtle placed his friends where they were to appear [for him], midway, and at the turn. Coyote was holding the signal bow for the start. "Ready!"

They started. Turtle pushed himself into the water while Bull just threw himself forward. Turtle's friends now put forth their best efforts to appear at the right times. They heard Bull coming, and now that Turtle which was stationed midway, came into view [surfaced], and said, "Here I am, going along!" Bull saw him and said to himself, "Gad! we are even, to here." He exerted himself the harder. Bull came to the turning place but as he did, he saw a short distance ahead the Turtle come into view. "Here I am, Bull. Now let us turn," said the Turtle to Bull. Bull became alarmed. "What is the meaning of this, to have such a one beat me?"

There he turned and exerted himself to the utmost. There again midway the Turtle surfaced a little farther ahead than before, and now Bull seemed to become fatigued. But when he saw the people crowded around the finishing place he ran with the last bit of strength he had. [M-m-m-m-m!] He ran like the wind. He was almost to the finishing place when Turtle, just a little ahead of him, pushed himself out of the water.

The people were surprised, incredulous. The buffalo bulls all bellowed; the cows wept. (From this came the holding dear of dead ones; and weeping and mourning. Now only a short time away was the coming of the human race, and then people would cheat one another even as Turtle initiated the practice.) The turtles now ate heartily; they settled themselves down to eating. . . . Thus it came to be said that turtle meat is very, very good for eating—for it is really Bull's meat.

Coyote and Fox Marry Husbands

NEZ PERCE

COYOTE AND FOX were short of food, and Coyote said, "Let us plan to get married to some man!" Fox answered, "But how can we marry men when we are men ourselves?" Coyote said, "That is easy enough! We will just put on women's clothes and the rest will only be good talking." So Fox agreed that it was a fine plan to marry some one that way. They dressed up in women's clothes, and went to see two young unmarried Wolves. They told these Wolf brothers that their parents had sent them out to try and find good husbands. Then the Wolves agreed to marry them.

Then with good talking Coyote told the Wolves, "Now, for five days you cannot really marry us, but instead must give us food to take home to our parents." The Wolf brothers believed what Coyote said, because they did not recognize him in that disguise. So for five days Coyote and Fox pretended to be girls, gathering food to take home to their parents.

At the end of this time Coyote did not know how to get out of the difficulty they'd gotten into. On the evening of the sixth day he said to Fox, "Be ready all the time, we shall leave for home tonight." Now the Wolves had two sisters who were dwelling near their brothers' camp. After dark Coyote went to the house of the girls; and when one of them went outside, he seized the other and violated her. This girl made a great outcry; and when Fox heard the cry, he jumped up and ran off. Coyote ran away also, and the Wolves never caught him.

The Umatilla Birdman

UMATILLA

THE FIRST MAN to fly over the Wallowa and Blue Mountains was E-tsa-wis-no. It was long, long ago. He had studied the swans in their flights overhead in the fall and the spring, and finally he felt sure that he could do the same thing. So he tried. Being of a persevering type, he bumped his nose and skinned his shins thousands of times in his efforts to imitate the swans.

"I can fly, if I try hard enough," was what he always said. He swung his arms and went through awkward motions for five years before he made any headway. Then he caught the knack of the thing, and finally one morning he could fly! So it came about that when the Spring migration of swans began the next year, E-tsa-wis-no went aloft to join the flight—without a word of farewell to his family!

The next fall he was seen flying North. Regularly, twice annually, for three years, he was seen overhead in company with the swans in their seasonal migrations, but after that he was seen no more. This is a true story. . . .

How Fish-Hawk Raided the Sioux

CAYUSE

A LONG TIME AGO, when many Nez Perce and Cayuse lived to the east, they used to go buffalo hunting. Once a man dreamed of the Sioux, he saw them in his sleep, and he told the young men, "Now I am going on the war-path day after tomorrow, and I shall travel to the Sioux." He was a tough man; many times he had fought and come out all right. His name was Fish-Hawk. Four Cayuse men and two Nez Perce men were going, the one named Fish-Hawk and one named Come-with-the-dawn and one named All-alighted-on-the-ground and one named Charging Coyote, and two Nez Perce men. Fish-Hawk took the lead, he held the pipe, he was the thinker in travels.

They all had red jackets, they were on the warpath, all six of them. They traveled and it snowed, it snowed like winter on the prairie. They traveled on horseback and they came upon the prairie, and went down into a canyon. Many Sioux lived close by there. Fish-Hawk stopped and he turned around towards his friends—"We've come right into camp, see, here are the tents, and they don't know we're here." Tents were all around, maybe two hundred or more, they saw the tents.

Then the Sioux discovered them and yelled in Sioux! Fish-Hawk said, "Brothers, think good, and take it easy—they are going to try and take us." And now they swept the Sioux horses along with them, they drove them along a little way, and then they all turned. "They are catching up with us," he told the others, the pipe-leader told them. "Younger brothers, move on from here, don't shoot yet, for now they will try and take us. Look, there is brushy ground ahead, there we will dismount, and soon they will try and get us. We shall not desert each other; look to your guns," and the Sioux chased them along.

Fish-Hawk, the people's chief in battle, turned his horse and he waved at the Sioux, he told them: "I am Cayuse, we all are; come on, you are three hundred or more. You are Sioux and you are just like old women, you never will kill us, we are Cayuse!"

So they yelled at the Sioux during the chase, and shot at them, they killed them as they went, and he told his brothers, the pipe-leader, "Now turn your horses loose," and they got off and they took off the bridles and took off their jackets and left it all behind and took only the guns and bullets into the brush, among the cottonwoods. He told them, the pipe-leader, he told them, "Younger brothers, look: we can dig trenches and fight well from there." They dug out the ground and crossed cottonwoods over the trenches and got under it all. They yelled at the Sioux, the Sioux yelled back at them and hurled insults, they yelled back again. They were killing Sioux.

Now one of the Sioux used up his bullets and he came up to them, one Sioux, a tough man, dog-disguised, he came towards them, he came up singing. Fish-Hawk said, the tough one, "Little brothers, now he comes, take good aim"—and they hit him close by the trench. He came on, and now he shot at Fish-Hawk with a bow and arrows. Fish-Hawk cried, "Little brothers, he shot me!" He got mad, the one named Fish-Hawk. He told them, "Friends, now watch your leader, now! He shot one of us, now know me, now I am going after him and I am going to drag him right into the trench"—and he stood up suddenly and threw himself out of the trench and they yelled, the Sioux, they shot at him, and he hopped, he grabbed the Sioux warrior by the legs and dragged him along, he threw him into the trench and he hit him. They took his bullets and gun, and scalped him.

Fish-Hawk told them, "Little brothers, maybe I am dying, now pull out the arrow"—and they pulled it out, and the pipe-leader, chief in war, breathed good again, but he was bleeding and getting weak and they tied up the wound. He started shooting again, he told them, "Little brothers, think carefully; look, they are trying to get us, try to shoot straighter," and they yelled.

He saw now that there was fire all around them, below and up above, and he told them, "Now, look, it's burning, they are trying to kill us by burning. Dig deeper now, we are going to be burned, they're scared and that's why they are trying to burn us to death. But we will never die of fire, we are younger brothers, tough ones with guns, they can't get us killed, and they will never kill us with fire."

So he told them, and when night came he gathered them in the middle of the thicket, he told them: "We killed many Sioux, now we're going, we're going out. We're in the midst of them but with my knowledge, soon we will get through anyway." And he told them, "A little wind will come up presently, now get ready, little brothers, let's travel!" And it came, the whirlwind, and they got out of the trench. When the fire flared up, they went down, they passed the Sioux all huddled up in a ditch, they passed by unseen, they traveled on.

Dawn came. The Sioux said, "Now, look, they're all burned up," and they went to the trench. When they got there they found nobody. The Sioux were surprised. "Where are they? How could they live? On which side of us did they pass?" They were greatly surprised, and as they went home, they cried on their way, they took many bodies home.

The Cayuse got out from the trench all right and from there they traveled without pants, shirt-less, pants-less, shoe-less—all they had were guns, and he told them, the chief, the pipe-leader, he told them, "Younger brothers, now we have traveled far, and one of us is getting cold and can travel no further." It was Charging Coyote; he told them, "Friends, now leave me, I will be too much bother, I'll stay right here. My forefathers died too, I'll just rest." Then the others told him, "No, friend, it's the same with all of us, without shoes, without pants, without shirts, somehow we will all get back."

Then they came upon a buffalo bull, and Fish-Hawk told them, "We have traveled far without eating, now kill it." And they killed two buffalo; from them they made shoes and pants and shirts, and they ate buffalo meat. But they had no tents, they got black from freezing and were awful to look at: thus they came back to their own tents.

This is all of the story about the raid on the Sioux: now they told it at the big war-dance at celebration-time, how this man, Fish-Hawk, the pipe-leader, went on the warpath, he was the man! "Only six of us, and you couldn't get us killed, only six, and maybe you were three hundred and maybe more. . . ." Thus they told the story, and now all the people know it. This is a true story, now there, we have made it, and it will always be the same story.

Laptissa'n and the Seven-headed Monster

NEZ PERCE

IN THE EARLY DAYS there was a chief who owned all kinds of property. He found the seven-headed monster running with his horses and cattle. This kept up for several years, and the monster grew bigger and bigger. The chief thought it gave him a big name to have such an animal running with his stock, so he didn't molest it. Finally the monster began to kill off the stock. Then the chief wanted to kill the monster, but he did not know just how to do it. He thought to himself, "Tomorrow I shall take half this band of Indians, and we shall just go and kill this monster."

So they went out to kill it, but when they came in sight of the monster, and fired at it, the monster attacked in turn, and began killing the Indians. It killed all those who had gone out against it, except for the chief himself. After this, the chief was afraid to attack a second time, and resigned himself to the loss of his stock. Then the monster stopped killing stock, and took to killing off Indians. It attacked the people in the village, and the chief made every effort to find a man who could win out over the monster.

Now there was a poor man in this band named Laptissa'n [Le Petit Jean]. This Laptissa'n told the chief that he would kill the monster if only the chief would furnish him with a mule. So the chief gave him the mule, and Laptissa'n went out. He did not know exactly what to do, but he began by riding round and round the monster on the mule. Finally he rode around so many times, that the monster grew weary watching, and fell asleep. Then Laptissa'n jumped off the mule, ran in, and cut the throat of the monster where the seven heads were joined into one neck.

Cry-Because-He-Had-no-Wife

NEZ PERCE

ONCE THERE WAS a little boy. He was an orphan. This boy cried
night and day, and would never be quiet. He cried until he grew
up. His grandmother asked him one day, "What makes you
cry?" He told her, "I cry because I want a wife." Now, the
grandparents knew of a girl in the east, so they sent him there.

As the boy was going along, he came to a giant's house. He
went in to see this giant, and the giant asked him to have breakfast with him. The giant had five roasts on the fire. He had four
large roasts and one small one. He said to the boy, "Pick out the
roast you want for breakfast." The boy picked out the small
roast. Now, the four large roasts were the legs of people that the
giant had killed. The small roast was venison. The boy knew this
from what his grandmother had told him, "Never eat too much."

After breakfast he went on. On the road he came to a great
rock cliff. Its name was Cliff-Giant, (Tiletlpiwaptama'wanat)
and it crushed people. The other giant had told him of this one,
and how to get by it. He had said to him, "Turn yourself into a
little dog, and very slowly follow the trail under the Rock-Cliff.
Keep your eye on the Rock-Cliff, and when you see it move,
run your best." He [the boy] did this and got by. Then he went
on his way again.

He could see at a distance the place where the girl lived. Until
he came in sight of this house, he had never left off crying. Now
the girl had a great stud horse that would kill people before they
reached the house. That was her guard. The boy picked up two
large stones and ran, crying, towards the house. The animal made
for the boy when he saw him coming. The boy spat all over one
of the stones, and when the animal came close, he threw the
stone behind himself. Then the stud horse stopped to stamp on
the stone, and the boy ran on. He was almost in reach of the
house before he threw the other stone. The horse stopped to
stamp on the second stone, and the boy reached the house and
jumped in.

He was in the house but a little while when the girl entered.
She knew him at once, and called him by name. She talked with
him, and asked him if he wanted a bath. He said he did. She built

a fire, heated water, and prepared him a bath. When he had taken the bath, he grew to man's size.

They stayed overnight at the girl's house. In the morning they started for his old home. When they reached it, his grandparents were very old, for he had been gone many years. The girl said to her husband, "You tell your grandparents to do nothing wrong [have sex] tonight. If they obey, I will give them a bath that will make them young again." In the morning the girl washed them with something, but they had not strictly obeyed her order, so they did not become young again. The next night they were both dead.

Then the young people set out again for the girl's home. They rode back on the stud horse, but he did not go very well. They made a whip out of smoke-wood. This whip said, "When the giant gets too close, throw me down, and I will tangle up his feet." They made a whip out of mud. This whip said, "Throw me down, and I will mire the giant." They made a whip out of slide-rock. This whip said, "Throw me down, and the giant will have trouble getting by." They made a whip out of red haw. This whip said, "Throw me down, and I will tear the giant's flesh." They made a whip out of some very high mountains. This whip said, "Throw me down, and the giant will not be able to get by me."

When they had finished all the whips, they started to pass the giant's house. The giant rushed out, and cried, "Give me your wife!" The boy answered, "Get me a cup of water, and I will give you my wife." When the giant went in to get the water, the boy whipped up the horse and hurried on. They made considerable distance before the giant came out. He almost overtook them, and they threw down the whip of smoke-wood. It tangled up the giant, and they got away again. When the giant almost overtook them the second time, they threw down the mudwhip, and the giant was mired. When the giant almost overtook them the third time, they threw the slide-rock whip, and the giant had great trouble getting by. When the giant almost overtook them the fourth time, they threw down the red-haw whip, and it tore his flesh. And when the giant almost overtook them the fifth time, they threw down the whip of high mountains, and he could not cross it. So they escaped the giant and reached home.

Red Willow

NEZ PERCE

A YOUTH HAD a very dear comrade (and fiancée)—a maiden. It came to pass that the maiden went in quest of a vision. "I am going for ten days and if I do not return then you will know that something has killed me."

Here was her fiancé, and when she went this youth followed her. He followed and killed her; shot her with an arrow. He could find no place to put the arrow. He tried to hide it but always on going away he could see it glowing red, glowing like blood. He hid it in many places but always he would see the red glow. There he said to himself, "Confound it! This is too much. Where shall I place it?" Thereupon he shot the arrow away and it stuck amid willows, and he saw it no more. Now he went home. There he began to weep, "My fiancée, my fiancée." But to himself he would say, "How could they suspect me of killing her?" Thus he sang and wept.

He had a younger brother who played about, spearing targets with arrows, and he, too, now began to sing, "My fiancée, my fiancée." Here he was spearing targets when his mother said to him, "What is this you say constantly?" —"I am only imitating my elder brother; I hear him sing often." The mother now said to the father, "It is likely that he has killed her." They had noticed, also, that he would go away for ten day periods.

Now the maiden's mother wept, opening wide her mouth, and looked toward the mountain to which her daughter had gone. . . . The old woman, the maiden's mother, wept. She wept with her mouth open, and a fly flew directly into it. She bit down on the fly quickly and burst it open; behold the fly was [stinking]! She said to herself, "My child is already dead."

Then a search was made for the maiden because the old woman had announced, "She is dead." They went to the mountains to search for the body. There they found it where he had tried to bury the maiden; they found her and saw that she had been shot. They searched for the arrow with which she had been shot, but never did they find the arrow. They took the maiden's body home and buried it there. They never found out who had killed her because the arrow was never found. From that it came to pass that the willow is red—of the maiden's blood.

Morning Song

NEZ PERCE

The herald rides all around the camp and sings—
  It is morning!
  It is morning!
  I wonder if everyone is up.
  We are all alive, be thankful!
  Rise up! Look sharp! Go see
  to the horses, maybe the wolves have killed one.
  The children are alive, be thankful!
  and you, older men
  and you, older women
  in other camps your friends are still living,
  maybe, but elsewhere some are sick
  this morning, and therefore their friends are sad
  and therefore the children are sad.
  Here, it is morning!

How Enga-Gwacu Jim
Met the Great Father

BANNOCK

"I was roasting some salmon on issue-day about twenty years ago. I told my family to eat and that I would join them later. This was against the advice of my familiar spirit (*bu'ha*). That night something spoke to me in a dream. I dreamt of a big war where fighting was going on close to me. Suddenly a hail-stone struck me and I could not get it out.

"From that time on I was sick, and ate very little for a month after my dream. My spirit did not help me any more. I felt as if I were going mad and was ready to die. The Sun spoke to me. He said, 'You are going to die. Put up a separate lodge for yourself. After your death, you will be restored to life if you desire to be alive again.' The Indians built me a separate lodge and left me there to die by myself.

"I was still breathing. I thought of seeing my dead father and mother, brother, and other relatives. I wished to die immediately. For three days and four nights I lay in the tent. At last on the fourth day, my soul (*mu'gua*) came out of my thigh, made a step forward, and glanced back at my body. The *mu'gua* was about as large as this (ten inches). My body was not yet lifeless. When the *mu'gua* had made three steps forward, my body dropped, cold and dead. I looked at it for some time; it made no movement at all.

"Suddenly something came down and went clean through my soul. My soul began to go downward. It did not ascend. I reached another world and followed a trail there. I beheld a helper of the Father (A'pö), who was making some dead men over again. I thought I might see the Father, but could only hear him. He was saying to me, 'You don't look very ill.' A kind of thin wire was making a noise at the time. The Father had a buckskin bag; out of its contents he makes everything. He tapped the wire three times. Then I was able to see his hand, which was as small and clean as a baby's. Then the whole world opened up and I could see the earth plainly. I saw everything there. I saw my own body lying there dead.

"The Sun told me I would be restored to life. I did not walk back and I don't know how I returned. Suddenly I was back alive. For a few moments, I had seen the Father. He was a handsome Indian. My familiar spirit left me when I fell sick and never returned after that. . . ."

Coyote and the Shadow People

NEZ PERCE

COYOTE AND his wife were dwelling there. His wife became ill. She died. Then Coyote became very, very lonely. He did nothing but weep for his wife.

There the death spirit came to him and said, "Coyote, do you pine for your wife?" —"Yes, friend, I long for her . . ." replied

Coyote. "I could take you to the place where your wife has gone but, I tell you, you must do everything just exactly as I say; not once are you to disregard my commands and do something else." —"Yes," replied Coyote, "yes friend, and what could I do? I will do everything you say." There the ghost told him, "Yes. Now let us go." Coyote added, "Yes, let it be so that we are going."

They went. There he said to Coyote again, "You must do whatever I say. Do not disobey." —"Yes, yes, friend. I have been pining so deeply, and why should I not heed you?" Coyote could not see the spirit clearly. He appeared to be only a shadow. They started and went along over a plain. "Oh, there are many horses; it looks like a round-up," exclaimed the ghost. "Yes," replied Coyote, though he really saw none, "yes, there are many horses." They had arrived now near the place of the dead. The ghost knew that Coyote could see nothing but he said, "Oh look, such quantities of service berries! Let us pick some to eat. Now when you see me reach up you too will reach up and when I bend the limb down you too will pull your hands down." —"Yes," Coyote said to him, "so be it that thus I will do." The ghost reached up and bent the branch down and Coyote did the same. Although he could see no berries he imitated the ghost in putting his hand to and from his mouth in the manner of eating. Thus they picked and ate berries. Coyote watched him carefully and imitated every action. When the ghost would put his hand into his mouth Coyote did the same. "Such good service berries these are," commented the ghost. "Yes, friend, it is good that we have found them," agreed Coyote. "Now let us go." And they went on.

"We are about to arrive," the ghost told him. "There is a long, very, very long lodge. Your wife is there somewhere. Just wait and let me ask someone." In a little while the ghost returned and said to Coyote, "Yes, they have told me where your wife is. We are coming to a door through which we will enter. You will do in every way exactly what you see me do. I will take hold of the door flap, raise it up, and, bending low, will enter. Then you too will take hold of the door flap and do the same." They proceeded in this manner now to enter.

It happened that Coyote's wife was sitting right near the entrance. The ghost said to Coyote, "Sit here beside your wife." They both sat. The ghost added, "Your wife is now going to prepare food for us." Coyote could see nothing, except that he was sitting there on an open prairie where nothing was in sight; yet he could feel the presence of the shadow. "Now she has prepared our food. Let us eat." The ghost reached down and then brought his hand to his mouth. Coyote could see nothing but the prairie dust. They ate. Coyote imitated all the movements of his companion. When they had finished and the woman had apparently put the food away the ghost said to Coyote, "You stay here. I must go around to see some people."

He went out but he returned soon. "Here we have conditions different from those you have in the land of the living. When it gets dark here it has dawned in your land and when it dawns for us it is growing dark for you." And now it began to grow dark and Coyote seemed to hear people whispering, talking in faint tones, all around him. Then darkness set in. Oh, Coyote saw many fires in a long-house. He saw that he was in a very, very large lodge and there were many fires burning. He saw the various people. They seemed to have shadow-like forms but he was able to recognize different persons. He saw his wife sitting by his side.

He was overjoyed, and he joyfully greeted all his old friends who had died long ago. How happy he was! He would march down the aisles between the fires, going here and there, and talk with the people. He did this throughout the night. Now he could see the doorway through which his friend and he had entered. At last it began to dawn and his friend came to him and said, "Coyote, our night is falling and in a little while you will not see us. But you must stay right here. Do not go anywhere at all. Stay right here and then in the evening you will see all these people again." —"Yes, friend. Where could I possibly go? I will spend the day here."

The dawn came and Coyote found himself alone sitting there in the middle of a prairie. He spent the day there, just dying from the heat, parching from the heat, thirsting from the heat. Coyote stayed here several days. He would suffer through the day but always at night he would make merry in the great lodge.

One day his ghost friend came to him and said, "Tomorrow you will go home. You will take your wife with you." —"Yes, friend, but I like it here so much. I am having a good time and I should like to remain here." —"Yes," the ghost replied; "nevertheless you will go tomorrow, and you must guard against your inclination to do foolish things. Do not yield to any queer notions. I will advise you now what you are to do. There are five mountains. You will travel for five days. Your wife will be with you but you must never, never touch her. Do not let any strange impulses possess you. You may talk to her but never touch her. Only after you have crossed and descended from the fifth mountain you may do whatever you like." —"Yes, friend," replied Coyote.

When dawn came again Coyote and his wife started. At first it seemed to him as if he were going alone yet he was dimly aware of his wife's presence as she walked along behind. They crossed one mountain and, now, Coyote could feel more definitely the presence of his wife; like a shadow she seemed. They went on and crossed the second mountain. They camped at night at the foot of each mountain. They had a little conical lodge which they would set up each time. Coyote's wife would sit on one side of the fire and he on the other. Her form appeared clearer and clearer.

The death spirit, who had sent them, now began to count the days and to figure the distance Coyote and his wife had covered. "I hope that he will do everything right and take his wife through to the world beyond," he kept saying to himself.

Here Coyote and his wife were spending their last night, their fourth camping, and on the morrow she would again assume fully the character of a living person. They were camping for the last time and Coyote could see her very clearly as if she were a real person who sat opposite him. He could see her face and body very clearly, but only looked and dared not touch her.

But suddenly a joyous impulse seized him; the joy of having his wife again overwhelmed him. He jumped to his feet and rushed over to embrace her. His wife cried out, "Stop! Stop! Coyote! Do not touch me. Stop!" Her warning had no effect. Coyote rushed over to his wife and just as he touched her body she vanished. She disappeared—returned to the shadow-land.

When the death spirit learned of Coyote's folly he became deeply angry. "You inveterate doer of this kind of thing! I told you not to do anything foolish. You, Coyote, were about to establish the practice of returning from death. Only a short time away the human race is coming, but you have spoiled everything and established for them death as it is."

Here Coyote wept and wept. He decided, "Tomorrow I shall return to see them again." He started back the following morning and as he went along he began to recognize the places where he and his spirit friend had passed before. He found the place

where the ghost had seen the herd of horses, and now he began
to do the same things they had done on their way to the shadow-
land. "Oh, look at the horses; it looks like a round-up." He went
on until he came to the place where the ghost had found the
service-berries. "Oh, such choice service-berries! Let us pick and
eat some." He went through the motions of picking and eating
berries.

He went on and finally came to the place where the long lodge
had stood. He said to himself, "Now when I take hold of the
door flap and raise it up you must do the same." Coyote remembered all the little things his friend had done. He saw the spot
where he had sat before. He went there, sat down, and said,
"Now, your wife has brought us food. Let us eat." He went
through the motions of eating again. Darkness fell, and now
Coyote listened for the voices, and he looked all around, he
looked here and there, but nothing appeared. Coyote sat there in
the middle of the prairie. He sat there all night but the lodge
didn't appear again nor did the ghost ever return to him.

Chief Joseph Speaks
in Washington, D.C.

NEZ PERCE

". . . My name is In-mut-too-yah-lat-lat, Thunder Traveling
Over the Mountains. I am chief of the Wal-lam-wat-kin band of
the Chute-pa-lu, or Nez Perce. I was born in eastern Oregon,
thirty-eight years ago. My father was chief before me. When a
young man, he was called Joseph by Mr. Spaulding, a missionary.
He died a few years ago. There was no stain on his hands of the
blood of a white man. He left a good name on the earth. He advised me well for my people. . . .

". . . Through all the years since the white men came to
Wallowa we have been threatened and taunted by them and the
treaty Nez Perce. They have given us no rest. We have had a
few good friends among white men, and they have always ad-

vised my people to bear these taunts without fighting. Our young men were quick-tempered, and I have had great trouble in keeping them from doing rash things. I have carried a heavy load on my back ever since I was a boy. I learned then that we were but few, while the white men were many, and that we could not hold our own with them. We were like deer. They were like grizzly bears. We had a small country. Their country was large. We were contented to let things remain as the Great Spirit Chief made them. They were not; and would change the rivers and mountains if they did not suit them. . . .

". . . In order to have all people understand how much land we owned, my father planted poles all around it and said:

'Inside is the home of my people—the white man may take the land outside. Inside this boundary all our people were born. It circles around the graves of our fathers, and we will never give up these graves to any man.' . . . My father sent for me. I saw he was dying. I took his hand in mine. He said: 'My son, my body is returning to my mother earth, and my spirit is going very soon to see the Great Spirit Chief. When I am gone, think of your country. You are the chief of these people. They look to you to guide them. Always remember that your father never sold his country. You must stop your ears whenever you are asked to sign a treaty selling your home. A few years more, and white men will be all around you. They have their eyes on this land. My son, never forget my dying words. This country holds your father's body. Never sell the bones of your father and mother.' I pressed my father's hand and told him I would protect his grave with my life. My father smiled and passed away to the spirit-land.

"I buried him in that beautiful valley of winding waters. I love that land more than all the rest of the world. A man who would not love his father's grave is worse than a wild animal. . . .

"[In Washington] I have heard talk and talk, but nothing is done. Good words do not last long unless they amount to something. Words do not pay for my dead people. They do not pay for my country, now overrun by white men. They do not protect my father's grave. They do not pay for all my horses and cattle. Good words will not give me back my children. Good words will not make good the promise of your War Chief General Miles. Good words will not give my people good health and stop them from dying. Good words will not get my people a home where they can live in peace and take care of themselves.

I am tired of talk that comes to nothing. It makes my heart sick when I remember all the good words and the broken promises. There has been too much talking by men who had no right to talk. Too many misrepresentations have been made, too many misunderstandings have come up between the white men about the Indians.

"If the white man wants to live in peace with the Indians he can live in peace. There need be no trouble. Treat all men alike. Give them all the same law. Give them all an even chance to live and grow. All men were made by the same Great Spirit Chief. They are all brothers. The earth is the mother of all people, and all people should have equal rights upon it. You might as well expect the rivers to run backwards as that any man who was born a free man should be contented when penned up and denied liberty to go where he pleases. If you tie a horse to a stake do you expect he will grow fat? If you pen an Indian up on a small spot of earth, and compel him to stay there, he will not be contented, nor will he grow and prosper. I have asked some of the great white chiefs where they get their authority to say to the Indian that he shall stay in one place, while he sees white men going where they please. They can not tell me. . . .

"I know that my race must change. We can not hold our own with the white men as we are. We only ask an even chance to live as other men live. We ask to be recognized as men. We ask that the same law shall work alike on all men. If the Indian breaks the law, punish him by the law. If the white man breaks the law, punish him also.

"Let me be a free man—free to travel, free to stop, free to work, free to trade where I choose, free to choose my own teachers, free to follow the religion of my fathers, free to think and talk and act for myself—and I will obey every law, or submit to the penalty.

"Whenever the white man treats the Indian as they treat each other, then we will have no more wars. We shall all be alike— brothers of one father and one mother, with one sky above us and one country around us, and one government for all. Then the Great Spirit Chief who rules above will smile upon this land, and send rain to wash out all the bloody spots made by brothers' hands from the face of the earth. For this time the Indian race are waiting and praying. I hope that no more groans of wounded men and women will ever go to the ear of the Great Spirit Chief above, and that all people may be one people. . . ."

Part Two

THE COLUMBIA

Wasco

Wishram

Tenino-Warm Springs

"Chinook"

Wasco basket *Courtesy of Thomas Burke Memorial*
Washington State Museum, cat. #2-4250

The Dalles. Drawing by J. M.
Stanley (from *Reports of
Explorations and Surveys*)

Columbia River petroglyphs
*Courtesy of Oregon Historical
Society*

ALONG THE GREAT DRY GORGE of the Columbia River from where it swings west between Oregon and Washington, down past Hood River toward the Willamette Valley, a rich Indian culture evolved on both sides of the river—at some sites, it appears from recent excavations, for as long as nine thousand years before the whites came.[1]

These Indians—mostly of Chinookan and Sahaptian stock—lived in and by the element of the "Great River of the West": it gave them their prime food, salmon; it brought the canoe trade from east and west and even from the Pacific that made river villages like Winquatt (The Dalles) famous all over the Indian West as busy, colorful, bountiful markets. The Columbia River Indians were primarily fishermen and traders, gregarious hard-bargaining folks who stayed home by the river, not nomads or warriors. So rooted to their villages were they, in fact, that some of their dialects seem to have lacked words for "North Wind" and "South Wind"—there being only prevailing east and west winds up and down the deep Columbia gorge.[2]

The only real threat to the security of the Columbia River Indians came in historical times, it seems, in the form of raids from the south and southeast by marauding bands of Shoshonean Indians, the so-called "Snakes."[3]

Hill of columnar basalt on the Columbia River (from Frémont, *Report of an Expedition to the Rocky Mountains*)

In this relatively stable, well-provided, strategically located population, the Indian arts of rock-carving, basketry, and story-telling flourished remarkably. Now, the great Bonneville, The Dalles, and John Day dams have inundated their village-sites and their traditional fishing rocks, at Celilo and elsewhere, and drowned their superbly executed rimrock petroglyphs (an impressive remnant is on display at the Winquatt Museum in The Dalles); and most of the people themselves now live inland south, up the Deschutes River on the Warm Springs Reservation, where as the Confederated Warm Springs Tribes they are progressively developing the land their ancestors used to visit seasonally on hunting and root-gathering expeditions.

All is changed, changed irrevocably—but, in stories like the following, the accents of another way of life along the cliffs and gravel-banks of the Great River—settled, agreeable, unwarlike, deeply social—can still be heard.

Wishram woman. Photograph by E. S. Curtis *Courtesy of Photography Collection, Suzzallo Library, University of Washington*

Tsagigla' lal. Columbia River petroglyph *Courtesy of Oregon Historical Society*

Columbia River petroglyphs *Courtesy of Oregon Historical Society*

"Dip-netting in Pools—Wishram." Photograph by E. S. Curtis *Courtesy of Photography Collection, Suzzallo Library, University of Washington*

Coyote at the Mouth
of the Columbia River

WISHRAM

COYOTE BEGAN at the ocean, at the mouth of the Columbia River, where lived an *at'at'a'hlia*, an evil creature who was constantly destroying people by tying them upon a baby board and sending them adrift into the foggy distance, with the command, "Go forever!" After a time the baby board came floating back to her, and upon it there was nothing but bones, for on its voyage it had been to a place of such intense heat that the flesh was melted away. On the shore sat many people awaiting their turn to be set adrift. Their hearts would have run away, but the power of the *at'at'a'hlia* held them there.

Then Coyote came among them, and after watching the evil one for a time, he told them, "I will try that, and soon I will return." So he was tied to the board, and as he started to drift out into the fog, the old woman said, "Go forever!" But all the people cried out, "Come back again!"

After a while the watchers could faintly see the board drifting closer, and they wondered if Coyote had been powerful enough to survive; and when it touched the shore they saw that he was alive, and all the people were glad. Then, to prove which was the stronger, the woman was placed on the board and sent out into the fog, while Coyote and all the people shouted, "Go forever!"

In time the board came drifting back with nothing but her bleached bones upon it. The people were happy that the evil one was destroyed, and they urged Coyote to take from their number a wife. But he said: "No, I do not want a wife. I am to travel up the river."

Coyote Frees the Fish

WISHRAM

COYOTE HEARD about two women who had fish preserved in a pond. Then he went to them as they were collecting driftwood from the river. He turned himself into a piece of wood (trying to get them to pick him up). He drifted along. But they did not get hold of him. He went ashore, ran off way yonder up river, and transformed himself into a boy. He put himself into a cradle, threw himself into the river, and again drifted along.

The two women caught sight of him wailing. They thought: "Some people have capsized, and this child is drifting towards us." The younger one thought: "Let us get hold of it." But the older woman did not want to have the child. Now it was drifting along. The older one thought, "That is Coyote." Nevertheless the younger woman took the child and put it in a canoe.

The two women started home towards their house. The child was wailing, and they arrived home with it. They took off the cradle from it and looked closely at it. As it turned out, the child was a boy. The younger one said, "A boy is better than drift-wood." And then she went and cut an eel and put its tail in his mouth. Then straightway he sucked at it and ate it all up. She gave him another eel, and again he sucked at it, (eating up) only half. Then he fell asleep, and half the eel was lying in his mouth. The two women said, "He is asleep; now let us go for some more wood."

And then they went far away. Coyote arose and saw them going far off. Then he made himself loose and seized their food. He roasted the fish on a spit; they were done and he ate. He caught sight of the fish, which were their food, in a lake. Then he examined (the lake) carefully, and discovered a spot where it would be easy (to make an outlet from it to the river). "Here I shall make the fish break out (from the lake), and then they shall go to the Great River" [*wi'mahl*—Columbia].

He made five digging-sticks, made them out of young oak. And then he put them down in that place. He started back home towards their house. Again, just as before, he put himself into the cradle. Again, there in his mouth lay the eel's tail. Again he fell asleep.

Now the two women arrived. "The boy is sleeping," they said, "very good is the boy, being a great sleeper." And then they retired for the night. Daylight came, the boy was sleeping. Again they went for wood. Again he saw them going far away. Then he got up and took their food. He roasted it on a spit and ate it all up. Then straightway he went to where his digging-sticks were.

He took hold of one of his digging-sticks. Then he stuck it

into the ground; he pulled it out, and the earth was all loosened up; his digging-stick broke. He took hold of another one and again stuck it into the ground. Then he loosened up the earth, and his digger was all broken to pieces. He took hold of another one of his digging-sticks. Again, he stuck it into the ground; he loosened the earth all up, and his third digger was all broken to pieces. He took hold of the fourth one; again his digger broke. Now at last he took hold of the fifth, and stuck it into the ground; he loosened the earth all up. And then the fish slid over into the Great River.

Now then the older woman bethought herself. She said to her companion, "You said, 'The child is good.' I myself thought, 'That is Coyote.' Now this day Coyote has treated us two badly. I told you, 'Let us not take the child, that is Coyote.' Now we have become poor, Coyote has made us so." Then they went to their house, and Coyote met them there.

He said to them: "Now by what right, perchance, would you two keep the fish to yourselves? You two are birds, and I shall tell you something. Soon now people will come into this land. Listen!" And the people could be heard, *du'lulululu*, like thunder rumbling afar. "Now they will come into this land; those fish will be the people's food. Whenever a fish will be caught, you two will come. Your name will be Swallows. Now this day I have done with you; thus I shall call you 'Swallows.' When the people will come, they will catch fish; and then you two will come, and it will be said of you, 'The swallows have come, Coyote called them so.' Thus will the people say: 'From these two did Coyote take away their fish preserved in a pond; now they have come.' " Thus did Coyote call those two.

Coyote and the Mouthless Man

WISHRAM

AGAIN COYOTE TRAVELED up the river. In the water he saw the canoe of a certain person, a man. He saw how the man dived into the water. He came up out of the water, his hands holding one sturgeon on that side and one sturgeon on this; he put the sturgeons down in the canoe. Then Coyote saw him count them with his finger, pointing about in the canoe. He thought: "When he dives, I shall take hold of and steal from him one of his sturgeons; let us see what he'll do."

The person dived under water. And then Coyote swam towards his canoe. He seized one of his sturgeons. He went and took the person's sturgeon with him, and hid it in the bushes. And then that Coyote seated himself there and hid. Then the person came up out of the water into his canoe; he put his sturgeons down in the canoe, again one and one. And then he counted them; again he counted them. Quite silently he counted them; [one sturgeon was missing].

And then the person pointed his finger out, first up high, then a little lower, again a little lower still, finally lower still, on the ground. There he pointed, where Coyote was sitting! Silently he held his finger there. Coyote tried to move to one side, there again was the finger. No matter which way Coyote moved, there was that finger pointing at him, Coyote. Now where his finger was pointed, that person went straight up to Coyote. Straightway he went to meet Coyote. . . . He kept pointing at him; Coyote kept dodging from side to side; the person kept him well in eye.

Coyote looked at the person [as he came up]; he was strange in appearance. As it turned out, he had no mouth; he had only a nose and eyes and ears. He spoke to Coyote with his nose; but he could not hear him; just deep down in his nose could be heard: "*Dnn Dnn Dnn Dnn*." In fact he was scolding Coyote in this way. Thus he said to him with his nose, "You are not good." Thus the person kept telling him; his heart was dark within him. Coyote thought: "Perhaps now this man desires the sturgeon; perhaps he is going to kill me. . . ."

And then the person went back to his canoe. Coyote made a fire when he had gone. He gathered some stones and heated them in the fire. And then they all became hot. He cut the sturgeon in two, cut it all up, and carefully made ready the stones. He laid the sturgeon out on the stones and steamed it; it was entirely done. And then he removed it and laid it down. Then the man who had no mouth came back; he met Coyote as he was eating.

And then [the person] took hold of that good well-done sturgeon. Then thought Coyote, "Wonder what he'll do with it!" [Coyote] looked at him; he took the good sturgeon. [The person] just sniffed at the sturgeon, then threw it away. And then Coyote thought, "It is not well." He went and brought the sturgeon back and brushed it clean. Now Coyote was thinking, "What is he going to do with it?" Once again the person took hold of it and did with it as before.

[Coyote] went up to him and looked at him closely. And then he thought, "I don't know what I shall do to make him a mouth." Secretly he took a flint and chipped it on one side; it became just like a sharp knife. And then he went up to the person with the flint secretly in hand and looked at him closely. In vain the man tried to dodge from side to side. Now Coyote put the flint down over his mouth. He sliced it open, and the person's blood flowed out. He breathed: "Haaaaa! Haaaaa!" Coyote said to him, "Go to the river and wash yourself."

When the person had come out of the water, he stopped and spoke to Coyote: "You do not seem to have steamed a large sturgeon." And then Coyote said, "Well, you would have killed me; you wanted the sturgeon for yourself. You got after me for the sturgeon."

Now the people [of the mouthless man's village] told one another: "There is a man whose mouth has been made for him." In truth, all the people of that same village were without mouths. And then they betook themselves to [Coyote]. He made mouths for all the people of that village. He called that village Nɪmɪshxa'ya [located below Castle Rock]. They said to him: "We will give you a woman." He said: "No! I shouldn't care for a woman; I'll not take one."

Coyote and the First Pregnancy

WISHRAM

. . . So COYOTE LEFT Nɪmɪshxa'ya, and a little above that place he saw a man turning somersaults, landing on his head, and yelling loudly, as if it hurt him. Coyote was curious, and going to see what it all meant, he found that the man had his ankles tied, and between his legs was a bundle of firewood.

"What is the matter, friend?" he asked. "My wife is about to have a child," the man answered, "and I am carrying wood for the house." —"But that is no way to carry wood," said Coyote. He untied the man's legs, cut some hazel-brush, and began to twist it into a rope, which he attached to the bundle as a pack-string. He swung the faggot on his back, passing the loop of the rope across his forehead.

"Take the lead, and I will carry this in for you," he said. So the man went ahead, and Coyote followed, bearing the bundle of fuel. "Here is my home," said the man after a while. Coyote threw down the load, and said, "That is the way to carry wood. Where is this woman who is to have a child?"

The man showed him a woman lying on a bed with a pile of robes wrapped around her hand. She did not seem to be pregnant, and Coyote unwrapped the hand, in a finger of which he saw a sliver embedded in a mass of puss. "Is this what is the matter?" he asked. "Yes," was the answer. "That is nothing; let me show you," said Coyote. He took a small sharp flake of bone, pricked the finger open, and pressed out the sliver.

"Now I will show you how to make a child," he said. He then did so.

Coyote remained a few days in that house, and the woman said she was soon to be a mother. In a short time the child was born. "That is your child," Coyote said to the man. "I give it to you."

Coyote's Carelessness

WASCO–WARM SPRINGS

COYOTE WAS going along, and he came to a river where five pretty sisters were bathing and washing clothes some distance from each other. "What pretty girls," said Coyote to himself, "I wonder how I can enjoy them all." He thought a little, and then turned himself into a baby laced up in a papoose-board, and set himself adrift on the river.

Pretty soon he drifted down to the oldest sister. "Oh, what a beautiful baby!" she said, and pulled it ashore and picked it up. Well, that Coyote turned back into himself before she knew what was happening, and he had his way with her; then he became a baby again and drifted down to the second oldest sister.

"Oh, my, what a cute baby!" she said, "I must save it!"—but when she picked it up it was that Coyote! And so he fooled two more sisters in the same way, until he got down to the last one, the youngest.

When she saw the baby drifting down she said, "There's something funny about this; let me see—" and she held the baby in the water with one hand and quickly unlaced it with the other. Sure enough, it was that Coyote! When he turned himself into a baby, he just forgot to change his penis too, and when the youngest sister saw he was no baby, she threw him far out into the river. He was careless, but she was careful.

Tsagigla'lal

WISHRAM

A WOMAN HAD a house where the village of Nɪxlu'ɪdɪx was later built [presentday Wishram, or Spedis]. She was chief of all who lived in this region. That was long ago, before Coyote came up the river and changed things, and people were not yet real people.

After a time Coyote in his travels came to this place and asked the inhabitants if they were living well or ill. They sent him to their chief, who lived up in the rocks, where she could look down on the village and know all that was going on.

Coyote climbed up to her home and asked: "What kind of living do you give these people? Do you treat them well, or are you one of those evil women?" —"I am teaching them how to live well and to build good houses," she said. "Soon the world is going to change," he told her, "and women will no longer be chiefs. You will be stopped from being a chief."

Then he changed her into a rock, with the command, "You shall stay here and watch over the people who live at this place, which shall be called Nɪxlu'ɪdɪx."

All the people know that Tsagigla'lal sees all things, for whenever they are looking up at her those large eyes are watching them.

Chief Mark Considers Monogamy, Warm Springs Agency, 1871

WASCO–WARM SPRINGS

"MY HEART IS warm like fire, but there are cold spots in it. I don't know how to talk. I want to be a white man. My father did not tell me it was wrong to have so many wives. I love all my women. My old wife is a mother to the others, I can't do without her; but she is old, she cannot work very much; I can't send her away to die. This woman cost me ten horses; she is a good woman; I can't do without her. That woman cost me eight horses; she is young; she will take care of me when I am old. I don't know how to do; I want to do right. I am not a bad man. I know your new law is good; the old law is bad. We must be like the white man. I am a man; I will put away the old law. . . . I want you to tell me how to do right. I love my women and children. I can't send any of them away; what must I do?"

A Wasco Woman Deceives Her Husband

WASCO

A MAN AND his wife and four children lived at Wasco. It was the time of year when the women were cutting grass to pack their dried fish in. One day, while this woman was getting grass, a man from Tenino came and talked with her. They fell in love with each other and planned to deceive the old husband. The woman said, "I will go to a creek and eat alder bark until I spit it up; he will think I am spitting blood. After a time I'll pretend to die." —"All right," said the Tenino man. She chewed the bark. At night she came to her house, apparently suffering terribly, and said, "I can't live. "What's the matter?" asked her husband. "Oh, I must have broken something inside." She had told the

Tenino man, "I'll die at daybreak. They will bury me, and you must be near to dig me up quickly."

At daybreak she died. Before dying she said to her husband, "When I die, take my cup and mountain-sheep horn dish and cover my face. Don't cover it all up."

The husband buried her soon after sunrise. As soon as he went away, the other man dug her up, and she went with him to Tenino. The old husband built a sweathouse, sweated five days, and mourned much. He did not know what to do with his children, they cried and worried so. One day he took the children out and made pictures on the rocks to amuse the youngest child —pictures of deer, birds, and weapons. To amuse his little girl he placed five stones in the road, one after another, and made holes in each stone.

Towards midnight of the following day the fire went out in his house, and in the village the fires went out in every house. Next day the father said to the eldest boy, "Go over to Tenino and get fire." The two boys started out. Towards sundown they reached Tenino, peeped into the door of a house, and the younger boy said, "That woman in there looks like our mother." The other boy looked and said, "It is our mother." Their father had made a stick of cedar bark for them with little cracks in it, good to hold fire; they crept up to the fire and lighted this stick. The mother had a little baby. She saw the two boys and asked them, "Does your little brother cry very much?" "Yes," said the eldest boy, "he cries all the time."

A few days after this the fire went out again. The boys went four times for fire; the fifth time they told their father that when they went for fire they always saw their mother. He said, "You must not talk that way." They laughed, and he scolded them, saying, "It is wrong to say that. Your mother is dead." They said, "No, she is not dead. We see her every time we go."

At last he went to her grave and found it empty. Then he went to Tenino, looked into the house, and saw her with the other man. She went outside for water, he followed her, touched her on the shoulder, and said, "Why have you done this?" She threw her arms around him and begged him to save her life. She said, "I'm sorry, and I want to live with you again. This man whips me all the time; I have no peace with him. I'll tell you what to do. When he puts his head on my lap and goes to sleep, you can slip in and cut his head off." This was done, and the man and his wife went home [to Wasco] together.

Next morning, when it was time for the man to get up, he still lay covered up. People came in, took the blanket off, and found that his head was gone. They could not find the head. They went up to Celilo and four different villages to hunt for it. At last they heard that the woman's husband had stuck it upon a pole at Wasco. Then they made war on the man and his people. When both sides were ready to fight, Coyote came along and asked, "What does this mean?" They told him. "No," he said, "I'll not have such a thing; this must end right here. A woman should never cause war. I'll end all such things. Right here you people of Tenino become rocks, and you Wascos be rocks." Both sides are still standing there to this day, all rocks.

The Deserted Boy

WISHRAM

SOME TIME LONG AGO the people said to the boy: "Now let us go for reeds." The boy was considered bad. So then they said: "Now you people shall take him along when you go for reeds." And then they said to them: "You shall abandon him there." So then the people all went across the river. They went on and arrived where the reeds were. And then they cut off the reeds and said to them: "If the boy says, 'Are you people still there?' you shall answer him, 'Ooo!'"

And then they all ran off; straight home they went, right across the river. No person at all was left on this side; they were all on the other side. And then that boy said: "Now let us all go home!" —"Oooo," said the reeds to him. He looked about long, but in vain; there was nobody. And then he too started to go home, he too went following behind them; he ran until he arrived at the river, but there were no people to be seen. So then the boy cried. And then he heard something, "Tlhh! Tlhh! Tlhh!" And then he turned his eyes and looked; he dried his tears. Now then he caught sight of a wee bit of fire in a shell. And then the boy took the fire and built [it] up. . . .

And further he caught sight of some string; also of that there was only a little. Straightway he took it. And further he went to the cache and saw five Indian potatoes. And then he thought: "My poor paternal grandmother has saved for me the Indian potatoes, and my paternal grandmother has saved for me the fire, and my maternal grandmother has saved for me the string." And then the boy made a fishline and he made a trap out of the string. He set his trap for magpies, and trapped them. Then he made a magpie-skin blanket. . . . He put it nicely about himself; when he went to sleep, he wrapped himself nicely in it.

And then he fished with hook and line and caught one sucker. Half of it he consumed, half he saved for himself. Next morning he consumed the other half. Then he went to fish again and caught two suckers; one he consumed, and one he saved for himself. Next morning he consumed the other one. Now next morning he went to fish again and caught three suckers. One and a half he consumed; next morning he consumed the other one and a half. Then again he went to fish and caught four suckers. Two he consumed, two he saved for himself. Next morning he consumed two all up. Now again he went to fish for the fifth time; the boy had now fished five times. He had now become a full-grown man.

And then he turned to look at his fish-line; behold! ground roasted fish was contained in a hollow vessel. He stood it up on the ground. And then the boy sang. Now then all the people were looking on at him, and then they said, "What has happened to him?" Truly, he became glad because he had caught roasted fish. Thus he sang:

"*Atse', Atse'!*
My feathered cloak waves freely over me!"
In truth, it was [the Merman's] virgin daughter that had given him [the fish] to eat.

Now then the boy had slept four nights; he slept through the fifth night. And then he awoke; a woman was sleeping with him. Very beautiful was the woman. Her hair was long, and she had bracelets reaching right up to here on her arms, and rings were on her fingers in great number; and he saw a house all covered with painted designs inside; and he saw that a mountain-sheep blanket covered over both of them, him and his wife. Truly, that woman was [the Merman's daughter], and she had given him [plenty] to eat; and plenty of Chinook salmon and sturgeon and blue-back salmon and eels, plenty of everything, she had brought. Now he married her.

Now the woman made food, and it became daylight that

morning. Then the two remained together quietly all day, and they remained together for a long time. And then spring came. And then the people found out that he lived with her. So then his paternal grandmother and his maternal grandmother went across the river straight to his house. And then he thought to himself: "The two old women are poor. Thus also on me did my paternal grandmother and my maternal grandmother take pity." So then he gave the two of them [something] to eat; he gave the old women salmon, and he gave them sturgeon. And then the two old women started home; they went across the river.

For a long time they were there. And then the story got about, and the people said, "Oh! There is much salmon and plenty of sturgeon and eels and blue-back salmon at the boy's." Now snow had begun to fall gently, gently. There was no food among the people; the people were hungry. And then the people said, "Let us too go to the boy." Now then his paternal grandmother and his maternal grandmother again went across the river first. And then they got close to the house. And then a great many people went across the river to the boy.

Now then the boy turned his head and looked; he saw the people crossing in a canoe in great numbers. And then he thought to himself: "It was not well thus when they abandoned me." Then, indeed, he caused an east wind to arise; a strong east wind arose and there was snow. All died in the water, the people were drowned. [Pitiless,] the boy thought to himself, "Thus they did to me, they abandoned me." And again others went across the river. And them also he treated as before; a strong wind blew, and snow fell. And again they died, twice the people died. And only the two old women remained. . . .

Little Raccoon and His Grandmother

WASCO–WARM SPRINGS

LITTLE RACCOON LIVED with his grandmother; he was her *k'utch* [paternal grandson], and she spoiled him. They were gathering acorns over the mountains, and one day she asked Raccoon what he wanted to eat for dinner. "Would you like some wapato?" she asked, and Raccoon answered, "No, I'm tired of wapato."

"Some jerky, then?" —"No, I'm tired of jerky." —"How about some dried fish-eyes?" —"I don't like dried fish-eyes!" So Raccoon's Grandmother grew angry and told him to just go out and find his own dinner. "But stay out of the acorns!" she told him.

Well, after awhile Raccoon came to the five pits where his grandmother was storing her winter's acorns. "I'm so hungry!" he said to himself, and after awhile he said, "Grandmother surely won't miss just one acorn." So he reached into the pit, under the dirt covering, and took out one acorn to eat—and then another, and then another, until pretty soon the pit was empty! "Now what shall I do?" he said, "Grandmother will be very angry." So he crapped once for every acorn in the pit, and then covered it all up. But he was still very hungry, and he went on to the second pit. "Well, maybe I'll just take one more acorn," he said, but after awhile that pit was empty too, and so he filled it up, as before, with his dung. Well, Raccoon just seemed to get hungrier and hungrier, and before long he had eaten every acorn in each of the five pits, and replaced every one with his dung.

After a while his grandmother went out to get some acorns for their supper. But when she reached into the first pit all she felt was little pieces of dung! "Somebody has been messing around here!" she said. So she went on to the second pit and reached in, and felt the same thing—and so on through all five pits. She was getting angrier and angrier. "I'll bet it was that Little Raccoon!" she yelled, and when she found him by the fire she grabbed a fire-stick [braided willow wands to carry live coals in] and whipped him from his nose to his tail. This is why raccoons have those stripes across their backs.

Little Raccoon ran away then, he thought he would go live with some friends in a village nearby. But when he arrived there everybody came out and jeered at him: "Ha ha, here comes that Little Raccoon; he stole all his grandmother's acorns and replaced them with his dung!" So Raccoon felt silly and went on to another village, but there again all the people ran out and ridiculed him, "Ha ha, here's that Little Raccoon, we've heard how you pilfered your grandmother's acorns and left her only dung!" He was ashamed, and went on to three more villages, but every time he arrived the people would come out and make fun of him. So Raccoon learned how stories about the mean things you do travel ahead of you, and he went off by himself into the woods.

Now about this time his old grandmother began to feel badly about whipping her little *k'ɪtch;* she felt sorry for him. So she set out to find him, but when she came to the first village, they told her that Raccoon had gone on to the next village, and so on, until she had visited all five villages without finding him. She was feeling pretty bad. Now Raccoon was up in a service-berry bush, eating berries, and he heard his grandmother coming up the hill, crying, "Oh my little *k'ɪtch,* my little Raccoon, where are you, where are you?" Raccoon yelled, "Here I am, Grandmother, just eating service-berries." Pretty soon she came up, nearly blind from crying so much, and she said, "My *k'ɪtch,* I'm so hungry, throw me some berries."

Now that his grandmother had found him, that Raccoon was feeling mischievous again, so he threw a whole handful of berries, leaves, and twigs right down her throat, and she began to choke. "Kak-kak," she cried, "my *k'ɪtch.* I'm choking; here, take my basket-hat and get me some water!" So that Raccoon climbed down, took the hat, and ran to a creek and filled it up, but he was feeling mean again so he poked a hole in the hat and by the time he got back he had only a little water. "Kak-kak!" cried the grandmother, "get me some more water!" So Raccoon went to fetch her water again, but he poked another hole, and brought even less water this time. He was obeying her, but not really. Each time he went he poked another hole into the hat and brought back a little less, and a little less, until the fifth time, when the grandmother could hardly talk, he brought her only one drop of water. And just as he handed her the basket-hat this time, she cried "Kak-kak-kak" once more—and turned into a blue-jay and flew off, scolding the way blue-jays do. Little Raccoon just sat down and cried; it was all his fault.

Wren Kills Elk

LOWER CHINOOK

THERE WAS WREN and his grandmother. Soon his grandmother said, "Oh, my grandson, I wish you would go out and hunt. I'm hungry. I want some meat." Wren asked, "What is it that you wish?" —"Well," his grandmother answered, "if you go out, go to one certain spot, then sit down and call for Elk."

Wren went out. He sat down upon a stump. He began to sing. He called for Elk to come. Soon Raccoon came along. Wren looked at him; he watched him. "Oh, this isn't any Elk!" Then he spoke to Raccoon, "I don't want you. I want Elk."

Wren called again. Another animal came. This time, it was Mink. Wren saw that it was Mink. He said, "I don't want you. I want Elk." —"I'm Elk," answered Mink. "No, you aren't," answered Wren. "Grandmother said that Elk was large."

Wren called again. Then Otter came. Otter said that he was Elk. But Wren answered, "I know that you are Otter. I don't want you." Now it was three that had come.

Wren called once more. He wanted Elk to come. He heard something coming. Pretty soon Deer came. "Maybe this is Elk," thought Wren. But it wasn't Elk. Wren found out who it was. It was Deer.

Then Wren called loudly, and sang. He called Elk. Soon he heard a loud crackling in the woods. Then Elk came. Wren wondered what he could do. "You called me," said Elk, "here I am." Wren wondered what he could do. "How could you ever kill me?" asked Elk; "you are too small." —"Oh, I'll jump on your neck, then crawl into your heart and cut it out," answered Wren. "No, you won't," said Elk, "I'll sneeze and blow you out." —"Then I'll crawl into your eye," Wren said. "I'll close my eye and smash you," answered Elk. "Well, I'll crawl into your ear then," Wren said. "But I'll shake my head and throw you out," Elk answered. "Then I'll watch until you open your mouth and get in that way," Wren said. "I'll spit you out," Elk answered.

Wren watched Elk. He turned around. Pretty soon he raised his tail. Wren jumped in. Elk shook and shook but he couldn't get him out. Wren crawled in a long way. He reached Elk's heart and cut it out. It took a long time. Elk jumped and ran, trying to get Wren out, but he couldn't. After a while he fell down. Then Wren crawled out. It was very hard to do. He was all greasy and bloody. He brought out some fat with him. He wondered what he could do with it to keep from getting it dirty. He was all greasy and bloody. Then he thought of skunk cabbage leaf. He went to a swamp and wrapped the fat up in a skunk cabbage leaf that he found there. Then he went home.

Wren's grandmother was making *tamanawas* [spirit power]. She was pounding the floor with a stick. She was saying, "I hope my grandson will come home soon." Then Wren came in. "Oh, I'm glad!" she said. "Yes, I'm home," Wren answered. He opened his package of grease. The woman was glad when she saw it. "We can't go after Elk this evening. We'll go in the morning," she decided. Wren was very tired. "You must lie down," his grandmother said. But she stayed awake all night, so they could be ready to leave early the next morning. She didn't really sleep at all.

Early in the morning she awakened Wren. She told him to wash himself. He was covered with blood. Wren washed. Then they started out. After a while they reached Elk. He was really there. Wren's grandmother was overjoyed. She started to sing,

"Grandson killed Elk!
Grandson killed Elk!"

Wren asked her how to skin Elk. "What?" she asked. "You—a hunter, and you don't know how to skin Elk?" Then she showed him. "Cut here and here, and here," she said. Then Wren skinned Elk. After he was skinned the old woman said, "You will have to dry the meat right here." —"But how do you dry it?" asked Wren. She showed him how to dry the meat. She put four sticks in the ground. Then she put two poles on the sticks. Then she put brush across the poles. After that she cut up all the meat and made it ready to dry. She put it all on top of the brush. Then she was finished.

She sent Wren to bring wood. She told him to get wood without any pitch; elder and bark. Wren brought the wood and made a fire under the meat to cook it. "Now, my grandson," the old woman said, "I want you to get some good hemlock; some small round sticks. Then we can turn the meat over so that it will dry quickly." The old woman was very glad. She took a bite of the meat over there, here, and over there. She was eating meat and grease once more.

The next day they started home. Wren wondered how they could take the meat. "We can't pack it all back, grandmother," he said. "Now, my grandson," she asked, "why do you say that you want to be a hunter? Go and find some cedar bark and cedar poles; poles that are easy to bend." Wren brought the bark and poles. The old woman put them together. She made a basket to carry the meat. Then she made a carrying strap. "It will be like that," she said; "that's how they will pack meat home. They will clean it all, saving everything. That's the way they will do it."

After the meat was taken care of, the old woman asked what

should be done with the hide. "Oh, I'll take that along," Wren answered. "All right, grandson, we'll fix it up for a blanket."
—"Oh, my grandmother, really?" Wren exclaimed. They rolled the hide up tight. Then they carried everything home. They packed it out.

When they reached home they made frames for curing the hide. They got bone scrapers. Every day, every day, they worked, scraping the hide. Then it was finished. It was nice and soft. The old woman said, "It will be like that for a long time from now. Somebody will have good luck at hunting. He will use the hide that way. He will waste nothing. He will save all the meat, and even the bones. The head will be saved. It will be put in the fire to burn the hair off. Then it will be scraped clean."
—"But what will be done with it?" asked Wren. "It will be saved for winter food. It won't spoil," the old woman answered. "The same will be done with the feet. They will be dried and saved. The grease will be stored too. It will be kept in bags made from intestines."

After a while Wolf came. He begged for some meat. "Oh, grandson," the old woman said, "we had a hard time to get this meat. We don't want to give it away." Wolf went away.

Wren and his grandmother went out. They got in a canoe and went down the river. Wolf went back to the house to ask for meat again. He wanted dried meat and grease. When he got there he found no one, so he went in and ate. He ate grease and dried meat. The old woman had put some wood on the fire before she left. Wolf put some fat on a stick and held it over the fire to melt it. The fat dropped on the fire. Wolf went out. He took some meat. Wren and his grandmother were in the canoe. Wren said, "Grandmother, someone is in our house. Let's go home." Wolf was afraid that someone would come. He took a lot of meat and left. Wren and the old woman returned. She saw what had happened. She saw drops of fat on the fireplace. She called Wren, "Come and see! The meat is nearly all gone." The fat was over half gone; the best meat was gone. Wren came in and looked around. Then he went outside. He saw tracks. "Come grandmother," he called; "Wolf's tracks are here. He was the one that took the meat."

The old woman came and saw that what he said was true.

The Elk, the Hunter, and His Greedy Father

WASCO

THERE WAS A MAN at Dog River [Hood River] in days gone by, whose wife was with child. Pretty soon she gave birth to a boy. While she was sick, the man carried wood, and one day a piece of bark fell on his forehead and cut him. When the boy was large enough to shoot, he killed birds and squirrels; he was a good shot. One day, however, his father said to him, "You don't do as I used to. I am ashamed to own you. When I was of your age, I used to catch young elks. One day when I killed a young elk, the old one attacked me and made this scar you see on my forehead."

Then the boy had a visit from an elk, and the elk said, "If you will serve me and hear what I say, I will be your master and will help you in every necessity. You must not be proud. You must not kill too many of any animal. I will be your guardian spirit."

So the young man became a great hunter, knew where every animal was—elk, bear, deer. He killed what he needed for himself, and no more. The old man, his father, said to him, "You are not doing enough. At your age I used to do much more." The young man was grieved at his father's scolding. The elk, the young man's helper, was very angry at the old man. At last [he] helped the young man to kill five whole herds of elk. He killed all except his own spirit elk, though he tried without knowing it to kill even [that one]. This elk went to a lake and pretended to be dead; the young man went into the water to draw the elk out, but as soon as he touched it, both sank.

After touching bottom, the young man woke as from a sleep, and saw bears, deer, and elks without number, and they were all persons. Those that he had killed were there too, and they groaned. A voice called, "Draw him in." Each time the voice was heard, he was drawn nearer his master, the Elk, until he was at his side. Then the great Elk said, "Why did you go beyond what I commanded? Your father required more of you than he himself ever did. Do you see our people on both sides? These are they whom you have killed. You have inflicted many needless wounds on our people. Your father lied to you. He never saw my father, as he falsely told you, saying that my father had met him. He also told you that my father gave him a scar. That is not true; he was carrying fire-wood when you were born, and a piece of bark fell on him and cut him. He has misled you. Now I shall leave you, and never be your guardian spirit again."

When the Elk had finished, a voice was heard saying five times, "Cast him out." The young man went home. The old man was talking, feeling well. The young man told his two wives to fix a bed for him. They did so. He lay there five days and nights, and then told his wives, "Heat water to wash me, also call my friends so that I may talk to them. Bring five elk-skins." All this was done. The people came together, and he told them, "My father was dissatisfied because, as he said, I did not do as he had done. What my father wanted grieved the guardian spirit which visited and aided me. My father deceived me. He said that he had been scarred on the head by a great elk while taking the young elk away. He said that I was a disgrace to him. He wanted me to kill more than was needed. He lied. The spirit has left me, and I die."

The Big-footed Man and His Son

WASCO

THERE WAS A CHIEF who lived near the mouth of the Columbia River. His feet were three feet long, his whole body was in proportion. He had a long house with five fireplaces. The house was nicely fixed, with fish and animals carved around on every side. He had a hundred wives—fifty beds on one side, and fifty on the other. A short distance to one side he had a house in which lived one hundred slaves. These slaves took great baskets every evening at sundown, brought sand from a bank at the seashore, and scattered it around the chief's house for fifty yards in width. Then they smoothed the sand perfectly; not even a mouse could move around the chief's house without leaving tracks.

This big-footed man was chief of all the people in that country. After nightfall nobody went near the chief's house. The chief went around his house each night to each one of his wives. About midnight he would be halfway around, and the sun would come up when he was with the last wife. He had a great many daughters, but not one son. [His name was Diabɩxwa'sxwas.]

News came to Diabɩxwa'sxwas that there was a chief's daughter in the Wasco country, and he made up his mind to go and buy her. He had fifty canoes filled with provisions and men to take him up the river. They landed near Wasco and came on foot to the village. He brought fifty slaves to give for the chief's daughter, twenty-five men and twenty-five women. Nädaiet was the name of the girl he had come for. They camped beside a bluff of rocks. He bought the girl; her people were willing to sell her, as he was a great chief. Whatever he asked for, he got. He took her home. Next morning, when he returned, he asked, "How many children were born while I was gone upriver?" —"Five girls." He had no sons, because he killed them as soon as they were born, for he did not want any one to be greater than himself.

Nädaiet bore him a child in time. The slaves brought sand every evening; it was perfectly level, so that no person could come near to meddle with his wives. After Nädiet's child was born, he asked, "What is it?" Five of the women had made a plan to deceive him, and they said, "It is a girl." They had been with their husband when he bought Nädaiet, and they sympathized with her. They put girl's clothes on the baby. The five women thought and cared for the child even more than the mother did. Word went out that the chief was killing all his sons. Everybody was angry.

The boy grew fast. He was large and heavy, and began to look like a boy; he was very wise. The girls were very large, too; at three or four they were as large as women. And it is from this that the Chinook people are so large and have such big feet.

The mother of the boy, as he grew older and began to show by his behavior that he was a boy, began to cry. She felt very anxious. The chief noticed this, and thought that she was home-sick. He said, "If you wish, you may take the child and go home to your father for a visit. I'll come for you." This was just what pleased the five women; they got a canoe ready, and the five women went with her. They told all not to tell about him, and they promised to keep the secret. As they got upriver out of sight of the old man, they took off the girl's clothes that the child was wearing, and put on a boy's. All that were with her [the mother] were delighted, and said, "The old man shall not be our master any longer." The boy was named after his father.

The others returned [to Diabɩxwa'sxwas], the mother remained at Wasco. The mother told the boy about his father and how many boys he had killed. The boy was angry, and hunted in the mountains for guardian spirits, so that he might get strength to fight his father. The fifth night he came home and said, "Mother, the five Thunders and Lightnings have given me their strength." His mother said, "That is not enough." He went again, came home the fifth day, and said, "I have the strength of five bands of Grizzly Bears." —"That is not enough." He went the third time, and said, "There are five bands of Elk, and the strength of them is mine; they promised it." —"That is nothing, get more."

The old chief was very bad among his people. He could walk on the water; when people were coming along on the water in a canoe, he could walk out and destroy them.

Now the boy's mother wanted him to get the power of running on the water so that he might overcome his father. She said, "Do not seek power any longer on the mountains, seek by the water." He went to the water and got the power of the five Whirlpools. His mother said, "That is not enough." When he came the fifth time, he said, "I have the power of the five long-legged Water Spiders. They said, 'We will give you strength to run on the water, as we do.'" His mother went to the water and saw him run on it; he already had large feet. Now she told him, "You had better look for still another power of something that runs on the water." He got the power of five bands of Yellow Flies running on the water. His mother said, "This is enough."

The old chief had not come for his wife and daughter, as he had intended to. The young man was now half grown, and was larger and stronger than his father. He gathered fifty canoes and men and weapons, took his mother, and went down to make war on his father for killing all his half-brothers. They landed on the side of the river opposite the house of the old chief, who sent his servants to ferry them over. He did not yet know who these people were. The young man told the men to remain with him, and all were glad to do so.

At night he walked over on the water to the other side, and got to the house just as his father rose up from one of the women. As his father went to the next woman, the young man lay down at the foot of the first woman's bed. All that night, as his father went from one woman to another, he followed him. The women all wondered how it was that he came a second time to their bed. They talked together and said, "It must be the young chief, our son, who has come."

The second night he [the young man] did the same. Next morning the chief saw tracks, measured them, and found that they were larger and broader than his own. He now suspected that he had a son, and told his people to get ready for war. The old chief brought fifty canoes with weapons and made an attack on the young man. He came with a Chinook Wind of great force, while the young chief brought the East Wind. The young man's canoes were urged forward by the East Wind, and the Chinook Wind drove onward those of the old man. When they met, there was a terrible crash; the canoes were broken and sunk. The young man drove the old chief all the way home, and a great many men were drowned.

Four days they fought this way, the East Wind driving the Chinook Wind. The fifth day the old man's strength began to fail him. The father and son did not fight in canoes, but on the water, hand to hand. As the old man's strength began to fail, he began to sink in the water; it would not hold him up any longer. He was overcome by his son and killed. The young chief liberated all his father's wives; only ten he took for himself. His mother went back to the Wasco people and lived with them. The young chief ruled his people well.

Wishram Canoe Song

The Battle of the Winds

WARM SPRINGS

THE BROTHERS of the Southwest Wind were always fighting with the brothers of the Northeast Wind and their sister, whose name was Tekstye.

Finally Tekstye's brothers were killed, and she ran away. But just as she reached the Columbia River, one of the Southwest Wind brothers caught up with her, and knocked her into the water.

Then he said to Tekstye, "From now on you will no longer be a person and go around freezing people. You can blow once in awhile, then I will come and overpower you. Rain will be your enemy too. You will blow and freeze everything, but then he and I will come; we will thaw out the ground, warm everything up, and make the earth green and beautiful again."

The Sun-Box

WARM SPRINGS

IN THE OLD TIME, the world was all dark. There was no sun out to give light; Eagle had it in a box, and he wouldn't let any of the other people come near it. He carried it in his claws.

Once in a while, however, he would open the lid of his box just a little, and then the world would become sunlit for a moment. Then all the others would say, "Oh, Eagle, give us sunlight all the time! We are tired of living in darkness!" But Eagle would just close his box and fly away.

But then one time, as he was lighting on a thorn tree, Eagle ran a thorn in his foot, and it hurt so badly that he yelled, "Oh brothers, come help me, I will die of pain and fever!"

The Crow, who was a doctor then, came and said, "All right, Eagle, I will heal you. I will pull the thorn out and cure the fever —but I can't work in darkness. I will have to open the sun-box, to see your wound clearly."

Eagle was suspicious, but the thorn was already festering, so he said, "All right, you can pull the lid back just a little—but if you profane my sun-box, I will call a curse on you!"

Right then Crow grabbed the box in his claws, flew up high with it, and, cawing in triumph, dropped it to smash on the rocks far below. The sunlight went free and filled the world.

Now, at night, when the night birds swoop and scream, the people say, "It's that Eagle, looking for his box of sunlight."

The Wishram Calendar

June—"Rotten Moon" [*fish spoil easily*]
July—"Advance-in-a-body Moon" [*salmon ascending the rivers*]
August—"Blackberry-patches Moon"
September—"Her-acorns Moon"
October—"Travel-in-canoes Moon"
November—"Snowy-mountains-in-the-morning Moon"
December—"Her-winter-houses Moon"
January—"Her-cold Moon"
February—"Shoulder Moon" [*shoulder-to-shoulder around the fire*]
March—"Long-days Moon"
April—"The-eighth Moon"
May—"The-ninth Moon"

The Girl on the Ice

WASCO

DURING A HARD WINTER among the people at Dog River . . . a great snowstorm set in. It snowed for seven months without stopping. The snow buried the tallest trees out of sight, and the people lived under the snow.

At the Cascades people were catching salmon; there was no snow there or at Winquatt. It snowed in just one place. The people under the snow did not know that it was summer everywhere else. The way they found it out was this:

A little bird came with a strawberry in its bill to an airhole they had made up out of the snow. They asked the bird what it was that had brought such a storm [to Dog River only], and the bird told them that one of the girls in the village had struck a bird. It was proved against the girl, and they offered her parents a great price for her. The parents would not sell her for a long time. At last the people bought her, and putting her on the ice as it floated down the river, pushed the ice into the middle of the stream. In that way they got rid of the snow. A few days later a Chinook wind came, bringing heat. The snow melted away at once, and things began to grow.

The girl floated on, day and night, down the river. Five years she floated. At the end of that time she came back up to the place where she had been put on the ice. When she returned, there was but a small piece of ice under her, just enough to hold her bones up. For she was almost gone, only skin and bones remained.

They took her into the village. She died. She was no longer accustomed to the smell of people, and died from the odor of them. After a while she came to life again, but it was a year before she could eat much.

Every summer after that she was nearly frozen to death, and went all bundled up; but in winter she was too warm, and would take off all her clothes, and go naked.

The Boy Who Went to Live with the Seals

WASCO

THE CHINOOK PEOPLE, who lived at the mouth of the Great River, moved some distance [upriver] to the east. At the end of the first day's journey they camped on the shore. One of the men had a little boy. After they had fixed the camp, he went with the boy to mend his canoe. After a while the boy disappeared. The father thought he had gone back to the camp. When he had finished with the canoe, he went to the camp and asked his wife where the boy was. She had not seen him. They went to the river, tracked him to the water, and all said that he must have drowned. Next morning the Chinook people moved on still farther up the river. The parents hunted everywhere for the child, but at last they too went on; they could not find the child.

Two or three years after this another party went up the river. On an island in the river there were a great many seals, and among them a boy. Word was sent to the parents of the lost boy. People went out and watched for the seals to come to land, so that they might see the boy. They watched until the seals came up on the island, one by one, and soon the island was covered. At last the boy came up out of the water and lay down by the seals. The people crept up, caught the boy, and took him to shore by force. He struggled to get away from them, and tried to return to the water. At first he refused to eat anything but raw salmon and other fish, and he would not talk; but by degrees he came to act like other human beings. Finally his parents got him back to his right mind, and he became very industrious. He carved bows and arrows and worked hard all the time.

As he grew up, he used to tell many stories of how he had lived down with the seals. He said that seals were just like people; they moved from place to place, camped at night, and would go as far as [Winquatt]. They moved around as the Indians did on land. The people had to watch him when he was in a canoe, for fear he would go back to the seals. The seals were always floating around when he was near. He always called them by name. His parents always covered his head when he was in a canoe. One day he threw the cover off, saw the seals, called them by name, said, "I am going!" and jumped into the water. He came to the surface far out, and cried to his mother and father, who were in the canoe, "I have a home down in the water. I will live there here-after."

A Boy and His Sister
Escape from an At'at'a'hlia

WASCO

Two CHILDREN went out to gather flint. . . . The little girl said, "Hurry and pick up flints; the *at'at'a'hlia* may come." And sure enough, she was right there. The moment the words were out of the girl's mouth, she looked behind, and there was the *at'at'a'hlia*. The brother and sister ran with all their might. The boy had one of the flints in his hand; he held it tight.

The old *at'at'a'hlia* caught them, put them in her great basket, and tied the mouth of it with buckskin strings. She was all spotted and striped, a terribly ugly looking creature, and very large. She lived on people, and was especially fond of eating children. She hurried along with the two children. The girl was larger than the boy; she sat on his foot in the basket. His foot was tender from an itch which he had on it; she hurt him greatly, and he said, "Sister, you hurt my foot where I have the itch."

The *at'at'a'hlia* said, "What is the matter? My children are burning up, surely." The girl heard what she said, and felt that she could frighten her. The girl repeated the *at'at'a'hlia*'s words: "Your children are burning up surely." The monster-woman was terrified at this, and said, "Somebody tells me my children are burning up." She called out their names on her fingers. The fifth time the girl called out very loud, "Your children are burning up!" The *at'at'a'hlia* put down the basket and ran towards home; but she came back, and hung the basket up on an oak tree, one of those near The Dalles on the Wishram side. The two children were hung up, and could not get out of the basket. The boy gave his sister the flint. She cut the strings of the cover, and they got out. They filled the basket with stones and dirt, and hung it up again; then they ran to the river.

The monster-woman hurried home, and found her children all safe, and said, "Oh, I thought you were burned to ashes! I have a nice pair of children out there for us," and she told how she had got them. Then she started back to bring the brother and sister. She pulled down the basket; it was heavy. She put it on her back, went home, and took it off. All her children got around it. She unstrapped it. Behold! there was nothing but stones and dirt. She knew they had got out and run away. She put the basket on her back and started after them.

The boy now made five rivers, for he was very powerful. The old woman jumped over the first river; she went over it so nicely that she said, "I must try that again." So she jumped over the first river five times. When she came to the second, she leaped over that too; high in the air she jumped this river five times. She jumped the third river five times; the fourth river the same way; also the fifth.

She saw the children now about a mile ahead. She sucked in her breath, and the children came in with it. They were almost in her jaws when she stopped, for she had to blow out again. That sent the children off about as far away as they were before. She drew in her breath again; they were nearly at her mouth, but she could not draw in another bit—she had to blow them away.

The children reached the Columbia River, jumped into a canoe, and pushed it way out. They told the crayfish, the turtles, and all the fish in the water, to eat her, and they told the big rocks to roll on her. When the old woman came to the river bank, she drew in her breath, and the canoe came almost to her hand; but then she had to blow out, and it went far out again. She tried many times to draw them in, but her breath was not long enough. Then she ran into the water and waded out part way. The fish began to eat her body all over, and the rocks came rolling down from the cliffs on to her. At last, barely alive, she waded out of the water, and the children escaped.

Arrow-Point Maker and Tobacco-Hunter

WASCO

THERE WAS an arrow-point maker on the right side of the Columbia, three miles below [Winquatt]. One day this man cut his finger with flint, so that it bled. He put his finger in his mouth, liked the taste of the blood, ate his finger off, then his hand, pulled the flesh from his arms, legs, and body, and ate it all. At last he had only a little bit of flesh left that was below his shoulders on his back, where he could not reach it. He was a skeleton now; nothing but his bones were left, only his heart hung in his body. He went to the next village and ate all the people. They could not kill him, nothing would penetrate his bones.

Now his wife, carrying a little son, escaped, went south, traveling over the grass, right on the tops of the blades of grass, so that he could not track her for a long time. But at last he found the tracks. The moment he found them, his wife knew it.

She traveled day and night in great fear. The husband gained on her, came nearer and nearer all the time. Far ahead of her was a blue mountain. She hurried on. When she reached the foot of the mountain, she saw a house, and went in. A very old man sat on one side making bows and arrows, and his daughter sat on the other side, making little tobacco-sacks.

The woman called him by a kinship-name, but the old man did not answer. The north wind, which had grown stronger, began to blow terribly, and almost carried the house away, threw down great trees. At last she begged so hard that the old man said, "Hide behind me." That moment the skeleton came in with a frightful wind, walked around the fire, and stamped on the old man's arrows, which broke into bits. The old man grabbed a long arrow-point and thrust it into the skeleton's heart. That instant the skeleton fell to the ground—a pile of bones. The wind stopped blowing when it fell. The old man said to the wife of the skeleton-man, "Come and throw these old bones outdoors."

There was plenty of tobacco growing on the hill above the old man's house. He made arrow-points all the time; and when his quiver was full, he would start out and return with it empty, but with tobacco in his hand. The old man and his daughter lived on smoke, neither ate anything; they lived on smoke from the kind of pipe that is straight. The old man always shot the tobacco; those whom he shot were the Tobacco people. When he brought home the tobacco, his daughter would put it into the little sacks, and they would smoke until all was gone. Then he would go off again on another hunt of these people.

The woman and child lived with the old man and his daughter for a long time. When the boy got old enough, he hunted squirrels for his mother. One day when the old man went out, the boy followed him. He saw the old man shoot up at a high rock bluff. The Tobacco people all lived in these high rocks. He crept close, sat behind the old man, took an arrow, and wished it to hit the tobacco. The arrow left his bow at the same instant that the old man's arrow left his bow, and five bunches of tobacco fell down.

The old man was delighted, and danced for joy; he had never shot so many in a whole day. "You are my son-in-law," said the old man, and went home. The daughter was glad that her father had so much tobacco. The old man said, "I don't know but that it is an [omen]." The boy laughed to himself. The old man said to his daughter, "This is your husband," and added, "The people of the future will be willing to give their daughters to a good hunter, and the girl must wait until the father and mother find such a man."

The old man now rested, and the young man hunted tobacco for him. He filled the house with tobacco. The old man was satisfied. Then the young man, his wife and mother, came to the Columbia River. When they came to the village where the young man's father had turned into a man-eater, they found only bones. The young man gathered up the bones, threw paint into the air five times, spoke five times to the sky, and the people all rose up as they were before the man-eater had devoured them.

When the mother was old, she had food given her every day by her daughter-in-law. She grew weak fast, and her son said, "It will be the duty of a daughter-in-law to care for her mother-in-law among the people to come." The mother said, "My daughter and I will go south, and we will be guardian spirits to medicine-women, and will give authority to women to smoke. When a women smokes, she will be a medicine-woman." The son said, "I will be a guardian spirit to help people. Those whom I help will be good hunters."

Two Brothers Become Sun and Moon

WASCO

A WOMAN and her two children lived below The Dalles. An old man lived some distance from them. One night the elder boy, who was about four years old, began to cry. The mother brought him everything there was in the house, but still he cried. At last she concluded to send him to the old man, whom she called Grandfather. She said to the boy, "Grandfather will tell you stories; go to him." The boy jumped up and ran off to the old man's house. The old man asked, "What do you want?" —"I want you to tell me stories." The boy lay down by the old man, who told this story: "Once there was a spring, and water flowed from it, and grass grew around it, *tawna, tawna*" [story, story].

"Oh," said the child, "that is very short!" —"No, that's a good story. It's long enough." The boy was angry and ran home. His mother said. "He must have told you a very short story!" —"He only said there was a spring, and water ran from it, and grass grew around it; then he said '*tawna, tawna*' right away!" The woman was provoked because the old man did not tell the boy a long story and keep him quiet. She went over and scolded him. He said, "I thought it was enough to quiet him, and that that was all that was wanted."

The boy cried again. The mother sent him again [to the old grandfather], and he told the same kind of story. The woman scolded him for not telling longer stories. This happened five times. Then the woman was very angry with the old man, and determined to move away, and she moved off some distance.

Now this boy's younger brother talked like an old man when he was not more than a year old. He would tell about many things which had been and would be. He had a very large stomach. When the elder boy punched it with his hand, it sounded strange, something like a bell. The elder boy was stupid, did nothing but cry and laugh. . . .

The father of the younger boy was Spider. The woman had left the father before the child was born, but he was constantly talking about his father. He would say, "My father is following us; he has gone up on a rock, and is looking for our fire; he has crossed the river." This made the woman very angry; she would shake the child, but right away again he would be talking about his father, Spider. He seemed to see him and to know all he was doing.

The elder boy dragged his little brother around all day in the sand and dirt, and nearly killed him. Next morning when the Spider Boy woke up, he said, "My father is going to kill himself because he cannot find us; he will heat rocks under a tree, then he will climb the tree and fall onto the rocks." "*Oali, oali,*" the child would sing, and so he went on day and night. He would rouse his mother in the night and say, "People over there are doing so and so," and he would sing "*Oali, oali,*" he would roll over against his brother, and the brother would kick him, but the child did not cry; he seldom cried. Again he would report, "I see a man hugging a woman over there." He looked everywhere, and saw everything that was going on in the world, and kept telling what he saw night and day. His mother and brother did not like him.

One day the mother told the elder brother to take the younger one outdoors and step on his stomach—"Then all of that big stomach will go off, and he will be like you." The boy took the child out, put him on his back, and stamped on his stomach. Immediately snakes, frogs, lizards, and everything of reptile kind came out of the boy and ran off. Then he got up and went into the house with his brother, and stopped singing "*Oali, oali,*" he never sang it again.

The mother told the boys to make bows and arrows, saying, "I'll give you five quivers, and you can fill them. I'll trim robes for you with shells; then I'll tell you what to do." The boys made the arrows. She trimmed beautiful robes for them, then said, "I want you to go out and kill Sun." In those days Sun never moved out of his tracks, always stood directly overhead, and no living thing could travel far and live, so great was the heat.

The mother said, "When you kill Sun, you can stay up there. One of you can be Sun, the other Moon." The boys were delighted. They started off and traveled south. When they got a little east of where Prineville [tak′si] now is, they wrestled with each other. Spider Boy was thrown, and at that spot a great many camas-roots came up. At every village they came to, they told the people where they were going; and all were glad, for all were tired of Sun and his terrible heat. Finally the boys turned and traveled east, until they were nearly overcome by the heat.

At last they came to a place from which, looking to the left, they could see a great ball of shining fire; they looked to the right, and there was a second ball of shining fire. They had gone up into the air, and had come to Moon's house; it was on the left side of Sun's house, not far away. Old Moon and his daughter lived there. Moon's daughter was very lame. She waited on the boys, brought them fruit of all kinds, huckleberries, and other things. The boys were amused as they saw her walk.

Moon's house was full of light, bright and dazzling. The boys ate, and then went out and came as near Sun's house as they could. It was so bright and hot that they couldn't get very close. They took their arrows and began to shoot at old Sun, who sat in his house. With their last arrow they killed the old man. Immediately there was no more strong light. They pulled out their arrows and said, "We cannot both be Sun, we must kill Moon, too." So they went back and killed Moon. Then they argued over which one should be Sun. The elder boy said, "I will be Sun. I am older than you are. You can be Moon and take his daughter." The younger brother agreed to this.

Now the people below were very anxious to know where the boys were, who had traveled to the east. As the heat grew less and less, they said, "It must be that the boys have done as they said."

Their mother knew that they had accomplished all they had wished for. Now they went through the sky together, and Moon followed Sun.

Coyote and Eagle Go to the Land of the Dead

WISHRAM

COYOTE HAD a wife and two children, and so had Eagle. Both families lived together. Eagle's wife and children died, and a few days later Coyote experienced the same misfortune. As Coyote wept, Eagle said, "Do not mourn: that will not bring your wife back. Make ready your moccasins, and we will go somewhere." So the two prepared for a long journey, and set out westward.

After four days they were close to the ocean; on the one side of a body of water they saw houses. Coyote called across, "Come with a boat!" —"Never mind; stop calling," said Eagle. He produced an elderberry stalk, made a flute, put the end into the water, and whistled. Soon they saw two persons come out of a house, walk to the water's edge, and enter a canoe. Said Eagle, "Do not look at those people when they land." The boat drew near, but a few yards from the shore it stopped, and Eagle told Coyote to close his eyes. He then took Coyote by the arm and leaped to the boat. The two persons paddled back, and when they stopped a short distance from the other side, Eagle again cautioned Coyote to close his eyes, and then leaped ashore with him.

They went to the village, where there were many houses, but no people were in sight. Everything was still as death. There was a very large underground house, into which they went. In it was an old woman [Frog] sitting with her face to the wall, and lying on the floor on the other side of the room was the moon. They sat down near the wall.

"Coyote," whispered Eagle, "watch that woman and see what she does when the sun goes down!" Just before the sun set they heard a voice outside calling, "Get up! Hurry! The sun is going down, and it will soon be night. Hurry! Hurry!" Coyote and Eagle still sat in a corner of the chamber watching the old woman.

People began to enter, many hundreds of them, men, women, and children. Coyote, as he watched, saw Eagle's wife and two daughters among them, and soon afterward his own family. When the room was filled, Nikshia'mchash, the old woman, cried, "Are all in?" Then she turned about, and from a squatting posture she jumped forward, then again and again, five times in all, until she alighted in a small pit beside the moon. This she raised and swallowed, and at once it was pitch dark. The people wandered about, hither and thither, crowding and jostling, unable to see. About daylight a voice from outside cried, "Nikshia'mchash, all get through!" The old woman then disgorged the moon, and laid it back in its place on the floor; all the people filed out, and the woman, Eagle, and Coyote were once more alone.

"Now, Coyote," said Eagle, "could you do that?" —"Yes, I can do that," he said. They went out, and Coyote at Eagle's direction made a box of boards, as large as he could carry, and put into it leaves from every kind of tree and blades from every kind of grass. "Well," said Eagle, "if you are sure you remember just how she did this, let us go in and kill her."

So they entered the house and killed her, and buried the body. Her dress they took off and put on Coyote, so that he looked just like her, and he sat down in her place. Eagle then told him to practice what he had seen, by turning around and jumping as the old woman had done. So Coyote turned about and jumped five times, but the last leap was a little short, yet he managed to slide into the hole. He put the moon into his mouth, but, try as he would, a thin edge still showed, and he covered it with his hands. Then he laid the moon back in its place and resumed his seat by the wall, waiting for sunset and the voice of the chief outside.

The day passed, the voice called, and the people entered. Coyote turned about and began to jump. Some [of the people] thought there was something strange about the manner of jumping, but others said it was really the old woman. When he came to the last jump and slipped into the pit, many cried out that this was not the old woman, but Coyote quickly lifted the moon and put it in his mouth, covering the edge with his hands.

When it was completely dark, Eagle placed the box in the doorway. Throughout the long night Coyote retained the moon in his mouth, until he was almost choking, but at last the voice of the chief was heard from the outside, and the dead began to file out. Everyone walked into the box, and Eagle quickly threw the cover over and tied it. The sound was like that of a great swarm of flies.

"Now, my brother, we are through," said Eagle. Coyote removed the dress and laid it down beside the moon, and Eagle threw the moon into the sky, where it remained. The two entered the canoe with the box, and paddled toward the east.

When they landed, Eagle carried the box. Near the end of the third night Coyote heard somebody talking; there seemed to be many voices. He awakened his companion, and said, "There are many people coming." —"Do not worry," said Eagle; "it is all right." The following night Coyote heard the talking again, and, looking about, he discovered that the voices came from the box which Eagle had been carrying. He placed his ear against it, and after a while distinguished the voice of his wife. He smiled, and broke into laughter, but he said nothing to Eagle.

At the end of the fifth night and the beginning of their last day of traveling, Coyote said to his friend, "I will carry the box now; you have carried it a long way." —"No," replied Eagle, "I will take it; I am strong." —"Let me carry it," insisted Coyote; "suppose we come to where people live, and they should see the chief carrying the load. How would that look?" Still Eagle retained his hold on the box, but as they went along Coyote kept begging, and about noon, wearying of the subject, Eagle gave him the box.

So Coyote had the load, and every time he heard the voice of his wife he would laugh. After a while he contrived to fall behind, and when Eagle was out of sight around a hill he began to open the box, in order to release his wife. But no sooner was the cover lifted than it was thrown back violently, and the dead people rushed out into the air with such force that Coyote was thrown to the ground. They quickly disappeared in the west. Eagle saw the cloud of dead people rising in the air, and came hurrying back. He found one man left there, a cripple who had been unable to rise; he threw him into the air, and the dead man floated away swiftly.

"You see what you have done, with your curiosity and haste!" said Eagle. "If we had brought these dead all the way back, people would not die forever, but only for a season, like these plants, whose leaves we have brought. Hereafter trees and grasses will die only in the winter, but in the spring will be green again. So it would have been with the people." —"Let us go back and catch them again," proposed Coyote; but Eagle objected: "They will not go to the same place, and we would not know how to find them; they will be where the moon is, up in the sky."

Song for Gathering Bones for Burial

WISHRAM

The "Stick" Indians

WARM SPRINGS

WHEN AN INDIAN is traveling up in the mountains in a lonely place and hears a certain bird singing, he knows it is probably a "stick" Indian. The stick Indians are spirits who live in high gloomy places, like Grizzly Flats [south of Mt. Jefferson] and upper Shitike Creek [southwest of Warm Springs Agency], and their favorite trick is to sing like a bird in the evening, when birds don't sing. If you follow the song, the stick Indian will lead you deeper and deeper into the woods—and you just won't come out, maybe you will lose your mind in there. Some Indians when they're out huckleberry-picking or hunting scatter matches all around their camp at night—they say the stick Indians like matches best of all, living in the dark.

Part Three

THE WILLAMETTE VALLEY

Kalapuya groups

Molala

Clackamas Chinook

Clackamas hazel root basket *Courtesy of Thomas Burke Memorial Washington State Museum, cat. #2–11840*

THE INDIANS *who occupied the Willamette Valley at the turn of the nineteenth century were living at the bullseye of the historical target that was "Oregon."* [1] *For the strategic country around the mouth of the Willamette River and the rich bottom land and prairies south to the head of the valley constituted the promised land at the end of the Oregon Trail, especially between 1845 and 1855: and as a consequence the Indians who lived here were the first in the Northwest to be displaced from their native grounds by settlers bent on farming.*

In fairness to those settlers, it should be pointed out that by the time they arrived in the valley in numbers, a series of epidemics, apparently introduced by earlier white traders and trappers in the

"Chinook Canoe-Burial" (from Kinietz, *John Mix Stanley and His Indian Paintings*) Courtesy of University of Michigan Press

1830s, had already ravaged the valley tribes and left large areas essentially unpopulated—an instance of disease serving as one of history's shock troops.[2] Would the "Oregon Country" have seemed so magnetic in the Midwest and the East in the 1840s, one wonders, if it had been still densely populated by natives?

The valley tribes represented here include the Clackamas Chinook, who occupied country around Portland and Oregon City, and in language and general culture were closely related to tribes of the Middle Columbia, represented in Part II. Melville Jacobs' 1929 discovery of a surviving Clackamas story-teller, Mrs. Victoria Howard, and their subsequent collaborations, may well —as Dell Hymes has said—strike future generations as the most important Northwest literary event of that time.[3] Certainly no Western Indian literature has been more fully and lucidly transcribed and interpreted as literature.

Kalapuya Indian (from Wilkes, *U.S. Exploring Expedition*)
Courtesy of Photography Collection, Suzzallo Library, University of Washington

Victoria Howard,
Clackamas storyteller

South of the Great Falls of the Willamette at Oregon City
were several groups of the Kalapuya Indians, speaking a dis-
tinctive language of their own. They were the Atfalati, around
the Tualatin Plains; the Mary's River Kalapuya, around Corvallis;
the Santiam Kalapuya, an upland people who lived on the two
branches of the Santiam River; and the Kalapuya proper, who
seem to have lived around present-day Eugene. A third valley
group were the Molalas, latecomers to the region. It is now be-
lieved that before 1820 Tenino Indians of the lower Deschutes
River drove the Molalas from their original homeland around
Tygh Valley and Sherar's Bridge on the Deschutes. The Molalas
crossed over the Cascades and settled down in the rugged country
southwest of Mt. Hood, in Clackamas County.[4] *The Molala*
language, now dead, was clearly Sahaptian, and most closely
related to the Cayuse.

The Indians of the valley clearly prized their homeland for the same reasons that their white successors did—for its generally temperate climate, navigable rivers, abundant fish and game, and fertile soil. Not that the Indians farmed, of course—the Kalapuya prophecy against plowing (p. 104) shows how alien the idea of tillage was to them—but their myths vividly reveal an appreciation of the prevailing natural bounty: camas and other staple roots and tubers, berries of all kinds, wild tobacco, grass for animals.

Theirs must have been an agreeable, well-provided-for, generally easy-going, interior *way of life. After the white settlement of the Valley was completed and the Indians were re-located on the Siletz and Grand Ronde reservations, they apparently had considerable freedom coming and going to favorite places—berry patches, hunting and fishing sites, and the like—and were reasonably well treated by the settlers.[5] The editor's grandfather, the late J. R. Mendenhall, who grew up in the 1880s near Willamina, used to tell of periodic visits at the family farm from a head-man named "Yamhill Joe" and his entourage en route to or from Grand Ronde.*

Still, in official dealings—governmental and religious—there is no denying that these valley Indians were ungenerously treated, and some historical and ethnographical texts have been included in this section to suggest how they expressed their anger and in some instances their contempt. In particular some of the early missionaries seem to have earned a fierce resentment; why, is perhaps indicated in this arch pronouncement on Clackamas and Kalapuya mythology by the Reverend Samuel Parker, who gospelized in Oregon in the late 1830s. "I am far from believing the many long and strange traditions with which we are often entertained. It is more than probable, that they are in most *instances the gratuitous offerings of designing and artful traders and hunters to that curiosity which is ever awake and attentive to subjects of this description. The Indians themselves would often be as much surprised at the rehearsal of their traditions, as those are, for whose amusement they are fabricated."[6]*

Fortified with hindsight, one can only wince at such lost opportunities—and appreciate all the more the efforts of men like Gatschet, Franchtenberg, and Jacobs—all non-Oregonians—to record and understand "the many long and strange traditions" which the Reverend Mr. Parker and too many of his successors in Oregon found unbelievable or inconsequential.

Coyote Builds Willamette Falls and the Magic Fish Trap

CLACKAMAS CHINOOK

COYOTE CAME to that place [around Oregon City] and found the people there very hungry. The river was full of salmon, but they had no way to spear them in the deep water. Coyote decided he would build a big waterfall, so that the salmon would come to the surface for spearing. Then he would build a fish trap there too.

First he tried at the mouth of Pudding River, but it was no good, and all he made was the gravel-bar there. So he went on down the river to Rock Island, and it was better, but after making the rapids there he gave up again and went farther down still. Where the Willamette Falls are now he found just the right place, and he made the Falls high and wide. All the Indians came and began to fish.

Now Coyote made his magic fish trap. He made it so it would speak, and say *Noseepsk!* when it was full. Because he was pretty hungry, Coyote decided to try it first himself. He set the trap by the Falls, and then ran back up the shore to prepare to make a cooking-fire. But he had only begun when the trap called out, "*Noseepsk!*" He hurried back; indeed the trap was full of salmon. Running back with them, he started his fire again, but again the fish trap cried "*Noseepsk! Noseepsk!*" He went again and found the trap full of salmon. Again he ran to the shore with them; again he had hardly gotten to his fire when the trap called out, "*Noseepsk! Noseepsk!*" It happened again, and again; the fifth time Coyote became angry and said to the trap, "What, can't you wait with your fish-catching until I've built a fire?" The trap was very offended by Coyote's impatience, and stopped working right then. So after that the people had to spear their salmon as best they could.

The Skookum's Tongue

CLACKAMAS CHINOOK

THE INDIANS living by the Falls became very rich anyway, and
built a large village on the west side of the river. Then a terrible
skookum who lived on the Tualatin River began to raid the
village. His den was about two miles away, but his tongue was
so long that he just stuck it out and caught the people with it
at will.

Before long, the village was nearly empty. When Coyote
returned there, he was very angry to see what the skookum was
doing. So he went to the monster's den and said to him, "You
wicked skookum; long enough have you been eating these people." And with one axe-stroke he chopped off the skookum's
tongue, and buried it under the rocks on the west side of the
Falls. The people returned to their village, and thrived again.

When the white men cut their canal around the Falls on the
west side, they merely exposed the channel made by Coyote for
the skookum's tongue.

The Skookum and the Wonderful Boy

CLACKAMAS CHINOOK

ON THE EAST SIDE of the Falls at about the site of Oregon City,
there was another large fishing village. Its chief was a great man
—but another skookum came out of the mountains to the east
and killed the chief and his whole village, except for the chief's
wife and their unborn son.

After the son's birth, the woman, wanting him to be strong,
took him to all the streams and lakes with spirit powers, and
bathed him in each one. This made him very strong, and he grew
up very fast. When the boy returned to the village beside the
Falls and entered his father's deserted lodge, he began to ask his
mother about the articles he saw there. She said, "This is the spear
with which your father used to catch the salmon; and this is the
axe with which he used to kill his enemies or chop wood; and
this is the bow with which he used to shoot arrows."

The boy took the axe and went out into the woods. Almost immediately he was met by the skookum. Driving his axe into a gnarly log so as to make a big crack in it, the boy said to the monster, "If you're so strong, hold this crack open for me while I take another cut." When the stupid skookum put his fingers in the crack, the boy pulled his axe, and the monster was caught fast. So the boy killed him easily.

Then the boy took his father's bow and shot an arrow into the sky. At the same time he called out, "As this arrow falls let those who died come to life," and so it happened. Just as the arrow fell back to earth, the old chief and all his people came up the river in their canoes. They landed at the rocks and began fishing as if nothing had happened. The boy was very happy and went down to meet his father, whom he had never seen before, but the old chief asked him, "Who are you? I am chief here!" and then hit him.

This made the boy very unhappy, and he climbed back up to the rocks above the Falls, and cried so much that his tears wore two big holes in the rock, which are there today. He finally decided that he could not help his people any more as a man, so he changed himself into a fish. But the noise of the river by the Falls bothered him, and he swam on up to the mouth of the Tualatin. But he couldn't rest there either, so he went on up the Willamette to the Molalla, and the Pudding River, and the Yamhill, still in search of quiet, until finally he reached the Santiam. Here he went to sleep in a quiet pool, and was discovered by Coyote, who turned him into a rock in the shape of a salmon.

This is why no salmon that climbs the Falls at Oregon City ever turns into these rivers to spawn, but keeps going upstream until it reaches the Santiam. Then when it sees the rock, it circles once in salute and goes on up the clear Santiam to spawn.

Badger and Coyote Were Neighbors

CLACKAMAS CHINOOK

Coyote and his five children lived there, four males, one female. Badger was a neighbor there, he had five children, all males. Each day they (all ten children) would go here and there. They came back in the evening. And the next day they would go out again. Now that is the way they were doing. They would go all over, they traveled about.

Now they reached a village, they stayed up above there, they looked down below at it, they saw where they (the villagers) were playing ball. And as they stayed there and watched, the people (of the village beneath) saw them now. They went to the place where they played ball. Now they (the villagers) played. When they threw the ball it was just like the sun. Now they stayed (above) there, they watched them playing. Sometimes it (the ball) would drop close by the ten children. Now the villagers quit (playing). Then they (the ten children) went back home, they went to their houses.

The next day then they did not go anywhere. All day long they chatted about that ball (and schemed about stealing it). They discussed it. Now their father Badger heard them. He said to his sons, "What is it that you are discussing?" So they told their father. "Yes," they said to him, "we got to a village, and they were playing ball. When the ball went it was just like the sun. We thought that we would go get it." Now then he said to his children, "What do you think (about talking this over with Coyote, too)?" So then they said to Coyote, "What do you think?" He said, "My children should be the first ones (to run with the ball), if they bring the ball." Badger said, "No. My children should be the first ones to do it." Coyote said, "No. My children have long bodies, their legs are long. They can run (faster than your children). Your children have short legs." So then Badger replied to him (Coyote), "Very well then."

Now the next day they got ready, and they went. They reached there. At that place one of them (the oldest son of Coyote) went immediately to the spot where the ball might drop. He covered (buried) himself at that place on the playing field. Then another (the next eldest son) buried himself further on, and another one (the third in age) still farther away. All four (sons of Coyote) covered themselves (with soil on the field). The last one farther on at the end (was) their younger sister. Now the (five) children of Badger merely remained (on the hill above the field), they watched.

Soon afterwards then the people (of that village) came there, they came to play ball. Now they threw the ball to where it fell close by him (Coyote's eldest son). He seized it. They looked for it, they said . . . , "Coyote's son is hiding it!" He let it go, and they took it, and they played more. Now it dropped close by him there once again. So then he took it, and he ran. The people turned and looked, they saw him running, he was taking the ball. Now they ran in pursuit, they got close to him, he got close to his younger brother (the second in age), he threw the ball to him. He said, "We are dying (going to be killed) because of the ball. Give a large chunk of it to our father." (His pursuers now caught up to him, and killed him.) Then the other (the second) one took it, and he ran too. The people pursued him, he got close to his younger brother (Coyote's third son). Now they seized him (the second son), and he threw the ball to his younger brother. So they killed all four of them. Now only their younger sister held the ball, she ran, she ran and ran, she left them quite a distance behind (because she was the fastest runner of all). She got close to the Badgers. Now as they seized her she threw the ball to them (the five Badger children), she said to them, "Give the biggest portion to our father (to Coyote). We have died because of the ball."

The Badgers took the ball. He (the first and oldest Badger child) dropped it when he picked it up. Another (the next to oldest) took it, he also dropped it when he picked it up. They (the pursuers) got to there, and stood there (watching the Badger children fumbling the ball). They said, they told them, "So those are the ones that would be taking away the ball!" They laughed at them. . . . They said, "Let it be a little later before we kill them!" Soon now they (the Badgers) kicked at the ground, and wind blew and dust and darkness stood there. Dust covered (everything), and the wind blew. Now the Badgers ran, they ran away with the ball. And those people pursued them. They got tired, they got thirsty (from dust and wind), they turned back to their home.

On the other hand those others (the Badgers) lay down (from exhaustion) right there when they had gotten close (to their home). And there they sat (and rested). Now they hallooed, they said to their father, "Badger! We left your children far back there!" Now they hallooed again, they went and told Coyote, "Back yonder we left your children." That is the way they did to them (they first deceived Badger and Coyote). Now Badger went outside, he said to his children, "Now really why did you do like that? You have been teasing and paining him (Coyote)."

Then they (the Badger children) went downhill (and entered the village), it was only Badger's children (who returned). They brought the ball with them.

Now Coyote tried in vain to drown himself. He did not die. Then he built a fire, he made a big fire, he leaped into it there. He did not burn, he did not die. He took a rope, he tied it, he tied it on his throat, he pulled himself up, once more he did not die. He took a knife, he cut his throat, (again) he did not die. He did every sort of thing that he intended for killing himself. He gave up. I do not know how many days he was doing like that. . . . Now he quit it, and he merely wept all the day long. (After a while) he gave that up (too).

Then Badger said to his children, "He has quit (mourning) now. So then cut up the ball for him. Give him half." And they did that for him, they gave him half. He took it, and he went here and there at the place where his children used to play. There he now mashed (into many pieces) that ball, at the place where they used to play. That was where he took it, he mashed it up, the ball was entirely gone (now).

Then they continued to live there, and Coyote was all alone. Now he went to work, he made a big loose pack basket. Then it was getting to be springtime, and when the leaves were coming out, now he got ready, and he went to the place where they had killed his children. He got to the (grave of the) first one (his eldest son). He picked ferns, he lined his pack basket with them. He got to the place where they had killed the first of his sons, he collected his bones, he put them into it (the basket), he laid them in it neatly. Then he got more ferns, he picked the leaves, he covered (the bones of) his son. Now he went a little farther, and he again got to bones (of his second son). Then he also put them into the basket, and that is the way he did again. He collected the bones of all five of his children.

Now he went on, he proceeded very slowly, he went only a short distance. Then he camped overnight. The next day he proceeded again, also very slowly like that. On the third day, then he heard them (talking to one another in the basket). They said, "You are lying upon me. Move a little." Then he went along all the more slowly. Now he kept going, he went just a short distance, and then he picked more leaves, he covered it all (with utmost care and constant replenishing with fresh leaves). And that is the way he did as he went along.

She (perhaps a centipede) would run across his path, she

would say to him, "Sniff sniff sniff! . . . Coyote is taking dead persons along!" He paid no heed to her. Now she ran repeatedly and all the more in front of him, again she would speak like that to him, "Sniff! Coyote is carrying dead persons along!" He laid his basket down very very slowly . . . , he got a stick, he ran after her. I do not know where she went and hid.

Then he packed his carrying basket on his back again, and now he went very very slowly, and he heard his children. Now they were chatting, they were saying, "Move around slowly and carefully! We are making our father tired." Then he was glad, and he went along even more slowly and cautiously. (He walked so very slowly that) he saw his (previous night's) campfire, and then he again camped overnight.

He went right on the next morning, and then that thing (the bug), ran back and forth across his path right there by his feet. Now he became angry. He placed his basket down, and again he chased it. I do not know where it hid.

On the fifth day then he heard them laughing. So he went along even more painstakingly. Now that thing went still more back and forth in front of him by his feet. He forgot . . . , he (much too abruptly) loosened and let go his pack basket. "Oh oh oh," his children sounded (and at once died from the shock of the sudden movement of the basket). All done, he finished, and he again put back his basket on himself. When he went along now he did not hear them talking at all. He went along then. They were dead now when he uncovered his basket. Only bones were inside it. He reached his house. The following day he buried them. He finished. . . . He wept for five days.

Then he said, "Indeed I myself did like that (and lost my children because of my doing). The people (who will populate this country) are coming and are close by now. Only in that one manner shall it be, when persons die. In that one way had I brought my children back, then the people would be like that (in later eras). When they died in summertime, wintertime, or toward springtime, after the leaves (came on the trees), they (all the dead) would have come back to life, and such persons would have revived on the fifth day (following a ritual like the one I attempted). But now his (any mourner's) sorrow departs from him after ten days (of formal mourning). Then he can go to anywhere where something (entertaining) is happening or they are gambling, and he may (then shed his mourning and) watch it."

Seal and Her Younger Brother Lived There

CLACKAMAS CHINOOK

They lived there, Seal, her daughter, her younger brother.
  I do not know when, now a woman got to Seal's younger
    brother.

They lived there,
  they would "go outside" in the evening.

  The girl would say, she would tell her mother:
    "Mother! something is different about my uncle's wife.
      It sounds like a man when she 'goes out.' "

  "Shush! your uncle's wife!"

A long long time they lived there like that,
  in the evening they would "go out."

  Now she would tell her:
    "Mother! something is different about my uncle's wife.
      When she 'goes out' it sounds like a man."

  "Shush!"

Her uncle and his wife would "lie together" in bed.
  Some time afterwards the two of them "lay" close to the fire,
    they "lay" close beside each other.

I do not know when at night, something came onto her face.
  She shook her mother,
    she told her:
      "Mother! something came onto my face."

  "Hmmmm. Shush. Your uncle, those two are 'going.' "

Some time afterwards now again she heard something dripping
    down.
  She told her:

"Mother! something is going t'u'qt'u'q.
  I hear something."

"Shush. Your uncle, those two are 'going.' "

The girl got up,
  she fixed the fire,
    she lit pitch,
      she looked where the two were lying:
        Oh! Oh! blood!

She raised her light to it, thus.
  In his bed her uncle's neck [is] cut, he is dead.
    She screamed.

She told her mother:
  "I told you something was dripping.
    You told me, shush, they are 'going.'
      I had told you something was different about my uncle's
        wife.
          When she would 'go out,' she would urinate with a
            sound like a man.
          You would tell me, shush!"
            She wept.

Seal said:
  "Younger brother! My younger brother!
    They are valuable standing there [houseposts].
      My younger brother!"
        She kept saying that.
But the girl herself wept.

She said:
  "I tried in vain to tell you,
    my uncle's wife would urinate with a sound like a man, not
      like a woman.
        You told me, shush!
          Oh oh my uncle! Oh my uncle!"
            The girl wept.

Now then I remember only that.

She Deceived Herself with Milt

CLACKAMAS CHINOOK

PEOPLE WERE living there. They were continually smoke-drying salmon and various things. There was one widow. They (fishermen) would come, they would come ashore there. Now she would be going about at that place. Right after they threw them (their catch of fish) ashore, she would get one or two to take with her. She smoke-dried them. Her house was full of food. In the winter they (other villagers) would get hungry, and then they would buy various things from her. That is how she had many valuables.

I do not know how long a time, and then she got one (large and fat) salmon, she butchered it well, she took out its milt. She thought, "Dear oh dear. It is nice. I shall not eat it." She wished, "Oh that you become a person." I do not know where she put it.

I do not know how long a time afterward, and then some person was sleeping beside her. She thought, "Oh my! I wonder where the person came from to me." She lay there for a while. Then she thought, "Perhaps he is not from here. Perhaps the person got to here from a long distance away." Presently as she was thinking about it, he then said to her, "What is your heart making you know? . . . You yourself said to me, 'I wish that you would become a person.'" She reflected. "Oh yes," she thought. "It just has to be that milt." She looked at him in the morning. "Goodness. A fine-looking man, he is light of skin." Now they remained there, I don't know how long a time they lived there.

Then some other woman began to steal him away from her. After quite some time then she (the other woman) took him away from her. She [the widow] continued to live there. When the other woman saw her, she would say, she would tell him, "Oh dear me. Your poor poor (former) wife! Look at her!" He would reply to her, "Leave her alone!" After quite some time then she laughed at her all the more. They (villagers) said to her (the deserted wife), "Dear oh dear. Why does your co-wife laugh at and mock you all the time?" She said, "Oh let it be!"

Now time after time when they (the married couple) were sitting there, she (the deserted wife) passed by them, she (the second wife) nudged her husband, she said to him, "Look at your (former) wife! Oh dear! the poor poor woman." He replied to her, "Leave her alone!" She laughed at her all the more. She (the deserted first wife) went along, she went back to them . . . and now she danced in front of them. She said (in the words of her song),

> "She deceived herself with milt,
> She deceived herself with milt."

The second wife nudged him. . . . "Oh dear! Oh dear! That poor poor wife of yours!" He continued to say, "Do leave her alone." The fifth time (when she had sung the song five times), she extended her spirit-power regalia toward the couple. The woman (the second wife) turned and looked, only milt lay beside her. She arose, she went away. That first woman took the milt, she threw it at her (the second wife). She said to her, "You are leaving your husband!" But that other woman went away. She pursued her. Again she took the milt, she threw it at the second wife, (saying) "This thing here is your husband!" She (the second wife) went back home, she reached her house, and there she remained, she stayed there. And that is what she continued to do.

Now I recall only that much of it.

[The everyday uses of such stories among the Indians is amusingly illustrated by this ethnographic footnote to the Milt narrative, as recorded by Melville Jacobs from Mrs. Victoria Howard:]

Our house at Grand Ronde Reservation was close to the road. When some white person would pass by, my mother-in-law would look at that white person, and she would laugh. She would say, "Dear oh dear it is a light one! Possibly it is Milt!" And then she would sing. This is what she would say in the words of the song,

> "Milt! She changed him into a man!"

A Girls' Game

CLACKAMAS CHINOOK

MY MOTHER told me how they used to play a game long ago. They would go get flowers, they would break off just the flowers, and they would tie them to a long rope. Then of as many of them as were there, one would stand a little apart. One of them hung the flowers on her, they placed them all over her, until her body was just covered with flowers. Then they danced.

One of these young girls would go to where that one was standing, and the one who was standing there would say, "Well, come! I see you are playing. What is the matter with your nose? it does not seem to be right. What is the matter with your eyes? one side is small. What is the matter with your head? it's crooked. What is the matter with your mouth? it is sort of twisted. Now you laugh! look at me! Don't make your eyes crooked." Until at last if the young woman would laugh at the one who did the talking, when she had not yet reached her, then she might laugh. "Now I have beaten you. Come now!"

The Kalapuya Way

SANTIAM KALAPUYA

THE GOOD OLD DAYS

This countryside is not good now. Long, long ago it was good country (had better hunting and food gathering). They were all Indians who lived in this countryside. Everything was good. No one labored (at hard labor for wages). Only a man went hunting, he hunted all the time. Women always used to dig camas, and they gathered tarweed seeds. Such things were all we ate. They gathered acorns, they picked hazelnuts, they picked berries, they dried blackberries.

PEOPLE SPOKE TO THE NEW MOON

Long ago when the people saw the (new) moon then they spoke to the moon. They said to it, "We are still (alive) here yet. We see you now that you have come out again, (and) we are still (alive) here yet."

MOSQUITO AND THUNDER

Mosquito was always telling it to thunder when the thunder said to him, "Where have you gotten this blood?" Then Mosquito would say, "Oh, I get it from this white fir tree. This is where I get this blood. There is a lot of blood in this white fir tree." [Hence Thunder, always "bloodthirsty," tends to strike white fir trees.]

A SHAMAN DREAMED THE EARTH BECAME BLACK LIKE PLOUGHED LAND

Long ago the people used to say that one great shaman in his dream had seen all the land black in his dream. That is what he told the people. "This earth was all black (in my dream)." He saw it in a dream at night. Just what that was likely to be he did not know. And then (later on) the rest of the people saw the whites plow up the ground. Now then they said, "That must have been what it was that the shaman saw long ago in his sleep."

MAKING BOWS AND ARROWS

Long long ago when the people made their bows they made them of yew wood. They made their bows of that. They split it, they scraped it with mussel shells, and with this sharp rock. That is the way they did it when they made their bows. They were good bows. Then when they were finished (scraping) they would warm it, and then they would rub on it grease which they had heated. Now when it became dry the bow would always be stout (strong), they say. That is the way they did. It was a good bow which they made. But as for these children's bows, they did not grease them. They just made them (without greasing them). When they were finished (making a bow) in the very same way they would make their arrows. When they were finished (making them), they would heat them, and then they would straighten them (still warm, using hands and teeth). They say that that is the way they used to do it when they made their arrows. That is how those old people spoke of it.

BLIND PEOPLE MADE ARROW POINTS

The people used to say long ago that the blind people made the arrow points. A blind person could do nothing, he could only make arrow points. He would do that all the time. That is what they used to say.

They always used to say, "His heart is not dead. Only his body has died. But on the other hand his heart will go across the ocean when he has become a dead person." They used to say it that way. And they would always say when they saw a flame (a light) burn, as it went along high above in the air in the night time, they would say, "Maybe someone now is pretty near death. It is the heart that is going along there in the night." Whatever they saw aflame going along up in the air, that is how they would always comment.

DREAMS ABOUT THE DEAD PEOPLE

Long ago my mother always said, "All of the people here once, when they (we) died, they (we) went across the ocean, to where all the dead people lived. When I die, all those people (relatives) of mine who have died (before me) I will see when I reach there (the land of the dead people). All those dead people are living there." That is how she always spoke. Then sometime later on when she was near death, she said, "Now maybe I am pretty nearly dead. Always a long time ago when I slept I would see my mother and my father in my dream. In my heart I knew that they had died long before. Always I would say (that) in my heart (I said it to myself) when I saw them (in my dream). However when I see them now in my sleep I do not say in my heart that they have died (long before). But it is (only) when my heart awakens (when I wake up) that I now know (realize) that they have died. And so that is how it always is with my sleep now. I do not (even) know that they are dead when I see them at night. Now I myself am perhaps nearly gone on to the land of the dead people to die."

The Four Creations

ATFALATI KALAPUYA

LONG AGO (in the myth age) there were people. There were many people, they filled this (Tualatin) country. There were many people everywhere. There was nothing of sickness. All the children who were made (born) became big. So then they accumulated (multiplied) for a long time. Now then five persons who were hunters went away, one dog accompanied them. Now they slept five times (five nights). When it became dark the dog left (them). Then one small girl (back at home) spoke to the dog, "How many (deer) have been killed (by the hunters)?" The dog did not speak. Again she spoke like this to it, "How many were killed?" She spoke to it five times in that manner, and then the dog spoke thus, "Five (deer) have been killed."

And now the earth turned over. All the people (of the first myth age) changed into stars (and they are still the stars today). Then there were no persons on the earth. Only the girl and the dog lived there. He made her his wife. Then she became pregnant, she gave birth to one dog and one human (child). And then again she became pregnant, she gave birth to one human (child and) one dog. From there on (from that time on) the people were made many (they multiplied again). Again the people multiplied, again the country filled up with people. Now one man spoke thus, "A great many people who are nearby now will arrive here, those who are the new people (to come here soon). It is better that we be no more in this country." (So accordingly) the headman went all over. He reached his house at length. Now then all those people (of this second myth age) were changed into pebbles. Here in the water (today still) are quantities of such small pebbles. Long ago those were the people (of the second myth age).

Long ago there was no water. Water was only pulled (sucked) from the trees. Now all (sorts of) people were again on the earth. The third (series of myth age) persons became many (they multiplied). Now then two women stole one infant, and they kept it all the time. It became large and dug roots. It turned into a girl. Then one flint boy found her, and he brought her to her mother. Then the two women (who had stolen the girl from her mother) became angry, they stood and danced (at their spirit-power dancing), they made rain (with their rain spirit-power), and then it rained twenty days. The earth was completely full (was flooded), the mountains sank, and then the (third myth age generation of) people died. Only one boy and one girl were left on the (flooded) earth (except also the two women who had caused the flood), flint (flint-boy) was the male. The man (flint-boy) put the girl in (under) his armpit, he hid her. Then the water went back (receded). He saw those two women, he took their ashes and blew them to skywards. (Thus) he made fog (mist and clouds). This is what he said, "You are not to go on the earth, you are to be clouds forever now. When the clouds become thick it will rain." Thus no one makes rain (now). All the persons (of the third myth age generation) became beaver, (they) changed to steelhead, (they) changed to all the kinds of things to live in the water. . . . Formerly they were persons, from here on now they lived in the sea. Formerly they were our own people (they were relatives of ours), the Water Beings, steelhead, crawfish, salmon, trout, mink, land otter, sea otter, seal, whales, the various things of the water.

After these three generations, then again people were made from the girl and the boy. Again they became many, the land filled up for the fourth time. Now then in one house poor ones were living, one woman, and one man. They had one child, a female child. Crow entered their house, it spoke thus, "Make an arrow, and make a bow!" The crow spoke like that to the man. When he had completed the arrow and the bow, then it spoke to him like this, "Hunt in the woods! Kill deer! Kill elk! Kill black bear! Kill panther! Kill wild cat! Kill grizzly! Kill that kind (such kinds) of things! Eat the flesh (of such animals)! Make blankets from their hide, all sorts of things from hide. They are good to wear. (Thus) make yourselves wealthy people [headmen]." That is what Crow said.

Now then he told the woman as follows, "Make (and) sharpen a stick, sharpen the end of a stick, and dig a hole (i.e., make yourself a digging stick). Get these camas, and get these potatoes, and get wild carrots, and all the edible things in the ground so that they may be eaten. (Then) you will be well off. Give me the child, I will take care of it. Bring me the child, I will take care of it." Now then the woman spoke as follows, "What will you do to it if you keep it?" —"It will rest on my wings." —"It might fall." The crow spoke thus, "It could not ever fall." —"Please try it (then)." So now he lay the child on top of his wings, he flew aloft, he flew down, he fluttered about high above. The infant never fell. "All right then," so the woman said. Now then the woman dug. And they stayed all the time at the house (there). Their food supply increased, and so they were well off. They lived (like that) for one year.

Now then Crow found a rock, a small rock (a pebble). He threw it into the fire. The child was playing (there). When the (heated) rock burst, [it] cracked to pieces . . . it (one fragment) hit the child's belly. Now then she (that one year old baby girl) became pregnant. Maybe (only) two moons . . . and she was about to give birth, (and then) she bore a male child. When she bore him she was only one year (old). He talked within five days when he was an infant, and in ten days he was walking, in fifteen days he was hunting birds outside, in twenty days he had killed a pheasant, in twenty-five days he had killed a fawn, in thirty days he had killed a large deer, and then in thirty-five days he had killed a small elk, in forty days he had killed a large elk.

Now then he spoke thus to his grandmother, "I am dying for water." That is what he told his grandmother. The woman spoke as follows, "There is no water." Now then the child said thus, "What has caused it to be said that there is no water?" The woman spoke as follows, "Always there has been no water. When the people were made there was always no water." The child spoke thus, "It is not good for there to be no water here. That is assuredly how the new people (the Indians to come here) will arrive; it will be good for water to be handy. How could you have waited to drink water?" The woman said as follows, "We have peeled the (bark from) trees, (and) there where we suck the water flows out." The child spoke thus, "That way is no good. I will look for water." The child spoke as follows, "Do you see the sun standing here?" —"Yes," was what the woman said. "Do you see the moon? There is where I will get water. If there is none there, I will go to the sun. Maybe they (the people there) are keeping the water." —"Very well," said the woman.

Now then he went along, he arrived at the house of the moon. The moon spoke like this, "Where do you come from?" The child spoke as follows, "I am merely going along. . . . I am looking for water." The moon said as follows, "The sun is feeling contrary (spiteful). The sun has a child. Go to it there. I will give you grass (some herb) that has a nice scent. The sun's child will smell it, and will (then) give you water." —"Very well. Give me my grass. . . ."

Now then he was given it. He reached the house of the sun. He saw the sun's female child. "Oh," she said to him, "You smell very much (very sweetly)." —"Certainly!" said the child, "I do smell (fine). Well then, give me (let me share) water." So then she took a wooden bucket, she went to fetch water from the next place (at the adjacent house). The boy said as follows, "Let us both go!" So then they went together to the next place. The

[boy] saw the water. A lake appeared. A canoe stood there, two paddles were lying in it. The [boy] said as follows, "Oh, (what) a fine canoe!" The sun's child said to him, "Get into it. Let us play." —"All right." The girl said, "Turn around (twist) the other way!" So then the [boy] got into it, he put the paddles into the water. He spoke thus, "Now let us go. Let us go all over." He spoke like that to the water.

The water moved along, it went all over, the water was started. First it became the ocean, and then it made streams, and then it made all the creeks, and now all the various types of waters were finished. "Now I have completed all the waters." That was what he said. "Now the water is fine. When the new people (the Indians to come) have arrived, there will be lots of water. They will not be poor in water." And so we are still living here now. (This is) the end of the myth people.

Kalapuya Ceremonial Song

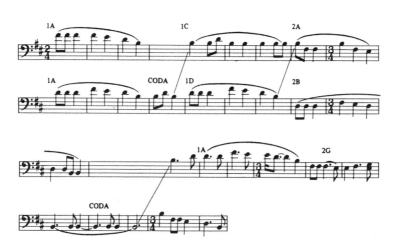

Amhuluk, the Monster of Wapato Lake

ATFALATI KALAPUYA

AMHULUK FOUND himself a place on Forked Mountain; he stopped there and has lived there ever since. Every living being seen by him is drowned there; all the trees there stand upside down in his stagnant water. His legs have no hair on them, his horns are spotted and huge. He keeps several kinds of dogs with him.

Three children were busy digging for *adsadsh*-root [?], when Amhuluk came out of the ground nearby. The children said, "Let us take his beautiful spotted horns, to make digging-tools out of them!" But Amhuluk came up fast and lifted two of the children on his horns; the oldest child managed to escape. Wherever Amhuluk set his feet the ground was sinking. When the boy reached home he said to his father, "Something dreadful has come near us, and has taken away my brother and sister!" Then he went to sleep, and his parents noticed that his body was spotted all over.

Immediately the father started out for Forked Mountain. He found the tracks of the boy who had escaped and followed them, skirting the mountain. There he saw the bodies of his children emerging from the muddy pool. Then they disappeared for a while, and then re-appeared on the opposite slope of the mountain. This happened five times, and finally the father reached the exact spot where the children had been drowned. There was a pool of water, with a mist over it, and in the mist he saw his children lifted up high on the horns of Amhuluk. With his hands he signalled to them, and the children replied: *"Didei, didei, didei,* we are changed, we are changed, we are changed!"

The father began to mourn, and stayed on the shore all night. The next day the mist came up again, and again the children rose up on the horns of Amhuluk. The father made signals again, and the children answered, *"Didei, didei, didei."* He made a lodge on the shore and stayed in it five days, and every day the children appeared to him as before. When they stopped appearing, the father went back to his family. His oldest son had died. The father said, "Amhuluk has taken the children. I have seen them;

they are at the Forked Mountain. I have seen them upon the horns of the monster; many trees were in the water, the crowns down below, the trunks looking upward."

Ptchiza' and the Seven-headed Snake

MARY'S RIVER KALAPUYA

ONE BOY LIVED together with his grandmother. He was poor, he was an orphan. One day the old woman made a bow that was small, and also an arrow. The child played with it, he merely shot (with it). At length wintertime came. Snow lay on the ground. The old woman poured ashes outside near the door. Now birds came there. At length the child killed one snow bird. He fetched it, he took it in, he gave it to his grandmother. His grandmother said, "Oh that is good eating, that sort of bird." Now he shot birds all day long. The old woman again made a bow and arrow, that were somewhat larger. The child killed snowbirds, and meadowlarks, and robins. He was doing that every day. Now his grandmother again indeed made another bow that was bigger, and arrows. And so the child would shoot birds the day long. The child always swam in the early morning.

He always kept one small stick, he whipped his hair with it, he always had it (for helping to dry his hair). At length one day that stick spoke to the boy. The boy was frightened. The stick said, "Do not fear me. I always want to help you. Which is the reason why I have shown my heart to you. You will become strong (with the help of me as your guardian-spirit) if you take my words (and obey me)." The boy said, "Very well indeed." And now the boy said, "If your heart is that way (towards me), then I will keep you like that for all time." The stick said, "That is how my heart is (towards you). Now you and I are one. Nothing will be too difficult for you." The boy said, "Very well indeed." Then the stick said, "Now I will give you your name. Ptchiza' [Le Petit Jean] is to be your name." The boy said, "It is well indeed." The stick said, "Do not ever leave me. Wherever you go, take me with you. That will be why you will be strong."

Ptchiza' said, "Very well indeed." Then the boy went back home.

Again he shot, he shot birds, they ate them. After a little while Ptchiza' said to his grandmother, "My bow is not strong." So then his grandmother made a bigger bow. Now he killed quail, and pheasant, and grouse. It was summertime now, that is what they ate. Then one day Ptchiza' said, "My bow is not strong." Again his grandmother made a bow, the bow was strong. She made a flint, she fitted it on the arrow's tip. With it he shot deer, and he killed them. They ate many deer now. He hunted all the time now, until he filled up five houses (with deer meat). Then he told his grandmother, "Now I will be leaving you. You have quantities of food." The old woman said, "It is well indeed. Seek your work (wherever you like)." Ptchiza' said, "That is what I want to do. I will leave you tomorrow for good."

In the early morning Ptchiza' swam, and then Ptchiza' went. He took with him his stick. They talked to one another. The stick said, "We will go in this direction. At the headman's (king's) house (castle) there we will be getting our work." Sure enough, they went there. When they had nearly gotten to the headman's house (to the king's castle), Ptchiza' sat down, he took out his stick, he placed it there, and he said, "What will we do now?" The stick said, "We will not do anything else. You are to take your job here from the headman (the king). After a while I will be telling you what, but not now," said the stick. Ptchiza' said, "That is well, then." So now they went along, and they reached the headman's house. Ptchiza' became bad (extremely dirty), he was covered with snot, and dust was puffing from his eyes, when he shut (and opened) them. Now they reached the headman's house. Ptchiza' got work. He took care of the horses' house (stables), and the cattle. That was his work. He kept outside (in the wood-shed).

He worked there perhaps so long a time, when his stick said, "Tomorrow the headman is going to deliver his daughter. The snake is going to eat up the headman's daughter. He eats up the headman's daughters all the time. If the headman did not give the snake his daughter, then he himself would be killed, and indeed all his people too. That is the reason why he gives his daughter to the snake. So tomorrow let us go, let us help him." To be sure, it was the next day, (and) the people all came together. They all had black feathers (mourning). All the houses' windows were black, their windows were closed (were draped) with black cloth. They did like that for two days, when they took the girl. Then they went with black horses, which were hung on to (hitched to) a small wagon. The girl was in it. . . .

Now Ptchiza' (and the stick) changed (transformed) themselves. [Ptchiza'] first made a bay horse of the stick. The stick gave him a long knife. Now when they went, the headman (and the people) were already gone. So they (Ptchiza' and his horse) then went along in the rear. They were just as if they were shadows. Half way along they caught up with people. Ptchiza' merely did like this with his hand, immediately the girl jumped up behind him, she rode behind Ptchiza'. They went on, they got to where the snake dwelt. He had already emerged from the water. The snake had seven heads. Ptchiza' and the snake fought, and the horse kicked and bit it. They cut off two of its heads. Then the snake said, "Really that is enough now! Indeed let us fight again tomorrow." Now it said, "You are Ptchiza'," the snake said. Ptchiza' said, "I do not know whose name that is."

The snake went into the lake. Ptchiza' got off, he cut off the tongues of the snake. And the girl took out her handkerchief, she gave it to Ptchiza', and also her finger ring. Some of the people were still going along. Ptchiza' and his horse went back, they met those people. Ptchiza' did that with his hand, the girl got into the (king's) wagon at once. Ptchiza' just passed by. Now the girl told her father, "Let us go back. Let us go to the fight tomorrow." The headman said, "Who is it who took you?" The girl said, "I do not know." Then they turned about, they came back, they arrived at the house (the castle).

Indeed the next morning they went away again to their fight. Ptchiza' went along in the rear. His horse was a chestnut now. So, they were going along in the rear, until they caught up with the people. He did the very same way again. He simply did that with his hand, the girl leaped at once behind, she rode with Ptchiza'. So they went along, they got to the snake. He had already come out from the lake. Indeed now they fought again, again indeed he cut off two of the snake's heads. The snake said, "Let us quit! Indeed tomorrow again!" Sure enough the snake went into the lake. Ptchiza' got down, he cut off the tongues. Again he tied it with a handkerchief of the girl. He had cut four now. He got on the horse, they came back. They met some of the people. Ptchiza' merely did like that with his hand, the girl got into the (king's) wagon immediately. Ptchiza' just came along. The girl said (to her father), "Let us go back. Indeed let us go again tomorrow to the fight." Sure enough the headman said, "Who is that?" The girl said, "I do not know." So they came back; they reached the house.

Again indeed the next day they went to their fight. Again in the very same manner Ptchiza′ now had a black horse. They caught up to the people. Ptchiza′ just did that with his hand, the girl rode behind Ptchiza′. They went along, they got there. The snake had already come out of the lake. They fought, again he cut off one of its heads. The snake said, "Let us quit! Tomorrow again!" The snake went into the lake. Ptchiza′ again cut off the tongue, he tied it up in a handkerchief. They went back. They met the people, they were coming along. Ptchiza′ merely did like that with his hand, the girl at once got into the wagon.

They did like that five times. The fifth time they went to their fight, they killed him. His last head was strong. They fought a long time. The snake kept saying all the time, "You are Ptchiza′!" Ptchiza′ said, "I do not know whose name that is." The snake said, "It is indeed you, Ptchiza′. You are going to kill me now. No one but you could kill me." Ptchiza′ said, "It is not my name that you are naming me by." As they fought, Ptchiza′ got tired, his horse got tired too, (and) the girl got tired. She nearly fell. They killed him at last. Ptchiza′ got down, he cut off his tongue, he tied it in a handkerchief too. He had now cut off seven of the heads. So then Ptchiza′ got on his horse, they went back.

The met the people coming along. Ptchiza′ told the girl, "Tell your father to burn the snake. Be sure not to forget it. You must tell it to him." The girl said, "Very well indeed." Then the girl said, "Who are you?" Ptchiza′ said, "You do not want to know who I am." Now then when they met the people, Ptchiza′ just did like that with his hand, the girl got into the wagon directly. Ptchiza′ indeed went along. The girl said, "Turn the horses around quickly! Let us follow him (to see) who he is who has been helping me. I want to know where he will go to." So they pursued, they whipped the horses, but they could not overtake him. Ptchiza′ was indeed however just like a shadow. That is why they could not tell (recognize) him. The people got back home then.

Now the next day the headman (king) said, "I want all the people to assemble in my house (palace). I want to find out what has helped me," the headman said. Ptchiza′ was working then, he took care of his (the king's) horses and cattle. That was his task.

Now all the people assembled. They talked it all over, they wanted to find out whoever had been helping them. After a while five men brought the (snake) heads. "Wonder where they got them from?" The girl said to her father, "That person who helped me said to me to tell you, 'Burn that snake.'" To be sure, the headman said to the people, "Haul a quantity of wood. We will burn up that snake." Sure enough, they hauled up a quantity of wood, and then they burned the snake. Never again will there be a snake like that, who lives in this land eating people. The headman burned up the snake. When it blazed up the fire got right to the sky. Then there was no longer a snake like that. They came back.

Now the people were coming together then. The five men arrived first. They said that they themselves had killed it. They bore its seven heads on a yellow-red dollar platter [golden plate]. All the people were talking about the heads, because the headman had said, that he himself wanted them to talk over those heads—even the children, even a single word (of comment), or two, or three, or as many as they might want to utter. For a long time the people were talking it over together at the headman's house. . . . Now those five men said, "We killed that snake." Then the headman said, "If you did kill it, then for that, one of you may marry my daughter." The girl asked for the finger ring, and her handkerchief. Each of those men showed a ring and a handkerchief, but the girl said, "This is not my handkerchief, nor my finger ring."

In a little while one person said, "You have not gone to fetch that one boy. He is the last one now. There are no other persons now (to seek)." The headman said, "Indeed have him come in. It is well if he too speaks about these heads of the snake." So sure enough they went to fetch Ptchiza'. His stick said to him, "Now they will come for you. Do not be going. Pretty soon they will come to fetch you. Before you go I will tell you (what to do)." Sure enough they came to Ptchiza'. He was told, "The headman wants to see you." Ptchiza' said, "Maybe no (I guess I will not be going)." So they went back.

The headman said, "Where is he?" —"He does not want to come." The headman said, "Go get him. He has to come." I do not know perhaps how many thousands of people were there. Then they went to get Ptchiza' again. He was told, "If you do not want to go, then we will take you along." Ptchiza' said, "Do not take me along. You go back. I will be coming along (after you)." So indeed those two men went back. Then Ptchiza′'s stick said. "Pretty soon after you reach the headman's house, he will say to you thus, 'Discuss this head!' You are to say as follows, that you do not know anything about it. But after a while you should speak concerning the tongue." Ptchiza′ said, "Very well." He took his stick, he put it into his pocket.

Now then he went, he arrived. The two of them (the messengers sent to Ptchiza′) had gotten back. The headman said, "Where is Ptchiza′?" They said, "He is coming." Soon afterwards Ptchiza′ got there. The headman said, "Everybody discussed this head. Now I want you to say something too, whatever you know about this head." Ptchiza′ said, "If that be your heart (desire), I will tell you a little something about that. I want nobody to go outside or enter." The headman said, "Guard all doors and windows." A couple of men guarded each door. Then Ptchiza′ said, "Headman! I do not know much about it. Every head that I myself saw had a tongue." Then the headman immediately investigated. He said, "Indeed yes." After a while Ptchiza′ took out his handkerchief, in it were tied up the tongues. He threw them on top of the eating place (on the table).

At once the girl ran up, she said, "This is my handkerchief, this is my finger ring. This is the one who helped me, which is why I am alive today." She held his neck, she ate [kissed] his mouth. Ptchiza′ was just full of [snot] still. Now then Ptchiza′ said, "Give me a small house (a room)." To be sure, the headman gave him a small house. . . . Ptchiza′ went into it then, he changed himself. When he came out he was much finer in appearance than any of the people. So then the headman said, "Now you are to take my daughter. You will become the headman." Ptchiza′ however said nothing. Then Ptchiza′ got married. All the people stood to dance (they danced). Those five men were put into the strong house (jail). Maybe they are in there yet.

Coyote's Swallowing Match with Grizzly Bear

MOLALA

COYOTE WAS going up toward Mt. Hood. He met Grizzly Bear. Grizzly Bear said, "Where are you going, Coyote?"

Coyote said, "I am going up country."

"Why are you going there?" asked Grizzly Bear.

Coyote said, "I am making the world."

Then Grizzly Bear said, "We must fight."

Coyote said, "No, we must have a swallowing match."

Grizzly said, "No! We must fight a duel."

Coyote said, "We will swallow stones."

Grizzly said, "Go ahead, we will swallow them."

Coyote said, "We must have them very hot."

"How many hot rocks?" asked Grizzly.

Coyote said, "You swallow first, then I will."

Then the Grizzly Bear swallowed a hot stone, "Now it's your turn," he said.

Then Coyote said, "Yes," and began to swallow strawberries, not rocks! He fooled Grizzly, he swallowed five strawberries. Then Coyote told Grizzly, "Now you must swallow five hot stones."

"All right," said Grizzly. Then he commenced swallowing hot rocks, they burst his heart, and he died.

Now Coyote sat down and studied. "Now I must go, I am going on forever. He is gone now, the world is going to last so long!"

He skinned Grizzly, then began cutting him up; he scattered his body in little pieces all over. Then to the Molala country he threw the heart. He said, "Now the Molala will be good hunters; they will all be good men, thinking and studying about hunting deer. They will think all the time they are on a hunt."

Indeed they know how to dodge out, those Molala.

The Indians Hear
a Treaty Speech in 1855

SANTIAM KALAPUYA

THE AMERICANS (troops) arrived. They spoke as follows, "qa'
yaqats! [chief's name] Now we will give you quantities of
money, (and) all sorts of things. So then you will not be poor.
All your tribespeople will be just like Americans. You will be
given everything—(property such as) cattle, horses, wagons,
blankets, breeches, hats, coats, overcoats, quantities of flour,
sugar, coffee. You will be given food for five years. The Americans will watch over you. They will make your fences. They will
plough your land. They will fence your land. They will make
your houses. They will build a hammer house (blacksmith shop).
A man will come who knows how to make all sorts of things (a
blacksmith). He will fix your wagon for you if it should break.
He will make the handle of your ground breaker (your plow).
He will just fix it (at cost). The great headman (the government
of the United States—symbolized in the President) will pay for
it. Whatever you may desire, he will make it.

"A trading house (a store) will be built. You may obtain
(there) whatever you wish. An iron house (a blacksmith shop)
will be erected, to repair what has gotten spoiled. Whatever sort
of iron thing you may want, you will not have to pay for it.
There will be erected a paper (book) house (i.e., a school building). Your children will speak (read from) the paper (book).
That is the way they will do like Americans. Twenty acres (will
be given to) each person (Indian), and as long as you remain on
the place, then it will be your own place. The great headman
(the United States and its President) will give it to you to be
your own place. After twenty years the (last) payment for your
place will cease, and then no one will (be necessary to) watch
over you. You will take care of your own heart (you will then
be no longer a government ward). That is how you will be
(then) just like an American. . . ."

[Note: Compare what the Indians understood they were being
promised in this 1855 speech, with what Chief Jo Hutchins com-
plained of lacking in the following speech fourteen years later.]

Jo Hutchins' Speech to Superintendent Meacham, Grand Ronde, 1869

SANTIAM KALAPUYA

"I AM WATCHING your eye. I am watching your tongue. I am thinking all the time. Perhaps you are making fools of us. We don't want to be made fools. I have heard tyees [chiefs] talk like you do now. They go back home and send us something a white man don't want. We are not dogs. We have hearts. We may be blind. We do not see the things the treaty promised. Maybe they got lost on the way. The President is a long way off. He can't hear us. Our words get lost in the wind before they get there. Maybe his ear is small. Maybe your ears are small. They look big. Our ears are large. We hear everything.

"Some things we don't like. We have been a long time in the mud. Sometimes we sink down. Some white men help us up. Some white men stand on our heads. We want a schoolhouse built on the ground of the Santiam people. Then our children can have some sense. We want an Indian to work in the blacksmith shop. We don't like halfbreeds. They are not Indians. They are not white men. Their hearts are divided. We want some harness. We want some ploughs. We want a sawmill. What is a mill good for that has no dam? That old mill is not good; it won't saw boards.

"We want a church. Some of these people are Catholics. Some of them are like Mr. Parish, a Methodist. Some got no religion. Maybe they don't need religion.

"Some people think Indians got no sense. We don't want any blankets. We have had a heap of blankets. Some of them have been like sail-cloth muslin. The old people have got no sense; they want blankets. The treaty said we, every man, have his land, he have a paper for his land. We don't see the paper. We see the land. We want it divided. When we have land all in one place, some Indian put his horses in the field; another Indian turn them out. Then they go to law. One man says another man got the best ground. They go to law about that. We want the land marked out. Every man builds his own house. We want some apples. Mark out the land, then we plant some trees, by-and-by we have some apples.

"Maybe you don't like my talk. I talk straight. I am not a coward. I am chief of the Santiams. You hear me now. We see your eyes; look straight. Maybe you are a good man. We will find out. Sochala-tyee—God sees you. He sees us. All these people hear me talk. Some of them are scared. I am not afraid. Alta-kup-et—I am done."

Part Four

THE COAST

Clatsop Chinook

Tillamook

Alsea

Coos

Chinookan wood bowl *Courtesy of Thomas Burke Memorial*
Washington State Museum, cat. #4616

THE MYTHS and stories of the Indians who lived along the Oregon Coast vividly reveal the omnipresence of the Pacific Ocean in their lives. To judge from texts like the following, the great ocean was the fact of existence, an endless imaginative provocation. The sense of place conveyed by casual references to windy headlands, roaring surf, damp littoral forests, coastal weather is so strong, the stories seem unthinkable in any other setting.

Givers of ostentatious "potlatches" like their cousins along the Northwest Coast of Washington and Canada, but lacking their material wealth and their superb pictorial art, the Indians of the Oregon Coast traveled little beyond the boundaries of their maritime world, content to harvest the rich year-round bounty of the sea and the tidal rivers. Salmon was the staple of their

Yaquina Bay Indians (from Nash, *Oregon: There and Back*) *Courtesy of Photography Collection, Suzzallo Library, University of Washington*

"On the Beach—Chinook." Photograph by E. S. Curtis *Courtesy of Photography Collection, Suzzallo Library, University of Washington*

Good Life (the story of Coyote's painful invention of the fishing rituals suggests how central the salmon was to their economy), but there were also herring, flounder, clams, crabs, oysters, seals, an occasional stranded whale—and, inland, deer and elk to hunt and camas roots to dig.[1]

Some of the tribes, notably those around the mouth of the Columbia, had very early trading contacts with white men— when Lewis and Clark and later the Astor party reached the coast overland, the Clatsops seem to have been dealing with Russian and possibly Spanish ships for several decades. The half century of American conquest and occupation initiated by Lewis and Clark saw almost all coastal tribes and bands moved out of their small villages and onto two crowded and heterogeneous reservations, the Siletz in Yamhill County, and the Grand Ronde in Polk and Lincoln counties. To appreciate something of the confusions of living on these reservations, one need only consider that the Siletz contained Indians speaking dialects of no fewer than six more-or-less mutually unintelligible language-groups: the Athapascan, Yakonan, Kusan, Takelman, Shastan, and Sahaptian! And the fate of the Coast Indians through the nineteenth century generally can be illustrated by these population estimates for the Tillamooks, once one of the most powerful tribes along the Oregon Pacific—1805: 2,200 (as estimated by Lewis and Clark); 1845: 400 (the terrible epidemics of the 1830s had run their course); 1849: 200; 1910: 25 . . .[2]

Beyond the literature of other regions in Oregon these stories persistently dwell on the possibility of other worlds, other mediums of life, and strange travels and transformations from one world to another. The imagination of the coastal Indian, living on the brink of the great unknown element of the Pacific, must have been deeply attuned to such possibilities—witness the transformations of the boy in "The Magic Hazel Twig" and the sea-change in "The Woman Who Married a Merman"; the voyages in "The Journey across the Ocean," with its tantalizing hints of real encounters with the Japanese or Chinese; the ultimate metaphysical journeys narrated in "The Girl Who Married a Ghost," and others.

Behind such weird episodes, there is always the compelling presence of the sea, both familiar and alien, indifferent giver of life, another, alternative medium of being, limitless—"the river with one bank," the Indians called it—the source of all change. So, in the historical text which concludes this selection, "The First Ship Comes to Clatsop Country," that "mysterious thing about which we have heard in tales" came out of the Pacific not unexpectedly—and so the terrible "sea-change" of white conquest was already upon the Indians of the Oregon Coast.

Charles Cultee, Chinook storyteller

South Wind Marries Ocean's Daughter

NEHALEM TILLAMOOK

SOUTH WIND [As'ai'yahahl] traveled in the winter. It was always stormy then. He had many different headbands. He would say, "I will put on my headband with which I run on trees. I will travel only on the limbs of trees." That was the time when the limbs broke off the trees. The limbs broke off and fell down when he walked on them. Sometimes he would say, "Now I will wear this headband with which I break off the tree tops." He had still another headband which he wore when he felled whole trees, just as if they had been chopped down. Very rarely he would start out saying, "This time I will wear the headband with which I pull trees up by the roots."

In his travels he always saw a beautiful girl on the ocean beach. She would be sitting by the waves at the edge of the beach. He was always attempting to catch her. But just as he almost touched her she would disappear. Ah, he thought about her. He wanted so much to catch her. He had seen her many times, but he did not know what kind of a girl she was. Finally Blue Jay told him, "Well, South Wind, do you still want to catch that girl?"— "Yes, aunt," he replied, "would you tell me how to do it?" She told him, "When you see her, if you attempt to catch her do not blink your eyes. Just keep staring straight at her until you seize her with your hand. Then it will be all right. You will have caught her. Do you know who she is?" —"No!" —"She is that Ocean's daughter. Ocean is the chief of chiefs." South Wind had often destroyed things for Ocean to receive.

He found her the next time he went forth. He did as he had been advised, and he caught hold of her. He took her home, he took her south. He made her his wife. That girl did not like it. She said, "Oh, I have never had a home like this! My bed at home is soft. I did not sleep on a hard bed at home." South Wind had a wooden bed. After a while he asked her, "Do you want me to take you home to your father? Shall we go and stay with your father awhile?" Yes, she wanted to go home. She was very pleased.

He took her home. He saw many different things there. His father-in-law had everything! All sorts of living things were his pets. Those whales and many unattractive animals were his pets. They talked together. South Wind said, "Well, we will work together for the remainder of time. I will destroy things for you, so you can possess them. You must do your part. When I travel, you will be angry and drift things and drown things. In that way we will work together forever." Then he took his wife to his own home again. She took her belongings from her father's place since she was to remain with South Wind.

South Wind had one wife already when he was trying to catch that girl. She was continually getting angry and jealous. She would decide, "I will leave. I am not going to live with him any more. I am going away." She would start in the night and travel, travel as long as she could. She would then think, "Well, I must be far away now." South Wind would arise in the morning and notice that his first wife was gone. He would look, there in the far corner of the room he would see her. There she would be, with her belongings scattered around, and her bed made there. She was never able to travel far enough to get out of South Wind's house. The whole world was South Wind's house!

That is ended.

The Exploits of South Wind

NEHALEM TILLAMOOK

[What follows, in digest or "abstract" form prepared by Elizabeth Jacobs, is a cycle of episodes in the career of the Tillamook Trickster and Transformer, South Wind. The language is that of Mrs. Jacobs.]

TRAVELING NORTH, South Wind turns Ice into April fish, brings an early spring, makes East Wind stop singing. He stretches his penis across Tillamook Bay, copulates with a virgin, is forced to ask Mountain Straw to cut off his penis, part of which now forms the bar in Tillamook Bay; the tip remains within the girl. At Bay City he finds a whale, induces Flint and Copper to fight in order to obtain a flint knife.

On the way to Kelches Point he encounters an old woman who

feeds him camas, he arranges to meet her again, cuts his penis into three parts which he transforms into dogs which also eat camas. The third time he meets her she gives him a bundle of bumblebees. Angry, he overtakes her, turns her into a rock. He arrives at the home of the virgin he has desecrated; pretending to doctor her he copulates with her again, splices the tip of his penis back in place, runs away saying that men shall never be paid for intercourse.

He sees a canoe with three people, one a virgin; interested in the virgin, he transforms himself into a baby, lies on a rock in the water, is picked up by the people, cries until the girl holds him, touches her vulva, exclaims that it is soft like an old woman's. At Bay City he transforms his penis into a clam digger, eats clams with a family, ordains that there shall be but one clam in each shell, and juice instead of oil. He induces the woman to stroke the clam digger and makes sarcastic remarks when she discovers that it is his penis. He avoids Stink Bug women who want to make him impotent, but he copulates with two girls who take him under the ocean with them. He escapes them, asks for rocks to shelter him as he sleeps in the sun, awakens enclosed by rocks, calls Woodpecker who breaks her bill trying to free him, calls Yellowhammer. When she has pecked a hole he reaches up and seizes her leg; she flies away insulted. He takes himself apart, throws body parts out of the hole; Sea Gull and Raven eat his eyes. He feels his way to Bald Eagle's house, pretends to be measuring the house, brags about his eyes, effects a trade with Bald Eagle, who then steals Snail's eyes and voice.

South Wind goes to Nehalem, names it, changes the Clatsop speech of the people to Tillamook, turns salmon into flounder, ordains that there shall be no Chinook salmon and no wild potatoes at Nehalem. He crosses Neahkanie Mountain, kills four monster women, three of whom he charms by rattling sea shells on his knees and inducing them to allow their knees to be hammered. He creates breakers on the ocean, kills other monster women by pretending he is having his power illness [a kind of psychic crisis?] which requires pitchwood and dry grass to be scattered in their house; he turns the house into rock, burns the women, ordains that nothing of their sort shall endanger people again on the mountain.

At Arch Cape he stops with Year Around who has twenty baskets of fish, representing the months of the year. He throws ashes on her fish to make them appear mildewed, causes sap to run in the cedar trees by striking them with his penis, transforms his feces into salmonberries, thus triumphs over Year Around, shortening the year to twelve months. He goes on, sleeps; five hunters knot his hair; he is frightened by his image when he drinks, discovers what it is, causes the five hunters to sleep, transforms them into wolves.

He approaches Double-bladed Knife, a powerful sky being who resembles a child, attempts to destroy him, finds himself paralyzed. The being awakes, makes South Wind name him, takes him to his sky home, warning him not to open his eyes. He advises him to sit by the lake where his wives will feed him; the first day South Wind does not obey instructions, goes hungry; after that they send wooden bowls of food to the top of the water for him. Though warned not to approach the lake at night when it is a house, he goes, finds the beautiful wives of Double-bladed Knife dancing with young hired men. The house is lighted by a moon which Bull Frog swallows and spits out.

Curious about the period of darkness, South Wind hits Frog with a rock. Frog spits out the moon, and the wives are discovered copulating with the hired men; South Wind leaves in anger. Double-bladed Knife puts him on a platform to be tried by the wives, warning him not to look up. Overcome by the magic of the wives of Double-bladed Knife, he looks up during the trial, is bounced an immeasurable distance. Lost a long time, he is discovered by the sons of Double-bladed Knife. Nearly starved, he insists on tasting Double-bladed Knife's oil, it causes him to swell, he defecates lizards and snakes which crawl back into the lake. Double-bladed Knife returns him to the beach because he cannot feed him.

South Wind encounters Wild Hen, kills and eats her children. Arriving at a house where a man is wearing a belt of live snakes, he insists on wearing it, is angry when it hurts him, makes a lucky bird of his feces, and tells the man to follow it up a tree to the sky. The man revenges himself on South Wind by inducing a whale to take him out into the ocean and keep him for months.

He goes to Fort Stevens, lives with a fisherman, Snake, who makes nets in his mouth; he obtains advice from his feces on how to clean and cook fish so that they will be plentiful. At the Columbia River he turns a man into a rock, makes the river too deep to be waded. Going upriver he is swallowed by a monster, wishes for the Fire Drill Carriers to be swallowed; they arrive, he builds a fire on the monster's heart, causes him to drink water until he bursts, then states that nothing of that kind shall happen in the future.

He discovers that he is pregnant, suffers horribly in childbirth, binds his penis with wild cherry bark to prevent its splitting, ordains that men will not bear children. Ashamed, he kills his daughter, goes along weeping, turns five young men into rocks because they laugh while he weeps. He meets his baby, kills her three more times, meets her again. The fourth time he stations her on the highest mountain [Hood?] to be his informant about the behavior of the people after he leaves.

He returns downriver on the Washington side, stations his feces to watch a fish-trap for him; she calls him when there are no fish; he kicks her and besmears his foot. He gets a small fish, makes twin daughters of its eggs. The girls steer and paddle crookedly, causing the river to be crooked. He offends them by calling them wives; they run away and become the Younger Wild Women. He returns south. . . .

Coyote in the Cedar Tree

CHINOOK

ONCE COYOTE was traveling from the country of the Tillamooks to the country of the Clatsops. Coyote passed the mountains and the headlands of the coast. Then he followed the trail through the deep woods. As he was traveling along Coyote saw an immense cedar. The inside was hollow. He could see it through a big gap which opened and closed as the tree swayed in the wind. Coyote cried, "Open, Cedar Tree!" Then the tree opened. Coyote jumped inside. He said, "Close, Cedar Tree!" Then the tree closed. Coyote was shut inside the tree.

After a while Coyote said, "Open, Cedar Tree!" Nothing happened. Once more Coyote said, "Open, Cedar Tree!" Again nothing happened. Coyote was angry. He called to the tree, he kicked it. The tree did not answer. Then Coyote remembered that he was Coyote, the wisest and most cunning of all animals. He began to think.

After he had thought, Coyote called the birds to help him. He told them to peck a hole through the Cedar Tree. The first to try was Wren. Wren pecked and pecked at the Cedar Tree until her bill was blunted. But Wren could not even make a dent. Therefore Coyote called her "wren." Then Coyote called the other birds. Sparrow came, Robin came, Finch came, but they could not even break the heavy bark. So Coyote gave each one a name and sent them away. Then Owl came, and Raven, and Hawk, and Eagle. They could not make even a little hole. Finally Little Woodpecker made a tiny hole. Then the big Yellow Woodpecker came and pecked a large hole. But the hole was too small for Coyote. So he saw there was no help from the birds.

Coyote began to think hard. After he had thought, Coyote began to take himself apart. He took himself all apart and slipped each piece through Yellowhammer's hole. First he slipped a leg through, then a paw, then his tail, then his ears, and his eyes, until he was all through the hole, and outside the Cedar Tree. Then Coyote began to put himself together. He put his legs and paws together, then his tail, his nose, his ears, and then his body. At last Coyote had himself all together except for his eyes. He could not find his eyes. Raven had seen them on the ground and had stolen them. Coyote was blind.

But Coyote did not want the animals to know he was blind. He smelled a wild rose. He found the bush and picked two rose leaves. He put the rose leaves in place of his eyes. Then Coyote traveled on. feeling his way along the trail. Soon he met a squaw. The squaw began to jeer, "Oh ho, oh ho, you seem to be very blind!"

"Oh no," said Coyote. "I am measuring the ground. I can see better than you can. I can see *tamanawus* [spirit] rays."

The squaw was greatly ashamed. Coyote pretended to see wonderful things at a great distance.

The squaw said, "I wish I could see *tamanawus* rays!"

Coyote said, "Change eyes with me. Then you can see everything."

So Coyote and the squaw traded eyes. Coyote took the squaw's eyes and gave her the rose leaves. Then Coyote could see as well as ever. The squaw could see nothing. Coyote said, "For your foolishness you must always be a snail. You must creep. You must feel your way on the ground."

Coyote Invents the Fishing Rituals

CHINOOK

COYOTE WAS COMING. He came to Got'ä't [Clatsop]. There he
met a heavy surf. He was afraid that he might be drifted away
and went up to the spruce trees. He stayed there a long time.
Then he took some sand and threw it upon the surf, saying:
"This shall be a prairie and no surf. The future generations shall
walk on this prairie." Thus Clatsop became a prairie.

At Nia'xaqsi [Neacoxie], a creek originated. He went and
built a house at its mouth. Then he speared a silver-side salmon,
a steelhead, and a fall salmon. Then he threw away the steelhead
and the fall salmon, saying: "This creek is too small. I do not like
to see steelhead and fall salmon here. It shall be a bad omen when
a fall salmon is killed here; somebody shall die. When a female
salmon or fall salmon is killed a woman shall die; when a male is
killed a man shall die." Now he carried only the silver-side
salmon to his house. When he arrived there he cut it at once,
steamed it, and ate it.

On the next day he took his harpoon and went again to the
mouth of [the creek]. He did not see anything, and the flood tide
set in. He went home. On the next day he went again and did
not see anything. Then he became angry and went home. He
defecated and said to his excrements, "Why have these silver-side
salmon disappeared?" —"Oh, you with your bandy legs, you
have no sense. When the first silver-side salmon is killed it must
not be cut. It must be split along its back and roasted. It must not
be steamed. Only when they go up river can they be steamed."
Coyote went home.

On the next day he went again, and speared three. He went
home and made three spits. He roasted each salmon on a spit. On
the next day he went again and stood at the mouth of the creek.
He did not see anything until the flood tide set in. Then he became angry and went home. He defecated. He spoke and asked
his excrements, "Why have these silver-side salmon disappeared?"
His excrements said to him, "We told you, you with your bandy
legs, when the first silver-side salmon are killed, spits must be
made, one for the head, one for the back, one for the roe, one for
the body. The gills must be burnt." —"Yes," said Coyote.

On the next day he went again. He again killed three silver-side salmon. When he arrived at home he cut them all up and made many spits. He roasted them all separately. The spits of the breast, body, head, back, and roe were at separate places. Coyote roasted them. On the next morning he went again. He speared ten silver-sides. Coyote was very glad. He came home and split part of the fish. The other part he left and went to sleep. On the next morning he roasted the rest. Then he went fishing again. He did not see anything before the flood tide set in. He went home. On the next morning he went again, but again he did not see anything. He went home angry.

He defecated and asked his excrements: "Why have these silver-side salmon disappeared?" His excrements scolded him, "When the first silver-side salmon are killed, they are not left raw. All must be roasted. When many are caught, they must all be roasted before you go to sleep." On the next morning Coyote went and stood at the mouth of the river. He speared ten. Then he made many double spits, and remained awake until all were roasted that he had caught. Now he had learned all that is forbidden in regard to silver-side salmon when they first arrive at [Neacoxie Creek]. He remained there and said, "The Indians shall always do as I had to do. If a man who prepares corpses eats a silver-side salmon, they shall disappear at once. If a murderer eats silver-side salmon, they shall at once disappear. They shall also disappear when a girl who has just reached puberty or a menstruating woman eats them. Even I got tired."

Now he came this way. At some distance he met a number of women who were digging roots. He asked them, "What are you doing?" "We are digging camas." "How can you dig camas at Clatsop? You shall dig some roots here, but no camas." Now they gathered only thistle roots and wild onions. He left those women and spoiled that land. He changed the camas into wild onions.

Then he came to Clatsop. It was the spring of the year. Then he met his younger brother the snake. Coyote said to him, "Let us make nets." The snake replied, "As you wish." Now they bought material for twine, and paid the frog and the newt to spin it. . . . It got day. Then they [Coyote and Snake] went to catch jack salmon in their net. They laid the net and caught two in it. Coyote jumped over the net. Now they intended to catch more salmon, but the flood-tide set in. So they went home. Coyote said that he was hungry, and he split the salmon at once. They roasted them. When they were cooked they ate. The frog and the newt were their cousins. The next morning they went fishing again with their net. Newt looked after the rope, the snake stood at the upper end of the net, Coyote at the lower end. They intended to catch salmon, but they did not get anything before the flood-tide set in. They went home.

Coyote was angry. He defecated and spoke to his excrements, "You are a liar!" They said to him, "You with your bandy legs. When people kill a salmon they do not jump over the net. You must not step over your net. And when the first salmon are caught, they are not cut until the afternoon." —"Oh," said Coyote, "you told me enough." On the next morning they went fishing again. When they killed a [jack] salmon they did not jump over the net. They laid their net twice. Enough salmon were in the net. Coyote ordered the newt, "Bail out the canoe, it is full of water." She bailed it out. Then they intended to fish again, but the flood-tide set in. They went home and put down what they had caught in the house. In the afternoon Coyote split the salmon. He split them in the same way as the silver-side salmon. He placed the head, the back, the body, and the roe in separate places and on separate double spits. They were done.

The next morning they went fishing. They did not catch anything. Coyote became angry and defecated. He said to his excrements, "Tell me, why have these [jack] salmon disappeared?" His excrements scolded him, "Do you think their taboos are the same as those of the silver-side salmon? They are different. When you go fishing for [jack] salmon and they go into your net, you may lay it three times. No more salmon will swim into it. It is enough then. Never bail out your canoe. When you come home and cut the salmon, you must split it at the sides and roast belly and back on separate spits. Then put four sticks vertically into the ground [so that they form a square] and lay two horizontal sticks across them. On top of this frame place the back with the head and the tail attached to it." Coyote said to his excrements, "You told me enough. . . ." [Poor Coyote blunders his way through seven more taboos, being excrementally lectured each time on how the salmon should be killed, how they should be distributed among the people—a crow must be allowed to carry one off beforehand—how at a certain place on the Washington shore the first salmon to be caught should be offered salmonberries, and so on. At last the lessons seem to run their course, and Coyote says:]

"Even I got tired. The Indians shall always do it in the same manner. Murderers, those who prepare corpses, girls who have just matured, menstruating women, widows and widowers shall not eat salmon. Thus shall be the taboos for all generations of people."

How Coyote Killed the Giantess and Herded the Salmon

CHINOOK

CRANE, COYOTE, and Heron lived together. Every day they went digging clams until the flood-tide set in. One day Coyote said: "How many [giant-women] do you have for your sweethearts?" Crane replied, "Two canoes full and some must walk." Coyote said, "How few sweethearts you have! I have five canoes full and some must walk." Heron remained silent.

Five days they dug clams, and the nights they slept on a prairie. When Crane was sleepy Coyote rose and cried, "A giantess is coming down to the beach!" Crane yelled; he had fallen asleep. Then Coyote said, "I have only deceived you." He did so often.

Now they fell asleep. Then [a giantess] came to the beach and put them into her basket. She put Coyote at the bottom, Crane in the middle, and Heron on top. She carried them inland. Now Heron awoke. He took hold of a branch and hung there. When the monster had gone a long distance Coyote awoke. He looked around but remained quiet. Then Crane awoke. He shouted, but Coyote said, "Be quiet, be quiet, the monster carries us away."

She brought them to her house and to her children. One she had lost. Then she said to her eldest daughter, "Go and get two spits; bring straight huckleberry sticks." Her daughter went out. Then Coyote said to Crane, "Bend your neck when she is about to roast you." When the spit was brought Crane bent his neck. Then she said to her daughter, "Bring a crooked spit." Coyote said, "When a crooked spit is brought, stretch out your neck." The girl brought a crooked spit, then Crane stretched out his neck. Five times the girl went; then she became tired.

[The giantess] said, "We will make them our slaves." In those days Crane's tail was half a fathom long. Coyote said to him, "Look here! We will deceive her. I shall sing my conjuring song and you will help me." They gathered pitchwood and when the house was full Coyote sang his conjuring song. He put a snake on as a headband. He said to Crane, "I will put the snake on your head as a headband." Crane shouted; he was afraid.

Now Coyote sang his conjuring song. Four nights they remained awake; on the fifth night [the monster-woman] and her children fell asleep. Then Coyote took a digging stick and rammed it into the ground so that only the handle remained visible. He tied the hair of [the giantess] and her children to the digging stick. Then he and Crane went out and set fire to the house. Crane's tail caught fire. Then Coyote said to him, "Stay on this prairie." Crane did so and the prairie caught fire. Then Coyote said to him, "Stay in this fern." He did so and it caught fire. "Stay in this dry wood." He did so and it caught fire. At last Crane's tail was wholly burnt. Then Coyote said, "Stay in the water." Thus Crane's tail was burnt. Now the monster [the giantess] caught fire. She said to her children, "Rise, Coyote will burn our house!" She tried to get up, but her hair pulled her back. She and her children were all burnt.

Now Coyote and Crane went up to Nιx′kəle′x. They went up the river to its rapids. There they built a house. Coyote made holes in the stones and said, "Perhaps fall salmon will jump into my holes. Silver-side salmon will jump into my holes. Calico salmon will jump into my hole. All kinds of fish will jump in." Crane made himself a harpoon shaft and a harpoon and stood near the water. When a male fall salmon or a silver-side salmon passed him, he speared them. He caught many fish. Then he split them. Every day he did so. Bad [spawning] fall salmon and female silver-side salmon jumped into Coyote's hole. Every now and then a good fish would jump into it.

Now their house was full of fish. The dry salmon of Crane was fat. When Coyote looked he saw that his salmon was all grey and no fat was on it. Coyote thought, "I will kill him and take his dry salmon." Now he sang his conjuring song and Crane helped him. Coyote had a large club. Crane stretched out his neck when he helped Coyote. Then he struck at Crane's neck, but Crane bent it. Coyote was ashamed because he had missed him. Crane put all of his dry fish into a basket. So did Coyote. They were angry with one another. Crane and Coyote were angry.

Crane carried his dry salmon on his back. He came back

several times until he had carried them all away. Coyote, however, was too lazy to carry them on his back. He placed all
those fish in a row. The trail led across the hill to Nɪx'kəle'x.
Coyote thought, "I shall try to drive them." He put roe into his
quiver which he hung over his shoulder. Then he began to drive
his fish. Crane had already gone down the river. Now Coyote
drove the baskets in which his fish were. When they came near
the water, they began to roll rapidly. The first basket arrived at
the river and rolled into it. The next one arrived at the river and
rolled into it. All rolled into the river. He ran after them in
order to hold them. He took hold of his fish, but he was pulled
into the river himself by the roe he had put in his quiver. Then
he took off his arrows and went ashore. All his fish had
disappeared.

Coyote said, "I think the people shall do thus: When they
move from one place to the other they shall not drive their food.
Even I could not do it. They shall work and become tired,
carrying it on their backs when they move." That is the story;
tomorrow it will be good weather.

The Man Who Lived with Thunderer

TILLAMOOK

ONCE UPON A TIME there was a man who lived at Slab Creek. One
day he went up to spear salmon. When he started out the sun
was shining, but soon dark clouds came up and it began to
thunder and to rain. Then it cleared up again, but soon a new
shower came on and the man was unable to spear a single fish. He
became angry and said, "What is that great thing that always
darkens the water and prevents me from seeing the fish?" He
went on and came to a tall spruce tree in which a large hole had
been burned out by lightning. He looked into it and discovered
a little boy. When he looked closer he saw the boy coming out.
As soon as he had stepped out of the hole the boy began to grow,
and soon reached a height taller than the spruce tree; his skin
was covered with feathers. Then he said, "Now you see how tall
I am. Don't look at me; I am the one whom you have scolded!"

Then the giant, who was no other than Thunderer [nixi'xunu], took the man's salmon spear and blanket. He leaned the spear against the tree and hung the blanket on it. He took the man under his armpit and flew with him towards the sky. When they reached a considerable height the man almost fell from under the Thunderer's armpit, and they descended again so that the man could regain his strength. Thunderer thought, "Where shall I put him to keep him from falling off?" He said to the man, "When we get up high again, close your eyes, so that the strong wind up there will not harm you." Then they flew up again and ascended in big circles.

Each flapping of Thunderer's wings was a peal of thunder, and when the noise stopped the man knew they had arrived, and he opened his eyes. On the next day Thunderbird told him to go and catch some salmon. The man went to the beach but did not see any salmon, although there were many whales swimming about. He went back to the house and said, "I do not see any salmon, but many whales are swimming about."

"Those are the fish I was speaking of," replied the Thunderer. "They are our salmon. Catch a few!" The man replied, "They are too large, and I cannot catch them."

They went out and the man saw that the people of Thunderer's country were catching whales in the same way as he was accustomed to catch salmon. Thunderer told him to stand aside, as he himself was preparing to catch whales. He caught the largest one and carried it up to a large cave which was nearby, and when he had deposited it there the whale flapped its tail and jumped about, violently shaking the mountain, so that it was impossible to stand upon it.

One day the man went up the river and saw many fish swimming in it. He thought, "I am tired of whale meat and I wish I could have some fish." He went back to the Thunderer's house and spoke to him, "Grandfather, I have found many fish, and I want to catch them." He made a fish spear, which he showed to the Thunderer; he looked at it, but found it so small that he was hardly able to feel it. It slipped under his fingernail, and he was unable to find it again. The main said, "How large are your fingernails! They are just like the crack of a log," and the Thunderer laughed.

The man made a new spear and went fishing salmon. Before he went the old man said, "Don't catch more than you are able to eat. You may take four or five." —"I cannot eat even one!" Then the grandfather laughed again and said, "If I should eat one hundred I would not have enough."

The man went out, caught one salmon, and brought it home. He was going to split it, but was unable to find a knife small enough for cutting the fish. Then Thunderer split a rock, as he thought, into very small pieces, but the smallest of these was so large that the man was unable to lift it. Then Thunderer broke it into still smaller pieces, and said, "I fear I have spoiled it, for it has become dust so fine that I cannot take hold of it." The man went out, but even then the smallest piece was so large that he was unable to lift it. After Thunderer had broken it again and the man had selected the smallest piece, he said, "It is still too large, but I think I must try to make use of it." Then the Thunderer told him how to cut the fish. He followed his commands and cut the fish, as the people of the Thunderer were accustomed to do.

He [the man] roasted it and ate it, but was unable to eat all. His grandfather [Thunderer] laughed and said, "Put it aside and go to sleep. When you awake you will be able to eat more." When the man awoke and wanted to continue eating the fish, it was gone. It had returned to the river from which he had taken it. He took his spear and went down the river to catch another salmon. There he saw one half of a fish swimming about. It was the one he had been eating. He caught it, roasted it, and finished eating it. The next day he caught another fish, and when he had eaten half of it and wanted to go to sleep he tied the remainder to a pole to prevent its returning to the river. But when he awoke he found that it had returned to the river. He had burned one side of the head of this salmon, and the next day on going to the river he saw the same salmon swimming about. It had taken some grass in its mouth and covered one side of its face, as it was ashamed to show how badly it was burned. Thunderer said, "Don't burn the salmon when you roast them, for they do not like it. They might take revenge upon you."

The next day the Thunderer again went whaling, and the man asked him to be allowed to accompany him, as he wanted to witness the spectacle. Thunderer granted his request, but when he came home in the evening he found that the man was badly hurt. He had been unable to stand on his feet when the whale was shaking the mountain, and was hurt by falling trees and stones. But on the following day the man asked once again if he could go along with Thunderer. He tied himself to a tree, but when

Thunderer came back in the evening to fetch him he found him again badly hurt, as he had been knocked about by the swinging trees.

Meanwhile the relatives of the man had been searching for him for over a year. They had gone up Slab Creek, where they found his spear and blanket leaning against a large spruce tree. They did not know what had become of him. They believed him to be dead, and his [wives] mourned for him.

One day while he was staying with the Thunderer he thought of his wives and children and longed to return. He said to himself, "Oh my children, are you still alive? There is no one to provide for you, and I am afraid you are dead." The Thunderer knew his thoughts and told him, "Do not worry, your wives are quite well. One of them has married again. I will take you back tomorrow." What Thunderer called the next day was actually the next year.

The following day he took the man under his armpit and put him under the spruce tree, from where he had taken him, and then flew back home. The man believed that he had been away only four days, but it had been four years. He did not go to his house, but stayed in the woods nearby. There his son found him. He asked the boy, "Who are you? is your father at home?" The boy replied, believing him to be a stranger, "No, I have no father; he was lost four years ago. For a long time they looked for him, and finally they found his blanket and his salmon spear." Then the man said, "I am your father. The Thunderer took me up in the sky, and I have returned."

Then he inquired after his wives, and the boy answered, "Mother is well, and all my brothers have grown up and are also well. Your other wife has married again, but mother remained true to you." Then the man sent him to call his wife. The boy ran home and said, "Mother! Father is in the woods!" His mother did not believe him, and whipped him for speaking about his [dead] father. Then the boy went out crying. He said to his father, "Mother did not believe me." The man gave him a piece of whale-meat and said, "Take this to your mother; I brought it from where I have been."

The boy obeyed, and took the whale meat to his mother, who said, "I will go with you, but if he is not your father I shall beat you." She accompanied her son and found her husband. He returned with her into the house, and she invited the whole tribe. The man danced and became a great shaman. For ten days he danced, and the people feasted. Then he told them where he had been and what he had seen, and said that whenever they wanted to have a whale he would get one. . . .

Thunderstorm Exorcism

ALSEA

The people would shout at Lightning
  Look sharp, jump back, my friend
  You can't hide behind me, my friend
Then the Thunder would roar,
the people would yell at him
  Look sharp, jump back, my friend
  You can't come in here, my friend
Then someone would go outside and dance
and beat the house with sticks and soon
all the people would be outside dancing
and while Lightning and Thunder were leaving
one man would sing all around the house
  The sky does not always act like this
  The Thunder only comes sometimes
  The sky is not doing anything bad
  It goes right on, this world

How the Coos People Discovered Fire

COOS

THE EARTH was full of people. All kinds of people lived in a mixed-up fashion. They had no fire or water. Whenever they wanted to eat, they would put the food under their arms (in order to eat it). They would dance with it, or the old people would sit on it. And when the food became warm, then they would eat it. Whenever salmon came ashore, they used to scoop it out.

In this manner, they had hardly any food. They were talking about fire all the time. "How would it be if we should go after fire?" —"Let us go." So they went. When they arrived, they found the fire burning; and one of them saw the water. The chief of the people (to whom they came) was sitting indoors. He was sitting sideways. "Halloo, cousin!" said the earth-chief. "Let us gamble (for the fire and water)!" The sky chief acted as if he did not hear. The earth chief sat down opposite him. After a short time the sky chief looked up and said, "You belong to a different tribe, so in what way are you my cousin? You must tell a story." But the earth chief answered, "You are older than I," and he went out. After a while he came back and said, "Halloo, cousin! Look! this here is your Indian cradle" [a pad of hide, for gambling on]. "Your Indian cradle is new, while mine is old. And here are your [gambling sticks], while there are my [gambling sticks]. Your [sticks] are new, but mine are old. Is it not so?" Then he put all these things before him. The sky chief looked at them, and said, "Indeed it is so, O cousin! Sit down here, we will gamble."

They began to play. The earth chief thought to himself, "With what shall I point at the player who puts his hands behind his back to mix up the gambling sticks? Suppose I put a piece of abalone shell into my eye? I will sleep in the inside part of my eye." Then he said to his followers, "You shall support me when I put my hands behind my back [to mix up the sticks]," and what he demanded was done.

Then he [the earth chief] pointed his finger at him (the sky chief) when he put his hands behind his back. Two men were supporting him. Thus things happened. Maggots began to eat up his (the sky chief's) anus, his face, his nose, his ears. Soon the maggots ate him up; but he did not notice it. He kept on sitting there. Two men were still supporting him from the back. He (the earth chief) had an abalone shell in his eye, and was sleeping in that inside part. Now it seemed as if the sky chief were looking at it. To his surprise, he saw an abalone shell in the other man's eye. By this time only bones remained of him, for the maggots had eaten up almost half of his body. The earth chief was sitting there for a while, and began to think, "With what shall I point at him? It seems that I ought to point at him with some very terrible thing." The sky chief still did not look at the maggots.

Only his bones, joined together, were sitting there. Still he did not look.

Now the earth chief said to his people, "Don't forget to seize the fire as soon as we win the game—And [somebody] take hold of the water." One of his men said, "I will run away with the water, and you ought to run with the fire." The earth chief said to the head man of the sky people, "Now it is your turn to put your hands behind your back." All the time he was thinking, "With what shall I point at him? It seems that nothing terrifies him. It will be very good if I point at him with a snake."

In the mean time the fire kept on burning. He (the earth chief) pointed at him (the sky chief) with a snake. But he (the sky chief) was on the lookout. The snake coiled around his thigh. Still he did not mind it. It crawled up to his waist and threatened to go into his mouth, all the while sticking out its tongue. Soon it was ready to enter his nose. The sky chief became afraid when he saw this. He shook off the snake and ran away. People were shouting at him.

The earth people quickly seized the fire. A very poor man ran away with the fire, while a little man kicked the water. They were running homewards. The man put the fire in his ear while running. As soon as the water was spilled, it began to rain. The fire was thrown into some willow-brush, and soon began to blaze. Thus they returned. From that time on, people have had fire; and from that time on, it has rained. Thus only the story is known. This is the end of it.

The Chetco

CHINOOK

LONG AGO a man lived with his dog at Point Adams, near the mouth of the Columbia. One evening the man and the dog were talking, where there was a loud knock at the door. It was a *chetco* monster! He wanted supper and a place to spend the night. So the Indian and his dog tried their best to be hospitable to their unwelcome guest.

In the night, the man awoke, and overheard the *chetco* jabbering and chuckling to himself about his plans to eat his hosts. The man decided to escape by digging a hole under the lodge, at the rear end. He put a piece of wood in his bed as a dummy, and told the dog that he would try to escape beyond Tillamook Head. The dog was to hide his escape tunnel by curling up on it, and lie to the *chetco* about where the man had gone.

When the *chetco* got up he grabbed at the man's bed, but found only the piece of wood. "Where did he go?" he asked the dog. The dog pointed upriver with his nose and said, "That way." So the monster ran upriver for several miles, before realizing that he had been deceived. He ran back to the lodge. "Dog, you tricked me!" he roared, and kicked him to pieces, thereby exposing the man's tunnel. The *chetco* ate the dog and then ran down the beach after the man. The monster was so big and lumbering that he made the sound of distant thunder as he ran along.

Reaching the mouth of the Necanicum River [at Seaside], the *chetco* met Kon-wak-shoo-ma, "Old Thunder," who ferried people over the river. Old Thunder's leg was very long, and when someone was to be ferried he would simply stretch it out across the river and the person would cross over. The *chetco* was carrying a big club made of bones of the dead. Now bones are evil things to the gods and spirits, so when Old Thunder saw the *chetco's* club, he said, "I will ferry you, but only if you do not touch me with that bone-club." The monster promised.

Old Thunder then swung his long leg over the river, and the *chetco* started across, but he was so intent on catching sight of the man that he accidentally touched him with the club. Instantly Old Thunder pulled his leg back, and the *chetco* fell into the river. As he was being swept out to sea, Old Thunder called to him, "You will go on out to sea, and from now on men will hear you roaring out there beyond the surf, and know what weather to expect. When you roar in the south, they will know that a storm is gathering, and when you roar in the north, they will know that a storm is passing away."

Wild Woman Ate Children

NEHALEM TILLAMOOK

PEOPLE WERE LIVING at Flower Pot, right near Bayocean. They had one daughter just in her basket cap [girlhood] and several other children who were small, none of them more than eight or nine years old. The maiden had a little baby brother to take care of. The people told those children the Indian rule, "Children must not eat when they are alone, when there are no grown people present." That older girl remembered that. But the smaller children, they often became hungry.

One day the children were all together in one of the houses. They were hungry, they said, "Our grown people have been gone too long. We are going to eat, we are hungry." They proceeded to eat. They broke off pieces of dried salmon eggs and ate them. They were all very fond of them, in those days. They passed the older girl a piece of those salmon eggs. She took it, but she would not eat it, she just held it in her hand. Those younger children ate, sitting by the fire they were keeping. The maiden carried her baby brother on her back. She walked about with him to keep him from crying. He himself was too small to eat dried salmon eggs.

Presently someone opened the door and came in. It was a woman the children had never seen before. She tossed about ten sharpened red huckleberry stakes into the house. She carried a basket of dry wood, rotten wood, with her. The older girl thought, "My! It looks to me as if she is that Wild Woman [hə'lgu] whom the older people speak of. They say that she acts this way. She uses those sharpened sticks for cooking little children." That woman built a roaring fire with that rotten wood. She seized each child and smelled its mouth. Those that had been eating salmon eggs she caused to be numb so they could not run out doors. That older girl was unable to run as well. The woman smelled of each child's mouth. She went to that maiden, noticed that she had not eaten any salmon eggs. She smelled of that little baby's mouth, he had not eaten any. Then she began.

She took away that older girl's voice so that she could not speak. In the same manner the baby was unable to cry. She took her stakes and inserted one in the anus of each child who had eaten salmon eggs. She put them around the fire to cook.

In the meantime the grown people were all clam-digging. It was not yet dark. They chanced to look toward the house. One said, "What can be happening? It looks as if that house is burning up. The whole house is smoking. We must go home, the children might get burned, they have not enough sense to run out if the house were on fire." They came home. Wild Woman saw those people coming. The children were not yet cooked enough to be eaten. She hastened away from there, she ran into the woods.

The grown people came in. There was that older girl walking about, unable to speak. There were those children staked around the fire, roasting. The people knew at once who had done that, they knew. That maiden could not talk to tell them anything. The next day the people put those children away [in burial canoes]. The father who had lost more children than anyone else said, "You people pack all of your things and leave." He said this to his wife as well. They did not want to go far away, they all went down to the sandspit to stay. There were houses there because it was a summer place for drying clams. They moved there.

That father said, "I will remain here, I will allow her to come to cook me." He knew her, he had her power, Wild Woman's. His wife did not like that, but he said, "Oh, I do not care. I want her to cook me. Do not leave any food of any sort except one piece of dried salmon eggs. She is more jealous of them than of anything else I can eat."

The man was there alone. He sharpened his knife as sharp as a razor. He gathered quantities of wood, kept a bright fire, and went without eating for four days. In the evening of the fourth day he ate those salmon eggs. Soon he heard a noise at the door. He knew that she was coming. She opened the door, she threw in a very large stake of red huckleberry bush, sharpened on both ends. She entered. She brought in that dry rotten wood. He sat up, watched her build up the fire. While she was doing that he got ready with his knife, he ran at her, grabbed her by the hair, he stuck his knife in her eyes. That was the only place she was soft. Those Wild Women are solid all over. Their flesh is not like a person's flesh, one cannot thrust a knife into them. He put her eyes out. He had a club in readiness. She was blind now, so he seized that club and clubbed her. She died. He put her in that great fire she had built. Then he tore the house down and made a larger fire.

Those others who had left had been watching every day. Now they said, "Well, that house appears to be burning." They wept, "He must be killed then." That Wild Woman was full of oil. The sky turned as red as if it too were burning. Then it turned black, pitch dark, though it was not yet night. At last when Wild Woman was nearly burned the man went down to the beach, got into the canoe he had kept there, and paddled down. He arrived at the place where his people were. He said, "I killed her when she was preparing to cook me. I put her eyes out, I mashed her after that, and I burned her."

No one has ever lived in that place since. Everyone is afraid of that place. After Wild Woman was dead that older girl could speak again. She described what Wild Woman had done, how she had smelled the children's mouths and cooked only those who had been eating. In the olden days [myth age] Wild Woman ate only lizards and poisonous things. But later on she ate children.

That is a kind of real happening. This story was told to children to keep them from eating when their parents were away.

The Woman Who Married a Merman

COOS

IN A VILLAGE named Takimiya there lived five brothers and a sister. Many men from different places wished to marry the girl, but she did not want to get married. It was her custom to go swimming every day in a little creek. One day, while returning from her daily swim, she noticed that she was pregnant. Her brothers demanded to know how this had happened, but she could not give them any answer, because she did not know.

After some time she gave birth to a boy, who was in the habit of crying all the time. Everything was tried to stop the baby's crying, but it was of no avail. Her brothers therefore advised her to put it outdoors. As soon as this was done, the baby stopped crying. After a little while the mother went out to look after her boy, and noticed, to her surprise, that he was eating some seal-meat, which was strung on a small stick. She looked around to see who could have given him the meat, but could find nobody.

So she took the child into the house. But the boy started to cry again, and would not let anybody sleep. Her brothers told her to take the child outside again, and advised her to conceal herself and watch it. A whole day she remained outside without seeing anyone.

Suddenly, towards evening, a man appeared and told her to follow him, because he was her husband. At first she refused to go with him, fearing that her relatives would not know where she had gone; but after he had assured her that she would be permitted to see her people again, she took the baby in her arms and followed him. They were going into the water. Her husband told her to hang on to his belt and to keep her eyes closed. She did so, and they arrived at a village at the bottom of the sea, which was inhabited by many Indians. Her husband was one of the five sons of the chief of this village. They lived there happy and satisfied.

The boy grew up in the meantime, and acquired the habit of playing with arrows. His mother would make them for him, and tell the child, at the same time, that his uncles, who lived above them [on the land], had lots of arrows. One day the boy asked his mother whether she would take him to his land uncles to get some arrows. To this the father of the boy objected, but he allowed his wife to go up alone. She put on five sea-otter hides, and started on her way early in the morning. As soon as her brothers saw her from the shore, they thought she was a real otter, and began to shoot at her with arrows. The otter seemed to have been hit repeatedly, but it would come up again, so that they did not know what became of their arrows. The otter was swimming up and down the river, followed by many people in canoes, all shooting at it, but nobody could hurt it.

Seeing the fruitlessness of their efforts, everybody gave up the chase—except the oldest brother, who followed the otter until it reached the beach. Coming nearer, he saw a woman moving around, and he recognized her at once as his lost sister. She told him that she was the sea-otter, and showed him the arrows with which they had been shooting at her. She said "I came here to get some arrows for my boy. My husband is the son of a chief. We are living not far from here. Whenever the tide is low, you can see our house right in the middle of the ocean. I brought you these sea-otter skins that you might exchange for some other things."

Her brother gave her as many arrows as she could carry, and she went back to her husband. But before going down into the water, she said to her brother, "You will find tomorrow morning a whale on the beach, right in front of your landing." And so it came to pass. The whale was divided among the people.

A few months afterwards the woman visited her relatives with her husband and child, and her brothers noticed that her shoulders were turning into those of a dark-colored sea-serpent. She stayed a little while, and then returned home. Long afterwards many of these sea-serpents came into the harbor; but the woman never came ashore again, and was seen no more. These sea-serpents had come after arrows, and the people kept on shooting at them, thereby giving them what they wanted. They never returned again; but every summer and winter they would put ashore two whales as a gift to their kinsmen above the sea.

Coyote and the Two Frog-Women

ALSEA

COYOTE WAS living there. He had no wife. Nobody wanted him. So one day he decided in his inner mind that he would go to the coast to look for dried salmon to buy. He went.

He was not gone long, when he came upon two frog-women who were digging in the ground for camas. Those two women called to him. "Where are you going?" He acted as if he didn't hear. When they had yelled at him for a third time, he seemed to pay attention. "What do you two want?" —"Nothing. We've just been trying to ask you a question." —"What is it?" —"Oh, where are you going?" —"I'm going to the coast to look for salmon." —"All right; are you going to leave us some on your way back?" —"Certainly," said Coyote. So he went on.

Now he was thinking in his inner mind, "I wonder how I am going to play a trick on those two?" He hadn't gone far when he saw some yellowjackets hanging on a branch. He went to the nest and took it off the tree, and closed it so that the yellowjackets could not come out. Then he put the nest into his basket. And after he put it into his basket, he opened the nest again, and then tied his basket tightly. Then after he had finished, he put it on like a pack, and went back to the two women.

Pretty soon he got back there, where those women were digging for camas. He did not seem to pay any attention to them. They shouted at him, "Hey, are you on your way home?" —"Yes, I am on my way home." —"How much salmon are you bringing back?" "Not very much." —"You promised to leave some behind for us two." —"All right, come and get it."

So they came up. Then he began to untie his pack. "You two put your heads inside this basket!" They did. Whereupon, after they had gotten their heads inside, he kicked his pack. The yellowjackets came out very angry, and stung the two frog-women, and they died. And after they were dead, that Coyote took off their vulvas, and went on. Now whenever he felt like intercourse, he would dig a hole in the ground, and put those vulvas there, and then do it.

Pretty soon those two women came to life again, and one of them began to examine herself. "My vulva is gone. How about you?" The other woman examined herself, and her vulva was gone! They agreed, "It was Coyote who played this trick on the two of us."

For this reason frogs, they say, have no female organs. So it ends.

The Magic Hazel Twig

ALSEA

FIVE BROTHERS were once living together. Their father was a very old man, and he wore a blanket made of the skin taken from the necks of elks. Each of the five brothers had children. One of these was a girl.

One day, the children took a hazel twig and began to twist it until it was soft. Only the inner part of the twig remained hard. This they separated and wrapped up in skins until it looked like a doll, which they gave to their younger sister. The girl took the doll and hid it away. Once in a while she would go to the hiding place to have a look at her doll.

One day when she took out her doll she found it had skin just like a human being. The next day the doll had a human face and even opened its eyes. On the third day it had legs and arms and looked just like a person; on the fourth day she found it smiling and raising its hands, and on the fifth day it was talking, and said: "You liked me when I was the heart of a hazel tree. Will you like me now after I have turned into a human being?" Then the next day, before daylight appeared, the girl went to look at her doll. As soon as she unwrapped the blankets the doll got up and walked around in the shape of a fine-looking boy.

Thereafter the boy ran around with the other children and became their playmate. One day one of the boys got into a fight with him, and he fought back. So that boy went home and told his parents that Teu'lsa was mean to him. Then Teu'lsa became ashamed and thought, "I guess they don't want me to be a person." So he took his foster grandfather's elkhide blanket and wrapped himself up in it until no part of his body showed. Then he lay down and refused to get up when called by his foster parents. On the third night they spoke harshly to him: "Here now! What is the matter with you? Get up!" But he answered, "No! Just leave me alone. I am getting to be different again."

The next night toward midnight they heard a noise as if some one were kicking, and pretty soon they heard the boy say, "Now I have split hooves already." Throughout the day he refused to come out of his corner. At night he spoke to the old grandfather saying, "Old man, look out! I have horns now." Then they became afraid of him and did not come near him any longer. They kept away from him. On the fifth night they heard him kicking around and trampling the ground, and pretty soon they saw him get up, looking like a natural elk. When they got up in the morning, he was standing in the shape of an elk.

After sunrise he tore the house down with his horns, and as he left he hooked the oldest brother and carried him off on his horns. The other people pursued him, shooting at him with arrows, but he did not seem to be hurt. Soon he turned on his pursuers and hooked another brother, leaving only three brothers. After awhile he got another one. Then the two remaining brothers began to cry, "That Teu'lsa has killed our elder brothers!" Still they kept on pursuing him, and as one of the remaining brothers was about to overtake him he turned on him suddenly and hooked him with his horns. This left only one brother, whose name was Mo'luptsɪni'sla.

Then Mo'luptsɪni'sla kept on following him all the way to Otter Rock [above Yaquina Head]. When they arrived there, the boy who had turned into an elk stopped and spoke to his pursuing brother, "Why don't you shoot me in the heart and kill me?" So Mo'luptsɩni'sla killed him. And while Teu'lsa was dying he said, "—Cut off my ears and nose and eyes and also all my sinews, and keep them." Then Mo'luptsɩni'sla followed these directions and put all those things into his quiver.

Then Mo'luptsɩni'sla climbed the mountain and came to a village. When the people living in this village saw him they said, "Here comes our brother-in-law." So he married one of the girls belonging to that village and stayed there for a long time.

One day his brothers-in-law asked him to accompany them to the place where they were working. So in the morning Mo'luptsɩni'sla took his quiver and went with his brothers-in-law. When they arrived at the place, he looked around and thought: "So this is what they are doing. They are gathering mussels." Then he helped for a long time. When the canoe was full, one of his brothers-in-law said, "Let us go out farther!" So they went out farther into the sea until they came to a rock. They left the canoe and climbed up on the rock, looking for some more mussels. After a while his brother-in-law said to him, "Wait here while we take the mussels to the canoe." So they left him.

Mo'luptsɩni'sla waited for them for a long time in vain. Then he climbed down, but when he came to the place where the canoe was, he found that he was alone. He did not know how to get back to the shore. He began to cry. After a while he remembered what Teu'lsa told him before his death. So he took out the ears and nose and eyes of the dead elk and spread them out on the rock. Then he took the largest sinew and lashed the rock with it. Presto! A canoe appeared in front of him. Then he placed the nose in the bow of the canoe alongside of the eyes and the ears, and the tail he commanded to act as a steersman. He himself stood in the middle of the canoe. Then the canoe started to move. It went very fast. As they went along the eyes of the dead elk acted as lookouts. Soon they were within sight of the shore.

When his brothers-in-law saw him, they said, "Here comes our brother-in-law." But he did not go ashore right away. He kept on floating close to the shore without landing. Finally he said to himself: "What am I doing here? I am going to go back to my own country." So he came ashore. As soon as he got out of the canoe he hit it on the ground and it disappeared. Then he put the nose, ears, eyes, and sinews of the dead elk back into his quiver and left his treacherous brothers-in-law for good.

This is all.

Xi'lgo and the Brother and Sister Who Married Each Other

TILLAMOOK

THERE WAS an old woman named Xi'lgo, and an old man who lived far up Nestucca River. The old man lived a little farther up than the old woman. He had no wife, and she had no husband. The old woman said, "I will go and try to find some children." She went down to the shore and sat down near a small lake, where she knew children used to go bathing. While she sat there waiting, two brothers and their sister came to the shore and began to play. After a while they took a bath, returned to the shore, and fell asleep. Then Xi'lgo, who carried a basket on her back, took one of the boys first, the girl next, and finally the other boy, threw them into her basket, and carried them away.

After a while the boy who lay in the bottom of the basket, and whose name was Taxuxsha, awoke, and on finding where he was, scratched a hole in the bottom of the basket, and escaped. He ran away, and for fear jumped into the sea, where he has lived ever since.

Xi'lgo did not notice his escape. When she reached home, she took the children out of the basket. They awoke, and did not know where they were. She led them into her house, and gave them a place to sleep. On the next morning she said, "If you wish anything to eat, you must go to an old man who lives farther up the river, and has a salmon-trap which is full every morning; there are both small and large fish in it." The children went, and saw the old man roasting salmon which he had fastened to a split stick and placed near the fire. He asked them what they wanted. "Do you want to eat salmon?" They replied, "Yes, we are hungry, and we came up here to eat. Xi'lgo sent us here."

When they had eaten, they said to the old man, "Tell us

something," and he told them a tale and gave them many instructions. Then they returned. They found the old woman near the fire, where she was heating stones. She asked the children, "Did the old man tell you a story?" and they replied, "Yes; he told us many tales, and gave us many instructions." Then she took the stones off the fire, placed skunk-cabbage leaves on top of the stones, and covered them with grass. When the skunk-cabbage was done, she ate it. Then she said, "You must go to the old man tomorrow morning and take him some skunk-cabbage; he will give you salmon in return."

The children obeyed, and took some skunk-cabbage to him; he gave them salmon in return, and told them stories. When the children returned, Xi'lgo asked them, "Did he tell you stories?" When she heard that the old man had done so, she became angry, took her knife, and said, "I will kill him." She went there, and lay down with the old man. After a while she returned and said, "I have killed him." Then the children thought, "Where shall we get anything to eat if the old man is dead?" Xi'lgo sang all the afternoon until late in the evening. On the following day she rose early and went out to get some skunk-cabbage. She returned before the children awoke and cooked it. She told them to take some of it to the old man. They thought, "Didn't she kill him yesterday? She told us that he was dead." Xi'lgo knew their thoughts at once, and said, "Where would you find anything to eat if I had killed him?"

Then the children went and found the old man roasting salmon as usual. He gave them some to eat, and when they were done he told them a story. On their return, Xi'lgo asked at once, "Did he tell you stories?" "Yes," they replied, "he told us a story." Then the old woman grew very angry. She took a long knife and said she would kill the old man. First they heard them talking for a long time. Then it became quiet. Again Xi'lgo lay down with the old man. Before going back she pulled her hair over her face, then she went back singing, "I have killed him; I have killed the old man! He spoke evil of me."

Early the next morning she rose and went to get some skunk-cabbage. She returned before the children were awake, and cooked it. She told the children to take some of it to the old man. They thought, "Didn't she kill him yesterday? She told us she had done so." Xi'lgo knew their thoughts at once, and said, "Where would you find anything to eat if I had killed him?" Then the children went and found the old man roasting salmon as usual. He gave them something to eat. Then the children said, "We have enough," and asked him to tell them something. The old man said, "What shall I tell you? She is fooling you, she is fooling you." Then the children thought, "How is she fooling us?"

They returned, and Xi'lgo asked them, "What did he tell you? Did he tell you stories?" "Yes," they replied, "he told us stories." Xi'lgo began to cry. "And what did he tell you? He has always abused my father." Then she took a knife and went out, saying that she was going to kill the old man.

When she left, the children were playing with shells. They arranged them in couples as husbands and wives. They saw her leaving, and they thought, "Did she say she was going to kill the old man? We will go and see what she is doing, and how she is fooling us." They took the shells along, all except one couple, and followed her to the house of the old man. They heard the old couple whispering together. They went to a chink in the wall, through which they peeped, and they saw them lying down together and talking. Xi'lgo cried at once, "How that tickles! I feel like someone is looking at me." She wanted to jump up, but the old man said, "Oh, don't be in a hurry."

The children ran away at once. When Xi'lgo came back to her home, she did not find them. She saw only the one pair of shells, which they had left. Then she said, "When you have grown up, you shall live as husband and wife."

The children went on and came to Clatsop, where they built a house. When the house was completed, the boy said to the girl, "Stay in that corner of the house, and I will stay in the one diagonally opposite." At night, when he was in bed, he heard the girl saying, "It [the rain] is dripping here." Then the boy said, "Put your bed in the other far corner." The girl did so, and after a short time she said, "It is dripping here." Then the boy said, "Move your bed a little more this way, to the middle of the long side of the house." After a short time she said again, "It is dripping here too," and he told her, "Come here to this side," After a short time the girl said again, "It is dripping here," and then he called her, and they lay down together. In due time she gave birth to a baby boy. The father and his son used to sleep on the roof of the house.

After a while Xi'lgo began to pursue the children. One day, when the young mother had gone picking berries, Xi'lgo reached the Columbia River, at a place opposite to where the house stood.

She saw the man and the boy sleeping on the roof. She called to them to take her across. The man did not hear her, and finally she became angry and said, "I wish you were dead." Then she went back home.

The man died, blood pouring from his mouth. At the time of sunset the boy awoke and began to cry. By this time his mother returned, and heard her child crying. She called to her husband, "Don't you hear our child crying? Come take him down." As he did not stir, she went up on the roof and saw the blood. She turned the body over and found that her brother was dead. Then she took her son up on her back, crying, "What shall I do?" She thought, "I will set fire to the house and burn myself." She gave her boy to a woman who lived close by, and then set fire to the house at one corner, and jumped into the flames.

After the fire had burned down, the woman who was to take care of the boy went and took a bone of the wrist of the woman and one rib of the man. She made a ball of the former and a bat of the latter for the boy to play with. She kept them at home until he was able to walk.

One day, when he was playing with his bat and ball, he happened to hit a girl who was standing by. She cried and said, "You have made me sick with your mother's and father's bones." Then the boy thought, "Are these my mother's and father's bones?" Crying, he went into the house of the woman who took care of him, and said, "A girl abused me, saying that those were my mother's and father's bones." Then the woman became very angry, and whipped the girl until she began to cry. She cried so long that her nose became thin and pointed.

The boy grew up, always thinking of his mother and father. He asked the old woman, "Who killed my mother and father?" She told him, "The one who killed them lives very far off, but if you want to go there I will help you." He wished to go, and the woman said, "A girl must go with you."

They selected a girl, and gave her a fine sea-otter skin to wear. The woman said, "Try to walk underground." She did so, assuming the shape of a mole. Then the woman told the boy, "Try to fly." He put a feather under his arm and flew away in the shape of an eagle. Then the two went to find Xi'lgo.

As they were going he told the girl, "When we reach a town I will fly in front of the houses, and all the people will come out; then you must go underground and steal all the dentalia-shells you can get hold of." When they came to a village he assumed the shape of an eagle. The people were all assembled in one house. One man who happened to go out saw the eagle, and called the people, saying, "See what is coming there!" They all rushed out, and among them was an old woman, who was no other than Xi'lgo. Meanwhile, the girl had assumed the shape of a mole, and had gained entry into the houses by burrowing underground. She stole all the dentalia she could lay her hands on. When Xi'lgo came out of the house, the eagle rushed down and took her up. Her hat fell down when he lifted her up, but he took her out to the ocean, where he tore her to pieces.

Then he joined the girl again, and they travelled on. Soon they came to another town. Again the people rushed out of the houses to see the eagle, and last of all there came an old woman, who was no other than Xi'lgo. The young man was surprised to see her still alive. He took her, carried her far out into the ocean, and tore her to pieces. When he snatched her up, her hat fell down.

He returned and met the girl, and they travelled on and met the Blue Jay [Wa'shwa'sh], who asked them, "What are you going to do with the old woman?" The young man replied, "I want to kill her. Do you know how I can accomplish it?" Blue Jay did not reply, and they left him.

After a while they came to a town, and again the people came out to see the eagle, and last among them an old woman, who was no other than Xi'lgo. Once more he took her up and tore her to pieces far out over the ocean, and her hat fell off as he lifted her up. He returned and met the girl, and when they were travelling again they again met the Blue Jay, who asked them what they were going to do with the old woman. The young man replied again, "I want to kill her." Then the Blue Jay said, "You must not take her body, but take her hat. You will find a small thing in the top of her hat. That is her heart. You must tear that and throw the pieces into the sea, then she will be dead." He followed this advice the next time, and succeeded in killing the old woman.

In every town where they had been the girl had taken dentalia, and now they divided it among themselves, and returned home.

The White Wife of Mouse

COOS

THE YOUNG MAN, Grey Mouse, traveled around, he journeyed all over. Even to places far away he would go. Then indeed once he saw a girl, a pretty girl, the girl's dress was white. "Aaah, I will have her for my wife."

He did marry her, and he took home his wife. Now he told her thus, "When I am away you are not to cook. And when I get back home then I will do the cooking for you. You might get hurt." So indeed his wife never cooked.

Once when her husband was gone, she said, "Oh, I will cook. I do not see why I should get hurt. Why, I would not get hurt." So then to be sure she cooked mussels, and then a barnacle on the mussel popped, it popped right in her eyes, and it killed her.

Now her husband got back home. "White one! Where are you?" Nothing answered him. So he sought her, and then he found her dead. Now he wept,

"My wife! my wife! my wife!
I told you all the time like that, I told you
you must not, you must not cook.
My wife! My wife!
You were so pretty, so pretty.
My heart is so sick that you died.
My wife! My wife!"

The Girl Who Married a Ghost

CHINOOK

THERE WERE Blue-Jay and his sister Io'i. One night the ghosts went out to buy a wife. They bought Io'i. (Her family) kept the dentalia (which they had given as a dowry), and at night they were married. On the following morning Io'i disappeared. Blue-Jay stayed at home for a year, then he said, "I shall go and search for my sister." He asked all the trees, "Where do people go when they die?" He asked all the birds, but they did not tell him. Then he asked an old wedge. It said, "Pay me, and I shall carry you there." Then he paid it, and it carried him to the ghosts.

The wedge and Blue-Jay arrived near a large town. There was no smoke (rising from the houses). Only from the last house, which was very large, they saw smoke rising. Blue-Jay entered this house and found his elder sister [Ioʼi]. "Ah, my brother," she said, "where do you come from? Have you died?" "Oh no, I am not dead. The wedge brought me here on his back." Then he went and opened all those houses. They were full of bones. A skull and bones lay near his sister. "What are you doing with these bones and this skull?" (asked Blue-Jay). His sister replied: "That is your brother-in-law; that is your brother-in-law." "Pshaw! Ioʼi is lying all the time. She says a skull is my brother-in-law!" When it grew dark the people arose, and the house became quite full. It was ten fathoms long.

[Blue-Jay] said to his sister, "Where did these people come from?" She replied, "Do you think they are people? They are ghosts." He stayed with his sister a long time. She said to him, "Do as they do and go fishing with your dipnet." "I think I will do that," he replied. When it grew dark he made himself ready. A boy (whom he was to accompany) made himself ready also. Those people always spoke in whispers. He did not understand them. His elder sister said to him, "You will go with that boy; he is one of your brother-in-law's relations." She continued, "Do not speak to him, but keep quiet."

Now they started. They had almost reached a number of people who were going down the river singing in their canoes. Then Blue-Jay joined their song. They became quiet at once. Blue-Jay looked back and saw that (in place of the boy) there were only bones in the stern of his canoe. They continued to go down the river, and Blue-Jay kept quiet. Then he looked back towards the stern of the canoe. The boy was sitting there again. He said to him in a low voice, "Where is your weir?" He spoke slowly. The boy replied, "It is down the river." They went on. Then Blue-Jay said in a loud voice, "Where is your weir?" And only a skeleton was in the stern of the canoe. Blue-Jay was again silent. He looked back and the boy was sitting again in the canoe. Then he said again in a low voice, "Where is your weir?" —"Here," replied the boy.

Now they fished with their dipnets. Blue-Jay felt something in his net. He lifted it and found only two branches in his net. He turned his net and threw them into the water. After a short while he put his net again into the water. It became full of leaves. He turned his net and threw them into the water, but some of the leaves fell into the canoe. The boy gathered them up. Then another branch came into (Blue-Jay's) net. He turned the net and threw it into the water. Some leaves came in and he threw them into the water. Some of the leaves again fell into the canoe. The boy gathered them up. (Blue-Jay) was pleased with two of the branches (which had caught in his net). He thought, "I will carry them to Io'i. She may use them for making fire." These branches were large.

They arrived at home and went up to the house. Blue-Jay was angry, because he had not caught anything. The boy brought up a mat full of trout to the house, and the people roasted them. Then the boy told them, "He threw out of the canoe what we had caught. Our canoe would have been full if he had not thrown it away." His sister said to Blue-Jay: "Why did you throw away what you had caught?" —"I threw it away because we had nothing but branches." "That is our food," she replied. "Do you think they were branches? The leaves were trout, and the branches were fall salmon." He said to his sister, "Well, I brought you two branches, you may use them for making fire." Then his sister went down to the beach. Now there were two fall salmon in the canoe. She carried them up to the house. Blue-Jay said to his elder sister, "Where did you steal those fall salmon?" She replied, "That is what you caught." Blue-Jay replied, "Io'i is always lying."

On the next day Blue-Jay went to the beach. There lay the canoes of the ghosts. They all had holes, and parts of them were mossgrown. He went up to the house and said to his sister, "How bad are your husband's canoes, Io'i." —"Oh, be quiet," she said; "the people will become tired of you." —"But the canoes of these people are full of holes!" Then his sister said to him, "Are they people? Are they people? They are ghosts." It grew dark again and Blue-Jay made himself ready. The boy made himself ready also. They went fishing again. Now he teased the boy. When they were on their way he shouted, and only bones were there. This he did several times until finally they arrived at the weir. Now they fished with their dipnets. He gathered the branches and leaves (which they caught), and when the ebb-tide set in their canoe was full. Then they went home. Now he teased the ghosts. He shouted as soon as they met one, and only bones were in the canoe. They arrived at home. He went up to his sister. She carried up (what he had caught); in part fall salmon, in part silver-side salmon.

On the next morning Blue-Jay went into the town. He found many old bones in the houses. When it grew dark (somebody said), "Ah, a whale has been found!" His sister gave him a knife and said, "Run! a whale has been found!" Blue-Jay ran and came to the beach. He met one of the people and asked in a loud voice, "Where is the whale?" Only a skeleton lay there. He kicked the skull and left it. He ran some distance and met other people. He shouted loudly; only skeletons lay there. Several times he did this to the people. Then he came to a large log. Its bark was perhaps *that* [gesture] thick. There was a crowd of people who were peeling off the bark. Blue-Jay shouted and only skeletons lay there. The bark was full of pitch. He peeled off two pieces, I do not know how large. He carried them home on his shoulder. He thought, "I really believed it was a whale, and, behold, it is a fir [log]."

He went home. When he arrived there he threw the bark down outside the house. He entered and said to his sister, "I really thought it was a whale. Look here, it is just bark." His sister said, "It is whale meat, it is whale meat; do you think it is just bark?" His sister went out and two cuts of whale meat lay on the ground. Ioʼi said, "It is a good whale, its (blubber) is very thick." Blue-Jay looked. A whale lay on the beach. Then he turned back. He met a person carrying bark on his back. He shouted and nothing but a skeleton lay there. He took that piece of bark and carried it home on his shoulder. He came home. This is what he did to the ghosts. In the course of time he had a lot of whale meat.

Now he continued to stay there. He went again to that town. He entered a house and took a child's skull, which he put on a large skeleton. And he took a large skull and put it on that child's skeleton. Thus he did to all the people. When it grew dark the child rose to its feet. It wanted to sit up, but it fell down again because its head pulled it down. The old man arose. His head was too light! The next morning Blue-Jay replaced the heads. Sometimes he did this to the legs of the ghosts. He gave small legs to an old man, and large legs to a child. Sometimes he exchanged a man's and a woman's legs.

In course of time they began to dislike him. Io'i's husband said: "These people dislike him because he mistreats them. Tell him he must go home. These people do not like him." Io'i tried to stop her younger brother. But he did not follow her. On the next morning he awoke early. Io'i was holding a skull in her arms. He threw it away. "Why do you hold that skull, Io'i?" "Ah, you have broken your brother-in-law's neck!" It grew dark. Now his brother-in-law was sick. A [shaman] tried to cure him, and he became well again.

Now Blue-Jay went home. His sister gave him five buckets full of water and said, "Take care! When you come to burning prairies, do not pour it out until you come to the fourth prairie. Then pour it out." "All right," replied Blue-Jay. Now he went home. He reached a prairie. It was hot. Red flowers bloomed on the prairie. Then he poured water on the prairie and one of his buckets was half empty. He reached the woods (and soon he came to a) prairie, which was burning at its end. He reached another prairie which was half on fire. "This is what my sister told me about." He poured the rest of the bucket out on the trail. He took another bucket and poured, and when it was half empty he reached the woods on the other side of the prairie. He reached still another prairie, the third one. One half of it was burning strongly. He took one of his buckets and emptied it. He took one more bucket and emptied one-half of it. Then he reached the woods on the other side of the prairie.

Now he had only two buckets and a half left. He reached another prairie which was almost totally on fire. He took that half bucket and emptied it. He took one more bucket, and when he reached the woods at the far side of the prairie he had emptied it. Now only one bucket was left. He reached another prairie which was completely ablaze. He poured out his last bucket. When he had gotten nearly across he had emptied his bucket. He took off his bearskin blanket and beat the fire. The whole bearskin blanket was burned. Then his head and his hair caught fire and he was burned.

Now Blue-Jay was dead. When it was just growing dark he came to his sister. "Kukukukukuku, Io'i," he called. His sister cried, "Ah, my brother is dead." His trail led to the water on the other side of the river. She launched her canoe and went to fetch him. She reached him. Io'i's canoe was pretty. She said to him, "And you said that canoe was moss-grown!" —"Ah, Io'i is always telling lies. The other ones had holes and were moss-grown, anyway." She said to him, "You are dead now, (therefore you see them differently)." —"Io'i is always telling lies."

Now she carried her brother across to the other side. He saw the people. They sang, they played *ιtlukum*, they played at dice with beaver teeth; the women played hoops; they played at dice with ten disks, they played *washakoa'i*. Farther in the town they sang conjurers' songs. Blue-Jay heard them. They were dancing kumm, kumm, kumm, kumm. He wanted to go to these singers. He tried to sing and to shout, but he was laughed at. He kept trying to shout but they all laughed at him.

Then he entered his brother-in-law's house. [He] was a chief; Io'i's husband was good-looking. She said, "And you broke his neck!" —"Io'i is always telling lies. Where did these canoes come from? They are pretty." —"And you said they were all moss-grown!" —"Io'i is always telling lies. The others all had holes. Parts of them were moss-grown." —"You are dead now, (therefore you see everything differently)" said his sister. —"Io'i is always telling lies." He tried to shout at the people, but they laughed at him. Then he gave it up and became quiet. His sister forgot him (for a moment). When she went to look for him, he was standing near the dancers. After five nights he entered their house. His sister opened the door and saw him dancing on his head, his legs upward. She turned back and cried. Now he had really died. He had died a second time.

How a Chinook Went to the Land of the Dead and Came Back

CHINOOK

"I WENT TO the ghosts. After some time I saw two persons carrying a stick on their shoulders. When I came near I saw that they were not persons, but posts of a house which carried a crossbeam. After a while I reached a person who hauled his entrails after him. Then I saw that it was a rush mat.

"After a while I came to a river. On the other side I saw a

large town, and I heard the noise of people building canoes. A person came to meet me, and I recognized my mother's relative who had recently died. He said, 'We waited for you; have you come at last? We heard you were coming. We have brought the girl for you whom you wanted to marry [the girl who died].'

"The grass where I stood was three fingers wide and as tall as a man. It waved and sounded like bells. The grass told the people on the other side who was coming. Then I saw the girl whom the people had brought, and I thought, 'I do not like her now; she looks just as her mother used to look.' I recognized my uncle among the people who came to meet me; he said, 'I brought some seal for you.' He gave me something that looked just like soap, and said, 'Eat this.' It tasted bad, and I did not swallow it, and he said, 'What will you eat? Why do you refuse what I give you?' I thought, 'I just came here, and already you are scolding me. I will return.' Then I turned around, and at once the sun struck my right side. Then I recovered my senses and found myself here."

The Journey across the Ocean

TILLAMOOK

ONCE UPON A TIME there were many people standing on the beach. They saw what they thought to be a whale drifting by, and many birds sitting on its back. Five brothers launched their canoe and went out to tow the whale to the beach. When they had been gone a little while and were approaching the thing, one of the men said, "That is no whale," but the others did not believe him. They went on, and when they were nearby they saw that it *was* no whale, but a canoe covered with whale skin on which birds were sitting. People from the other side of the ocean, the Tlxuɪna'i, were in it. When they [the brothers] saw this, they turned back as quickly as possible.

The people from the other side of the ocean pursued them. The brothers had just about gotten to the beach, when the other canoe overtook them. One of the five brothers jumped ashore, but the pursuers caused the water to draw back from the beach, and thus drew the canoe back out to sea. They took the four brothers who had remained in the canoe and began to return to their own country. They hunted whales while crossing the ocean, but whenever they were unsuccessful they cut pieces of flesh from the men they had captured and used it for bait. Finally nothing but their bones remained. Three of the brothers died, but the last, although nothing but his bones remained, was still alive [when they arrived].

The man who had escaped ran up to the house calling, "The men from the other side of the ocean have taken my brothers!" He went to the top of Bald Mountain, at the mouth of Salmon River [just south of Cascade Head] where he stayed twenty days fasting. Then he dreamed of his brothers. After this he returned to the village and asked all the people to go with him across the ocean to see what had become of his brothers.

They fitted out their largest canoe and started out the next morning. At nightfall they stopped far out at sea. The mountains of their home had disappeared from their view. Early in the morning they travelled on and stopped again at night-time. Thus they travelled for many days, steering towards the sunset. Finally they saw the land at the other side of the ocean. They found a kind of wood which they did not know. It looked like reed, but was as tall as a tree. They went ashore, and the man who had escaped from the canoe said, "I will go alone and look for my brothers."

He went along the beach and finally found a house. He waited until the following morning, and then he saw smoke rising from the roof. He opened the door a little way and peeped into the room. He saw a few old blankets. There was no living person to be seen. Cautiously he entered, and saw that there was something stirring about under the blankets. He was frightened and about to run, but he took heart and looked more closely. He found the bones of his brothers under the blankets.

They said, "Have you come, brother? You cannot help us now. We cannot move, and you cannot restore us to our former lives. But let us take revenge on these people. Take some of them back with you across the ocean. Every day their women go out to gather skunk-cabbage. Two go in each canoe, and when they return they will all come ashore and carry the skunk-cabbage up to the house. One will stay in her canoe. She is the chief's daughter. Her garments are covered with dentalia."

The man left the house, returned to his canoe, and told his

people what he had seen and heard. On the following day they hid in the woods. The women returned from gathering skunk-cabbage, and one girl remained in the canoe. Then they launched their canoe, bailed it out, ran up to the girl, captured her, and left the shore. They put her in the bottom of the canoe. She said, "Treat me well. I shall not attempt to run away." They returned across the ocean, travelling in the daytime and resting at night. They had been unable to take along the brothers whom the Tlxuɩna'i had captured, as they were nothing but bones, which would have brought bad luck to their canoe. On the third day at nightfall they began to see the mountains at the mouth of Salmon River, and on the fourth day, at sunset, they reached their village. There the last brother married the daughter of the Tlxuɩna'i chief.

After a while she was with child. She used to go out to the beach, look towards the sunset, and say, "Where the sun sets is my father's house." Every day she did the same thing. One night the people went out to see what she was doing. They did not find her at the place where she was accustomed to sit, and on coming toward the spot they saw her walking down the river on the surface of the water. She reached the sea and went over breakers and over waves back to her father's house. They were unable to bring her back.

After she had arrived at her father's house she gave birth to a boy. When he began to grow up, he made a bow and arrow and shot birds. One day his mother told him that his father was a chief in a village on the other side of the ocean. She said, "I came back before you were born. I was pregnant with you for ten months. It may be that your father will come here some day looking for me. If you should ever see a man who does not belong to this side of the ocean, think that he is your father. Ask him where he comes from, and treat him kindly."

After a number of years the man asked his people to accompany him once more across the ocean. He wished to look for his wife. He filled his canoe with precious skins and blankets and started out.

On arriving on the other side he hid his canoe in the woods, left his people in charge of it, and went alone to look for his wife. He hid behind a hill under some bushes, where he was able to see all that was going on, while he himself was invisible. Finally he saw a boy coming, playing with bow and arrows. The boy tried his strength, shooting as far as he could, and then gathering up his arrows. One arrow fell close to the man, who took it up. The boy ran after the arrow, and found his father.

He asked, "To what tribe do you belong? You do not belong here." The man replied, "I belong to the other side of the ocean." Then the boy said, "Mother told me that she had carried me for ten months when she came here. She told me that if I should see a stranger I should treat him well, because he might be my father." Then the man was glad and said, "I am your father."

He said to the boy, "Go home and tell your mother I am here. Is your grandfather at home?" —"No; they have gone whaling," replied the boy. He returned to the house and found his mother sitting with many other women. He stepped up to her and whispered in her ear, "I found Father; he wants to see you," and then ran out of the house again. In order to avoid suspicion, the woman did not stir until midnight, when all the other women were sleeping, and then went out to see her husband. She said, "Have your people come with you?" He said, "Yes, they are waiting for me in the canoe."

She said, "Call them; I will give them [something] to eat." At first they were afraid lest her father might kill them. But she reassured them, and called them in. Finally they hid their bows and arrows and knives under their blankets and entered the house. After they had eaten, the woman's father returned, and when he saw the strangers he grew angry, but his daughter took him out of the house, and told him, "This is my husband. I love him. You shall not murder him. They are going to give you many fine presents." Then they became good friends. The strangers gave him many skins and blankets and dentalia shells. After a while they returned home, accompanied by the woman and her son. Her father gave her beautiful clothing and many dentalia to take with her.

The Revenge against the Sky People

COOS

A MAN LIVED in kiwε'εt. He had an elder brother, who was always building canoes. Once he was working on a canoe, (when) a man came there to him. "What do you do with your canoes after you finish them?" —"I always sell my canoes." He kept on working, with his head bent down, while the man was talking to him. Alongside the man who was building lay his dog. All at once he [the stranger] hit the neck of the man who was building, and cut off his head. He took his head home.

The man who was building did not come home, and they went out looking for him. He lay in the canoe, dead, without a head. The little dog was barking alongside the canoe. The dog would look upwards every time it barked. Straight up it would look. So they began to think, "(Someone) from above must have killed him!" Then the next day the man's younger brother looked for him. The young man shot an arrow upwards, and then would shoot another one. He was shooting the arrows upwards. Every time he shot, his arrow would join (to the other); and as he kept on shooting this way, the arrows reached [down] to him.

Then he climbed up there. He went up on the arrows. He saw people when he had gotten up, and he asked, "From where do you come?" They were taking home a man's head. "We are [going to dance] for it," they said. They were taking home his elder brother's head. They said to the young man, "At a little place [nearby] the wife of the killer is digging fern-roots. Every forenoon she digs fern-roots there." So he went. He did not go very far. Suddenly, indeed, [he saw] a woman digging fern-roots. There was a big river.

So he asked the woman, "Do you have your own canoe?" —"Not so." —"Who ferries you across the river?" —"My husband ferries me across." —"What do you do when he ferries you across?" —"He does not land the canoe. I usually jump ashore." —"What does he do afterward?" —"He usually turns back. Then, when it is almost evening, I go home. He again comes after me. A little ways off [shore] he stops the canoe. Then I jump in with my pack. I get in there all right." —"What do you do with your fern-roots?" —"I usually dry them." —"What do you do with your fern-roots after they are dry?" —"I usually give some of them to all the people who live here. A little ways off in the next house, there live an old man and an old woman. I never give them any fern-roots." —"What do you usually do?" —"Then I cook the roots in a big pot." —"What do you do (then)?" —"I stir them with my hands." —"Doesn't your hand get burned?" —"Not so." —"Does your pot boil? Don't you ever say 'It hurts my hand!'?" —"No, it doesn't hurt me." —"What does your husband do when you lie down?" —"I lie a little ways off from my husband." —"Does your husband usually fall asleep quickly?" —"Yes, he usually falls asleep quickly."

Now he asked her all [these questions], and then killed her. He skinned the woman, and put on her hide. Indeed, he looked just like the woman. Then he took her load and packed it. He saw the husband coming. The husband was crossing. A little ways off in the river he stopped the canoe. Thus he [the young man] was thinking, "I wonder whether I shall get there if I jump! I will try it from this distance." He packed the load and jumped. One leg touched the water. He pretty nearly did not get there. Thus spoke the man [husband], "Is that you, my wife?" Thus he spoke: "I am tired, this is the reason why I almost did not get (there). My pack is heavy." He [the husband] did not think about it any more.

Whatever the woman had told him, the young man (did it) that way. He made only one mistake. He gave fern-roots to those old people. He opened their door. The two old people saw him when he entered. They did not take the fern-roots which he held in his hands. Then one [of them] shouted, "Someone from below gives us something!" They did not hear it in the next house.

When the thing he was cooking began to boil, he stirred it with his hand. "Ouch! It burned my hand!" The husband heard it. "What happened to you?" —"My finger was sore, this is the reason why I [yelled]." And he [the young man] was looking at the head that was fastened to the ceiling. It was his elder brother's head. He cried there because he saw his elder brother's head. The husband said: "You seem to be crying." —"There is so much smoke, my eyes are sore." He [the husband] no longer paid any attention to it.

Now it got to be evening. The woman was going upstairs. Thus spoke the [husband's little brother], "My sister-in-law (looks) like a man!" His grandmother said to him, "The women where she comes from (look) just like men. You must keep quiet!" Nobody again thought about it. From everywhere people (came) there to the murderer to help him. They were dancing for the head. For it they were dancing. Blood was dropping (from) the head (that) was hanging (there).

Then it got (to be) evening and they went to bed. . . . She [the "woman"] had a big knife under her pillow. The husband went to bed first. The woman was walking outside. She bored holes in all the canoes in the village. Only in the one in which she intended to cross she did not bore a hole. As soon as she was finished, she went inside. Then she went to bed a little ways from her husband. At midnight the husband was fast asleep. She got up on the sly. She cut off the head of the husband, and seized her elder brother's head. Then she ran away, and crossed over alone in the canoe.

His (the husband's) mother was sleeping under their bed. The blood dripped down on her, and the old woman lighted a torch. "Blood! Blood! What have you done? You must have killed your wife!" She heard nothing. So everybody woke up. Then they saw the man lying on his bed, without a head. His wife had disappeared, and the head that was hanging from the ceiling was gone. "The woman must have killed her husband." —"It was not a woman," [said the little boy].

Then they followed him. [They] shoved the canoes (into the water), but they kept on filling up with water, and they could not follow him.

Then [the young man] went down on his arrows, on which he had climbed up. Then he returned there (home). He brought back his elder brother's head. He assembled all his folks. Now, it is said, they were going to join his elder brother's head. Now they commenced to work. A small spruce tree was standing there. Against that small spruce tree they were joining his head. They danced for it. His head climbed a little bit on his body, and then fell down. Four times it happened that way. His head would go up a little bit, and then fall down again. The fifth time, however, his head stuck on. . . . Then he [the young man] said to his elder brother, "Now you are all right. . . ."

These are the Woodpecker people; this is why their heads are red today. The blood on their necks, that's what makes the head red. [Someone] said to them, "You shall be nothing. You shall be woodpeckers. The last people shall see you."

The First Ship
Comes to Clatsop Country

CHINOOK

THE SON of an old woman had died. She wailed for him for a whole year and then she stopped. Now one day she went to Seaside. There she used to stop, and she returned. She returned walking along the beach. She nearly reached Clatsop; now she saw something. She thought it was a whale.

When she came near it she saw two spruce trees standing upright on it. She thought, "Behold! it is no whale. It is a monster!" She reached the thing that lay there. Now she saw that its outer side was all covered with copper. Ropes were tied to those spruce trees, and it was full of iron. Then a bear came out of it. He stood on the thing that lay there. He looked just like a bear, but his face was that of a human being. Then she went home. She thought of her son, and cried, saying, "Oh my son is dead and the thing about which we have heard in tales is on shore!"

When she (had) nearly reached the town she continued to cry. (The people said), "Oh, a person comes crying. Perhaps somebody struck her." The people made themselves ready. They took their arrows. An old man said, "Listen!" Then the old woman said again and again, "Oh, my son is dead, and the thing about which we have heard in tales is on shore!" The people said, "What can it be?" They went running to meet her. They said, "What is it?" —"Ah, something lies there and it is thus. There are two bears on it, or maybe they are people."

Then the people ran. They reached the thing that lay there. Now the bears, or whatever they might be, held two copper kettles in their hands. The people were arriving. Now the two persons took their hands to their mouths and gave the people their kettles. They had lids. The men pointed inland and asked for water. Then [the] two people ran inland. They hid themselves behind a log. They returned again and ran down to the beach.

One man [of the people from the town] climbed up and entered the thing. He went down into the ship. He looked about in the interior; it was full of boxes. He found brass buttons in strings half a fathom long. He went out again to call his relatives, but they had already set fire to the ship. He jumped down. Those two persons had also gone down.

It burned just like fat. Then the Clatsop gathered the iron, the copper, and the brass. Then all the people learned about it. The two persons were taken to the chief of the Clatsop. Then the chief of the one town said, "I want to keep one of those men with me!" The people almost began to fight. Now one of them [sailors] was returned to one town, and the chief there was satisfied. Now the Quinault, the Chehalis, and the Willapa came. The people of all the towns came there. The Cascades, the Cowlitz, and the Klickitat came down the river. All those of the upper part of the river came down to Clatsop. The Quinault, the Chehalis, and the Willapa went. The people of all the towns went there. The Cascades, the Cowlitz, and the Klickitat came down river. . . .

Strips of copper two fingers wide and going around the arm were exchanged for one slave each. A piece of iron as long as one-half the forearm was exchanged for one slave. A piece of brass two fingers wide was exchanged for one slave. A nail was sold for a good curried deerskin. Several nails were given for long dentalia. They bought all this and the Clatsop became rich. Then iron and brass were seen for the first time. Now they kept those two persons. One was kept by each [Clatsop] chief, one was at the Clatsop town at the cape.

Klamath basketry tray *Courtesy of Thomas Burke Memorial Washington State Museum, cat. #2–1597*

*THE INDIANS who were at home in Oregon's southwest
quarter inhabited an ecologically well-favored, richly diverse
country, ranging north to south from the dense mixed forests of
the Umpqua drainage to the dry wasteland of the Tulelake Lava
Beds, and east to west from Crater Lake in the Cascades and the
Klamath country with its open tamarack-thicketed valleys and
marshes, to the deep overgrown gorges of the Rogue River, and
on to the austere Pacific shoreline, south of Cape Blanco.*

"The Chief—Klamath." Photograph by E. S. Curtis *Courtesy of
Photography Collection, Suzzallo Library, University of Washington*

Klamath burial site (from *Reports of Explorations and Surveys*)
Courtesy of Photography Collection, Suzzallo Library, University of Washington

*Such environmental diversity is paralleled by a striking heter-
ogeneity in the Indian people who lived here. At least five quite
distinct language groups are represented—Athapascan (Upper
Umpqua, Tututni-Joshua, and others), Lutuamian, a distant
branch of Sahaptian (Klamath, Modoc), Yakonan (Lower
Umpqua), Hokan (Shasta), and Takelman, the last a real
anomaly, as its speakers, the Takelma (who lived around Grants
Pass), were wholly surrounded by Athapascan groups. In terms
of cultural features, too, diversity prevails—for example, the
Modocs and Klamaths practiced cremation; all other tribes in the
area buried their dead. In general, the Modoc religion followed
the way of California tribes in emphasizing a shamanistic priest-
hood; the Klamath religion was much more "protestant." [1] The
Klamaths coexisted with the Modocs, but fought bitterly with*

"Klamath Warrior's Head-Dress." Photograph
by E. S. Curtis *Courtesy of Photography
Collection, Suzzallo Library, University of Washington*

"In the Forest—Klamath." Photograph by E. S. Curtis *Courtesy of Photography Collection, Suzzallo Library, University of Washington*

the nearby Takelma and other Indians of the Rogue River country. And so on—it is a special pity, considering the detailed ethnological work done on the Klamath by Leslie Spier and on the Modoc by Verne Ray [2] that so little is known about the very different ways of the Indians living to the west.

Certainly, as a populous, wealthy tribe, with trade connections with Indians to the north and south, the Klamaths dominated this region; but it was the Modocs who made history. In 1870, led by Kintpuash, "Captain Jack," they withdrew from the reservation established for them and the Klamaths, and moved toward Tulelake across the California border; and in 1872–3, in the lava beds south of Tulelake, about fifty Modoc warriors (with their families) held off fifteen hundred Army and Indian troops for over six months. This was the "Modoc War." The ringleaders, those who weren't executed, were shipped off to "Indian Territory," Oklahoma, where Chief Joseph and his Nez Perce would also be sent for their territorial defiance, six years later.

"Gathering Wokas—Klamath." Photograph by E. S. Curtis *Courtesy of Photography Collection, Suzzallo Library, University of Washington*

Overall, the official contacts between the Indians of the Oregon Southwest and the white men have been unhappy. In the 1850s an influx of miners into the gold fields around Jacksonville led to atrocities on both sides, and Indians in this region played a major part in the uprisings that shook Oregon Territory in 1855–56. Almost a century later, in 1954, the Bureau of Indian Affairs (acting, it seems, on behalf of lumber interests as well as supremely misguided government policy) succeeded in "terminating" the Klamath Reservation, buying off the Indians for large sums of money which, predictably, did not last long—and then the "declassified" Klamaths had nothing. Only now is this bureaucratic atrocity being corrected through reparations and restorations of some tribal lands.[3]

The cruel irony of all this is that the Klamaths—expert weavers, stone carvers, and boat builders (for use on Klamath Lake)—were a stable, well-to-do tribe, with an unusually deep and detailed sense of "home," as their mythology reveals. Beyond all other Oregon tribes, perhaps, they celebrated the natural features of their land—beds of the yellow water-lily or wokas *that was their staple food, eddies in streams, rock-piles, cliffs and points along Klamath Lake—in animistic beliefs and traditions, many of them weird and frightening. As Leslie Spier observes, "There is hardly a mile of Klamath territory but has its mythical references. Everywhere there are personages of the folk-tales, now transformed to rocks by Crow's laughter. Spirits are legion and in many cases are localized, so that one looking over the countryside finds it rich in religious connotations."*[4]

Thus the Klamath world was open, and intelligible, in Eliade's term;[5] *where every landmark has its identity in a story, to know the stories is to be imaginatively "at home"—I do not mean merely "at ease"—as most of us now will never be.*

Creation of the Klamath Country

KLAMATH

THERE WAS NO LAND, only a great lake. Kamukamts came from the north in a canoe. It floated along. It stopped. He shook it, but could not move it. He looked down, and in the water he saw the roof of a house. It was the house of Pocket Gopher. Gopher looked up. Then Kamukamts went down into the house, and they talked.

Kamukamts said, "You had better be thinking of what is the best thing to do."

"Yes, I am thinking of that now," replied Gopher.

"If you can plan anything better than I can do, you shall be the elder brother," promised Kamukamts. "What kind of food are we going to have?"

Gopher opened his mouth to yawn, and fish, roots, and berries came forth.

"It seems that you will be the elder brother," said Kamukamts.

That night Gopher caused his companion to sleep, and he burrowed under the bottom of the lake and made it bulge up into hills and mountains, which raised their tops above the surface. In the morning he said, "You had better go and look around!" When Kamukamts went out he was astonished. Gopher asked what should become of his house, and Kamukamts replied, "It will always remain as the oldest mountain" [Modoc Point].

"What will our children have for amusement?" asked Kamukamts. They played the game of throwing spears at a mark. They threw them, and their targets were hills. Kamukamts' spear knocked off the top of Bare Island, and so it is today. Then they invented all the other games.

Gopher asked, "What will live on the mountains?"

"Mountain lions, bears, elk, deer." Kamukamts named all the animals, both beasts and birds.

"What will grow in the mountains?" asked Gopher.

"I will walk over the earth and see what I can do," replied Kamukamts. So he went about and selected homes for the different tribes, and in each territory he placed something which was to characterize that particular tribe, such as obsidian in the Paiute country, marble in the Shasta country, and tules in the Klamath country. Then he looked about and saw smoke.

Kamukamts said, "What is the matter, I wonder? I see smoke here and there."

And Gopher replied, "You have beaten me. You are the elder brother." For he knew that the smoke was from the fires of people brought into being by Kamukamts. They listened, and heard the sound of people talking, and of children laughing and playing. The people increased very rapidly, and the animals and plants on the mountains multiplied.

Modoc Prayers

PRAYER TO A ROCK PILE

"My good helper, stone pile, you give me good luck. I am going out to hunt now. I give you this [stone]. Help me to have good luck hunting deer. That is what I want you to do."

PRAYER TO A SLAIN ANIMAL

"I want you to know, all you animals. Open your eyes. Find this man [mythical human being] who killed this animal. Find out what happened to this [specified] animal who is our friend, and whom this man killed. We'll go out to meet him; let him kill us. We don't want to live when this big animal, who is our brother, is dead. All of us animals will meet this man and find out what became of this animal."

GRACE FOR FIRST MEAL AT A NEW SUMMER CAMP

"We are glad to be here. We are going to give our food to this our country. Make us strong; make us lucky. Keep the women in good health so that they may dig camas and other roots in plenty for the Winter. Sun, you give us what we want so that we may be happy. Sun, you are all-knowing. You want us to have a good time and to live well. Now, great Sun, you know everything because you are over us."

"Earth, look up to me, know who I am; I will ask you for my wants. Give me all that I ask when you hear. I am a man. I want to know all these things: the right way to do. Teach me what I am to do. You know better than I, so I ask you to tell me as much as I, a man, may know. Help me in all things I do on this earth. You are my land, I was reared on you. I want to know everything so that I may be like others. I want to know all man's ways and do things in the right way.

"Also you, my sun, you see me every night and day. Give me light so that I may see everything. The sun is with me so that I can do all that a man can do. I want plenty to eat and drink. Give me all that and I'll be like your child. You are over all. Some men do wrong, some men do right. I want to do right. In many ways I see people pulled down by another's hand. I want you to put your hand upon me so that another can not pull me down. I want to live on this earth under your care. I know that you have given me already that which I live on. I ask you about all that I need. What I use you know about. I know what you have done for me already, since I was old enough to know. How good I have felt when the sun has shone upon me and warmed me on a cold day. I am very thankful for your care. You made all that on earth which is my food. So I just want to say: Gaze down upon every man living under you. You know what they need. Give it to them. Then we shall live on this earth. Give us a good life, a strong life, plenty of everything, good times; and allow all of us to be what you want us to be. You are our great sun, so we ask you to give us strength."

The Rainmaker

MODOC

GA'HGA [HERON] and his brother lived together. They were so small that people called them "the two little Ga'hga brothers." The elder brother was blind, but he was a great doctor; he could see everything, by the help of his medicines.

One day a man came to the Ga'hga brothers, and said, "A great many people are going to snare deer. They have made bark ropes and tied them between trees; now they are ready to drive the deer in. They want you to come and help them."

The elder brother was married. He had a nice-looking wife and a little boy. He said to his wife: "You must pound seed and get ready to go with my brother. I don't want to take my medicines there; I will stay here by the fire with our boy. I can't look out of my eyes. Maybe the deer would kill me."

The woman pounded seed; she left some for her husband and little boy to eat, and took a bagful for herself and her brother-in-law. Ga'hga got out his medicines and watched his wife and brother. He sat by the fire, but he followed them all the way to where the people were driving in deer. As he watched them he got jealous and mad, for he saw that his wife and brother were fond of each other. When they came home, they brought a fawn. The woman cut it up, roasted the meat, and gave some of it to her husband; he kicked it away. She gave him some *wədjək* [weed like mustard] to eat; he tasted it, spat it out, and threw the rest into the fire.

She said: "The people were kind to me today; they gave me the fawn and asked me to come tomorrow," and she began to pound seed and get ready to go.

The next day when the woman and her brother-in-law were starting off, Ga'hga said: "I know what kind of stuff you are feeding me! I know you are making sport of me. You don't fool me. You can do what you like; I don't care for you any longer, but I will make you feel sorry." They didn't answer, didn't say a word to him.

That day Ga'hga's sister came to see her little nephew. Ga'hga said: "I want you to get me a straw plate."

"Why do you want a straw plate?" asked his sister.

"Get it for me, I want it."

She wouldn't get him the plate till he told her what he was going to do with it, and he wouldn't tell. She was afraid of him; she knew he was mad about something.

After a while old man Kehkaäs [Stork] came; he was kin of Ga'hga. Ga'hga asked him for the plate and he gave it to him, and said, "Your brother is stealing your wife. All the people at the deer hunt say so. But you must keep quiet; you mustn't get mad. You are old and blind; your brother is young, and your wife is nice-looking."

Ga'hga screamed, he was so mad. He called his sister and said, "Lead me to the hunt!"

She was so scared that she had to do as he told her. He took the straw plate, and the three started. When they got to the place, his sister said: "Sit down here, away from the snares; then you will be safe."

"No," said Ga'hga, "I am going where my wife is."

"Don't be a fool," said his sister. "She doesn't want you; she has another man."

Ga'hga took the plate from under his arm, and sat down on it. About midnight his sister asked: "What are you doing? Why don't you lie down and go to sleep? Why are you sitting on that plate and keeping awake all night?"

"Keep still and let me alone," said Ga'hga. "Stay here by me; I am going to punish those people." Then he got up and began to dance on the plate and to call out: "Ho! ho! ho!"

Right away the rain came down, but Ga'hga didn't get wet. He kept shaking himself and calling: "Ho! ho! ho!" Each time that he called, it rained harder. There was deep water everywhere, but the plate was dry and the ground around it was dry. The people got as wet as though they had been swimming.

Ga'hga's sister said: "You shouldn't get mad and act in this way; you will kill everybody!"

He didn't listen to what she said; he called, "Ho! ho! ho!" and danced faster and faster. The people were almost drowned; the water was up to their arms. Still Ga'hga kept shaking himself and dancing and calling: "Ho! ho! ho!"

When the people saw that Ga'hga and his sister were dry, they said to his brother: "You have done this. You have made Ga'hga mad. You have taken your brother's wife," and they threatened to kill him.

He said, "I don't want her. I am going to die; I am freezing."

The people caught hold of the woman, dragged her along in the water, and threw her down in front of her husband. He stopped dancing, and right away it stopped raining.

The people said, "You shouldn't be mad at us. We didn't do this. We don't want to die; we want to go home. You should feel sorry for us and dry up the water."

Ga'hga was sorry for them. He danced on the plate, but he didn't call "Ho! ho! ho!" The water began to go away, and soon the ground was as dry as it had been before the rain, and everyone went home except Ga'hga and his wife and his brother.

Ga'hga sat on his plate; he wouldn't get up and he wouldn't speak. His wife got mad. She pushed him, and asked, "Why don't you get ready to go home?" He didn't answer: then she took hold of him, jerked him up, threw him on top of the load of meat on her back, and went home.

His brother went off in the mountains; he was afraid of Ga'hga, and afraid of the people; for they hated him, and the woman didn't care for him any longer.

Ga'hga was so jealous and cross that he drove his wife away. His sister took the little boy, and Ga'hga stayed alone. Maybe he is dead and maybe he is living. Doctors who have him for their medicine can make rain whenever they want to. It is a good medicine. When any one has it, they can look through a man's body just as we look through a window.

The Wildcat Brothers

MODOC

FIVE SLOÄ [WILDCAT] BROTHERS and their two sisters lived together. All the brothers were married, except the youngest. That one was beautiful; he had long blue hair, and his face was white and bright. His father and mother kept him in a basket under the ground. Every night his mother brought him out, washed his face, combed his hair, and gave him nice things to eat; then put him back before his brothers and sisters were awake.

The sisters hadn't seen him since he was a little baby, but the eldest sister liked him so well that she wouldn't marry anybody else. Each night she lay on the ground near the hole where his basket was. The eldest brother didn't like that. He said, "Our sister has no sense. She acts as if she were no kin of ours."

There were many people in the Sloä village. One day all those people went off to hunt deer. When they came together to roast meat, Wəlkətska [Marten] said to Blaiwas [Eagle]: "Why doesn't your son marry Sloä's sister?"

"I will try," said Wəlkətska. He told old man Yaukəl to ask Sloä's mother if he could have her daughter.

That evening Yaukəl said to old woman Sloä: "You must be tired of keeping your daughter after she is old enough to marry. The chief's youngest brother wants her. He will give you nice things for her."

The old woman told her daughter that Yaukəl said Wəlkətska wanted her. Her father said, "You are growing old; the chief's son is a nice-looking young man; you should marry him."

The girl was mad; she said to her mother: "If you want him in the house, you can marry him yourself; I don't want him." The girl was cross. She wanted to make everybody do as she liked.

The next morning, after the brothers had started off to hunt, and the sisters had gone to swim in the river, the father and mother took their youngest son out of the basket to bathe him and give him roots to eat.

He said, "My sister uncovers my basket and talks to me. I want you to hide me in some other place."

Out in the [lake] there was a little island as big as a house; the eldest brother made a place there to keep his blue-haired brother. While he was making the place nice, he pretended to be off hunting; when it was finished, he carried his brother there and hid him under the ground. One day, when he took roots to the island, his little sister went with him to watch that her older sister didn't follow them. They went home after dark, for they didn't want their sister to see which way they came.

The elder sister spent all of her time out of doors, swimming and gathering wood. The third time the brother went to the island, he left his little sister there to take care of her brother and keep the elder sister away.

For five days the sister hunted for her brother. She hunted everywhere—over the mountains, under the rocks, and out on the flats. Then she said, "I wonder where my little sister has gone. If I find her, maybe I will find my brother, too."

When she asked her mother, the old woman said, "You sister is in the south, with your brother."

"Why did you stop bathing my brother and why have you carried him away?" asked the girl. "Someday I will kill you all."

When she had hunted everywhere else, she went to the island, and there she found tracks, then she knew that her brother and sister were somewhere on the island. She pulled up the tule grass and looked under each blade of it, but she couldn't find them.

When the little girl saw her sister coming straight toward the island, she took a spear of tule grass and scraped it out with her finger nail, made it like a canoe; then she put her brother in it and they went under the water, went home.

When the elder sister couldn't find them, she knew that they had seen her and had gone away. That made her mad. She said: "We will see who is the most powerful!" When she got back to dry land, she lay down and rolled over and over on the sand, and cried "Wah-ha-ha! Wah-ha-ha!" Then she sat up on her knees and began to travel fast; all time calling out "Wah-ha-ha!" Right where she had rolled and along the trail she traveled, fire roared and blazed up to the sky. She went around the village where her father and mother lived and each minute she called: "Wah-ha-ha!" "Wah-ha-ha!"

The whole place began to burn. The people were terribly scared. Gak turned to a crow and flew up to the sky; Blaiwas became an eagle; Witwakis turned himself to a hawk and fled away. Tskel [Mink] and Wa'manik [Bull Snake] and Ke'is [Rattlesnake] and their kin went deep under the ground and were saved. All the other people, and the girl's own family, except her little sister, were burned up.

The little girl was like her sister; she was powerful, could do anything she wanted to, and she got outside the ring of fire.

The eldest sister took her brothers' hearts, put them on a string and tied the string around her neck; then she swam back to her island. She was glad now.

The little sister wandered around and cried, she felt so lonesome. At last she stopped crying and began to watch her sister when she swam in the lake. The sister would call in different ways, sometimes like a duck or a water bird, sometimes like an animal, but she always looked like a woman. Once, when she had been all day swimming and dancing in the water, she went to the island and right away fell asleep. The little sister made her sleep.

Then the girl took a spear of tule grass, changed it into a canoe, and went to the island; she cut the strings of hearts from her sister's head and put it in her bosom: then she cut her sister's head off and went back to land.

The head went back to the body, and the woman was alive again. She made a mournful noise, like an animal crying.

The little sister heard her, and said, "Cry all you want to; you can't kill me!" She took up a handful of ashes, threw them toward the island, and said, "You can never burn people up again. You will always live in the water. When the coming people taste of you, they will say, 'This meat doesn't taste good,' and they will spit it out."

The young woman heard what her sister said. She was mad; she made a motion up and down with her hands; they were turning to wings. Right away she became a [loon] and swam off.

The little sister got dry grass from the mountain and spread it down on the ground where each house had been. In one day there were as many houses as there had been before the fire. She gathered all the bones she could find and put them in a basket of boiling water; then she said to herself, "I mustn't get up when they call me. No matter what they say, I must lie still and not answer." She rolled herself up tight in a mat and lay down.

At sunset the people began to come out of the basket. Each person went to his own house and soon the houses were full again. The five brothers came back to life. Their father was the last one to get out of the basket; he stepped on the little girl's feet, and then she got up. Her brothers and father and mother were lying by the fire. She saw smoke coming out of all the houses and she knew that everybody was alive. Then she was glad, and all the people were glad.

Frost and Thunder

MODOC

Gowwa′ [SWALLOW] and Wähütus [?] were married to the same woman; she was kin to Gowwa′.

One day the two men went hunting and left their wife at home. While they were gone Wus [Fox] came along, and said to her, "Come to my house and be my wife. I have a big house and lots of nice blankets and beads. Why do you stay here with these men? They are poor."

"I don't want to go with you," said the woman. "Gowwa′ and Wähütus will come right away. If you stay here, they will kill you."

"I am not afraid of those men," said Wus. "I am stronger than they are; I can kill them." She couldn't make him go away.

When the men came, each had a deer on his back. "Cook some deer meat," they said to the woman. "We are hungry." They didn't see Wus.

She said, "A man is holding me; I can't get up."

"You are fooling us; nobody is holding you. Hurry up and cook for us."

When the woman didn't move Gowwa′ got mad and went toward her to jerk her up; then he saw Wus holding her down. The fire had gone down, and it was dark in the house. Gowwa′ punched the fire and said to Wähütus, "There is somebody over there with a nice skin on. We'll kill him and make a blanket." They caught Wus and pulled his skin off, then they threw him out.

The next morning, when Gowwa′'s mother went for water, she saw Wus and she felt sorry for him; she went to a swamp, and got cattails and wrapped them around him. Right away the cattails turned to nice fur. Wus was cured; he went home.

That day, while the two men were off hunting, Lok [Bear] came and stole their wife. She was afraid of him and had to go. There were five Lok brothers, all living in a house under the rocks.

When Gowwa′ and Wähütus came home and found their wife gone, their old mother-in-law said, "Lok, a big, nice-looking man, came and carried her off."

The next morning Gowwa′ and Wähütus started for Lok's house. As they went along they practiced killing each other to see how they were going to kill Lok. Gowwa′ killed Wähütus and went on a little way alone. Wähütus came to life and overtook Gowwa′. Then Wähütus killed Gowwa′ and went on. Gowwa′ came to life and caught up with Wähütus. So they kept on until they got to Lok's house.

Gowwa′ climbed to the top of the house. Wähütus went in at a hole on one side.

The five brothers were lying by the fire; one jumped up, tore Wähütus into little pieces, and threw the pieces out. Wähütus grew together, came to life, and ran into the house. Five times Lok killed Wähütus, tore him to pieces, and threw the pieces out; each time Wähütus ran in again.

Gowwa′ stood on the top of the house and waited. When they had killed Wähütus five times, he crept down and began throwing flint at the brothers. He was a great doctor, and right away all five of the brothers were dead. Then Wähütus and Gowwa′ took their wife and went home.

The next day while they went off hunting Yahya'haäs
[Thunder] came and stole their wife, and carried her off to his
house. Whenever Yahya'haäs saw a nice woman, he took her; he
stole everybody's wife. Five great rocks were around his house,
and he lived underground, in the middle. The name of the
house was Hwalɩs; nobody but Yahya'haäs could get into it.
There were many women there; he carried them in on his
shoulders.

Wähütus and Gowwa' didn't know how to get their wife back.
At last they sent to all the people in the world and asked them to
come and help break the rocks around Yahya'haäs' house.
Everybody came, and each man tried, but no one could break off
even a small piece of a rock.

Then Tsasgɩps [Frost] came. He was such a small man they
had forgotten him. He said, "I can break those rocks."

The people didn't listen to him; they kept on trying to break
them. Then somebody asked, "What does that little fellow say?
He talks all the time!"

"He says that he can break these rocks," said Blaiwas [Eagle].

Then the men began to talk about Tsasgɩps, and to say,
"Maybe he had better try. Maybe he is a *kiuks* [medicine man]
and can do something."

The people got him ready, sprinkled him with white paint, so
he was all white spots in front. He made, with his mouth, a noise
like blowing; the first rock crumbled to pieces. He made the
same noise with his mouth and struck against the second rock;
the rock fell into small pieces. He broke all five rocks in the same
way. Then the people killed Yahya'haäs with arrows, but his
spirit went up in the air and became Thunder. They shot a great
many times at the spirit as it flew up, for they saw it rising, but
they couldn't hit it; they missed it every time.

Thunder and Eagle Boy

MODOC

FIVE BLAIWAS [EAGLE] BROTHERS started off to hunt for deer.
When they got to the top of the first high mountain, they took
out their fire-drill to make a fire. As they turned the drill they

talked to the mountains, to the trees, to the rocks and the bushes, and asked for good luck, but they forgot to ask the drill to keep Yahya'haäs [Thunder] away. They made a fire, cooked their meat, and then got ready to hunt. When they were leaving the camp, they hung their dry meat and their seeds on a tree where they could get them when they came back in the evening.

After they had gone some distance, one of the brothers said: "That is the place where Yahya'haäs comes. He starts from the east; when he sees any one he walks slowly, but he can go around and come up in front of a person. [He has only one leg.] He can disappear like a flash. Sometimes his face is painted red, and he carries a red cane with red feathers on the end of it. Maybe he will come while we are gone and will eat our meat and seeds." The men were sorry that they had forgotten to tell the drill to keep Yahya'haäs away.

Just then one of them looked east, and said, "There he is; he is coming now!"

The men were scared; they didn't dare to run away, so they sat down and waited. When Yahya'haäs came to them, he said, "Well, well, I thought I would never see people again, but I see them now. I am glad you are here. Why don't you start a fire?"

"We forgot our drill."

"I thought people never forgot their drills. What are you here for?"

"We came to hunt for deer and rabbits."

"I have looked around all the morning," said Yahya'haäs; "I have been everywhere, but I haven't seen a deer track."

"We may as well give up hunting and go home," said one man to another.

"Can't you feed me smoke?" asked Yahya'haäs.

"We have no tobacco."

"This earth will make people trouble if they don't carry a fire-drill and tobacco," said Yahya'haäs. "If you can't feed me with smoke, you must wrestle with me."

"We have no pipe or fire-drill to make smoke with," said the oldest Blaiwas brother. "How can we feed you with smoke when we can't start a fire? We are in a hurry. We didn't come here to wrestle or play games, we came to hunt."

"This is my way," said Yahya'haäs. "If people don't feed me smoke and make me glad, I wrestle with them and throw them; then I am glad. Will you feed me smoke?"

"We can't," said Blaiwas. "We have no tobacco."

"Then we will wrestle," said Yahya'haäs.

The men didn't want to wrestle; they said they didn't know how. But Yahya'haäs kept talking about wrestling, talked till half a day was gone.

Yahya'haäs was red from head to foot. His red cane was sharp at both ends, and on his back was a red quiver of red, sharp-pointed arrows.

At last one Blaiwas said to his brothers, "We had better wrestle with him. It is just as well for us to die here. If we start for home, he will kill us."

Yahya'haäs fixed a place for his leg and piled up stones on a cliff above the lake. The eldest brother was chief; he was the first man to wrestle. He said, "Be strong, my brothers, you can't save yourselves. If he throws me over the cliff into the lake, don't get weak. Be strong and all die together." Then he sent a young boy to the village to tell the people that Yahya'haäs was going to kill him and his brothers.

Right away Yahya'haäs threw him over the cliff. As he sank in the lake, his bones boiled up to the top of the water, washed against the rocks, and rattled terribly.

Yahya'haäs threw over one man after another. As each man sank, he turned to bones and the bones floated against the rocks, struck hard and made a great noise.

In Blaiwas' house there was an old medicine woman. She woke up, and said, "I dreamed that I saw people crying and putting ashes on their heads. Our men have been killed. At noon tomorrow we shall get word of it."

"Women always have bad dreams," said Tusasa's [Skunk]. "There is nobody in the world strong enough to kill the five brothers."

At noon the next day a boy came along the trail; he was crying and screaming. When he got to Blaiwas' house he said, "The five brothers are killed. By this time not one of them is alive." He went to the next village and told the same news.

Tusasa's threw dirt on his head and rolled in the ashes. The people cut off their hair and mourned. The next morning they said, "Let us go and see the place where our men were killed."

Blaiwas' little boy was sleeping by the fire; his sister shook him, and said, "Wake up and wash your face; we are going to see the place where Yahya'haäs killed our people."

When his face was washed, the boy said, "Fix my feet; I want to go too."

"You are too small," said his mother. "Why do you want to go?"

"I want to die with my uncles. I am lonesome; I don't want to live any longer."

"You are too small to go. Yahya'haäs could take you up with one finger and throw you over the cliff."

"I am going where my uncles were killed," said the boy. "Paint me with red paint right in the center of my head, where my thoughts come in and teach me."

They painted him and got him ready to go. Tusasa's cut a long cedar tree, tied it on his head, and went with the others. He started off as if going to gamble; he laughed, jumped, and whooped. The people said, "Yahya'haäs will hear you and he will kill us all."

"It won't be hard for me to kill Yahya'haäs," boasted Tusasa's. "I will throw him over the cliff quickly." Then he said to the boy, "Why are you here? I shan't need your help. You are too small to go to the mountains; you had better go home."

The boy didn't look at Tusasa's; he said to his mother, "You must stop crying. I want all the people to stop crying and follow me." He went ahead.

The people looked at him and stopped crying. When they got to the lake, Yahya'haäs was not there, but he was not far off. The people hunted for the place where the men had been killed, but they couldn't find it. Then the little boy said, "Here it is! Yahya'haäs is coming. You can't see him, but I can. He will soon show himself in the east."

Tusasa's said, "I will be the first man to wrestle with him; I will throw him in the lake."

The people said, "It is bad to make fun of our chief and the men that were killed here. You will make trouble for us."

Right away they saw Yahya'haäs coming from the east. He had on a pale yellow coat that rattled as he hopped along. He had a yellow cane, and his face was painted yellow. When he came to the people, he said, "I like to see men and women. I don't like to walk around and see no one; it makes me lonesome. Will you feed me smoke?"

"We have nothing to make smoke with," said one of the men.

"Did you come to play with me?" asked Yahya'haäs. "I like to wrestle. The last man I saw threw me, and went away somewhere."

The little boy sat on the edge of the cliff; he didn't say anything, just looked at the water. At last he began to see men swimming around under the surface; then he saw the five brothers and lots of other men . . . his own people. He felt strong and glad when he saw them.

Tusasa's said, "You want to fight, don't you? You think you can kill Yahya'haäs, don't you?"

"Let the boy alone," said his mother. "Don't make fun of him; maybe he can teach us things."

Yahya'haäs kept asking the men to wrestle with him. At last they said, "We may as well get killed here. If we start for home, he will follow us." And they began to wrestle. Soon every man was over the cliff, except for Tusasa's. One man was very strong; he nearly broke Yahya'haäs' leg. Yahya'haäs screamed out, "That is not the way to wrestle. You shouldn't twist my leg."

"It is right for me to throw you any way I can," said the man. "You have killed a great many of my people." Yahya'haäs laughed, and threw the man—took him up with one hand, and flung him over the cliff.

When Tusasa's began to wrestle, he held tight to Yahya'haäs. "Look out! Don't hold me so tight!" said Yahya'haäs.

"I have always seen men hold tight," said Tusasa's, and he clung tighter. But Yahya'haäs loosened his hold and threw him into the lake.

The little boy told the women to go home, then he sat there alone.

"Why do you sit there so long?" asked Yahya'haäs. "I wonder if such a little fellow can wrestle. Come and try." Yahya'haäs caught hold of the boy and began to throw him up and play with him.

"Why do you make fun of me?" asked the boy. "Wait till you get through." He caught hold of Yahya'haäs, twisted his leg, broke it off, and pushed him to the lake.

Then the boy called, "Come out, my people. Come out of the water!"

There was a great noise, then all the men came out of the lake. The boy called to them, "Don't look back! Don't look back! If any man looks back, he will die!" As they climbed up the cliff, the boy stood on the edge and said to each one, "Don't look back. If you do you will die." When all were up he followed them and kept calling out, "Don't look back! Don't look back!"

Yahya'haäs came out of the water and screamed to the people, "You haven't thrown me yet! I am standing in the same place. Why do you run away. Come back and throw me!"

The boy said, "Yahya'haäs is dead; that is his spirit. It will kill us if we look back." They were far off, but still they heard the call, "Come back and wrestle! Look back and see me! The boy lies; he didn't throw me. Men don't run away. Come back!"

The boy said, "Don't look back!" He talked to the spirit without turning his face towards it. He said, "You will not treat my people in this way again; but you will always live [as Thunder]. You will always be on the mountains and by the water; you will walk around by the lakes and rivers; but you will never be a person again."

Then the boy said to his people: "It is hard work to live in this world; we will be birds [eagles] and live in the air." That moment they all became birds. The boy is a medicine bird. Doctors often see him, and he helps them cure sick people.

Yahya'haäs is a great medicine; if a doctor has him for a medicine, he can cure a dying man.

Chief Allen David of the Klamaths and Captain Jack of the Modocs Make Peace at Fort Klamath, December 1869

ALLEN DAVID: "I see you. I see your eyes. Your skin is red like my own. I will show you my heart. We have long been enemies. Many of our brave muck-a-lux (people) are dead. The ground is black with their blood. Their bones have been carried by the coyotes to the mountains, and scattered among the rocks. Our people are melting away like snow. We see the white chief is strong. The law is strong. We cannot be Indians longer. We must take the white man's law. The law our fathers had is dead. The white chief brought you here. We have made friends. We have washed each other's hands; they are not bloody now. We are friends. We have buried all the bad blood. We will not dig it up again. The white man sees us. Soch-e-la Tyee—God is looking at our hearts. The sun is a witness between us; the mountains are looking on us.

"This pine-tree is a witness, O my people! When you see this tree, remember it is a witness that here we made friends with the Mo-a-doc-as. Never cut down that tree. Let the arm be broke that would hurt it; let the hand die that would break a twig from it. So long as snow shall fall on Yainax mountain, let it stand. Long as the white rabbit shall live in the manzanita, let it stand. Let our children play round it; let the young people dance under its boughs, and let the old men smoke together in its shade. Let this tree stand there forever, as a witness. I have done."

CAPTAIN JACK: "The white chief brought me here. I feel ashamed of my people, because they are poor. I feel like a man in a strange country without a father. My heart was afraid. I have heard your words; they warm my heart. I am not strange now. The blood is all washed from our hands. We are enemies no longer. We have buried the past. We have forgotten that we were enemies. We will not throw away the white chief's words. We will not hide them in the grass. I have planted a long stake in the ground. I have tied myself with a strong rope. I will not dig up the stake. I will not break the rope. My heart is the heart of my people. I am their words. I am not speaking for myself. I speak their hearts. My heart comes up to my mouth. I cannot keep it down with a sharp stick. I am done."

The Klamath Calendar

SPRING AND SUMMER

In the month of the little finger the Indians dry the large suckers, kill gudgeon at the Bridge of Slanting Rocks, kill fish at the fish-dam when they are jumping. Now they will be leaving home soon; they prepare dry fish, go after *ipos*, gather *kol*; they dry camas, bake it, roast it, eat it raw.

In the thumb-month they put dried camas underground; now they start off for Klamath Marsh to gather *wokas*-seed. They gather it for five days, they let it ripen for six days, they grind the seed, winnow it, make flour. Only women gather *wokas;* the men hunt mule-deer and antelope. Now they will row to the island and camp there, at Skull Place, at Thunderbolt, at Drowned Snake, at Slope Steps; they put the canoes away in the lake bottom. . . .

In the index-month they haul home the *wokas*-seed. We will go there, all of us will carry it. We must rest one day, our horses will be sore. We will scrape up moth-chrysalids, gather pine nuts, sweet resin, blackberries, black cherries, wild gooseberries, huckleberries. . . .

AUTUMN

In the thumb-month at berry-time mares foal; the Indians return, their gathering finished. The women dry berries by the fire, they drink red huckleberry juice, and boil the berries. . . .

In the index-month in the sweat house they dance, there will be a feast in the winter house. Now a man will haul hay, and we will stack it up in fine stacks. "Where shall I stack it?" —"In two stacks, in long stacks heap it up. You must help me tomorrow too—four days you must help me."

WINTER

In the midfinger month the leaves fall. In the ring-finger month it is snowing. In the month of the little finger it snows heavily. In the thumb month the lake is frozen. In the index-month it rains much, they dance in the house. . . .

The Crater Lake Myth

KLAMATH

. . . I WILL TELL about Yamsi, where that Weasel lived long ago. And old Marten lived with him. . . . They camped there. And they went to get water always, having gone a little ways to some well. That well of theirs was good, there. And that Weasel used to keep going after water. Now then once he went after water.

And he said, "What a be-e-eautiful girl is sitting there on the bank," he said. "At our well. A lovely girl—with long, long hair," he said.

Then that Old Marten said, "Just be calm!" he said. "You don't know who she is," he said. "But *I* know her," he said. "That girl is evil. If you want a woman, then get married to that one-eyed one who is digging (roots) over there." Lying down he said thus, for he saw everything that was happening even very far away. That Old Marten—he knows so much. Then he said, "There are many women there digging camas root," he said. "And you take that one, who is one-eyed, having just one eye," he said. "Having just one eye, she is industrious," he said. "She is nothing at all, of whom you spoke."

"Why do I have to take one like that?" (Weasel) said. "I don't want that kind," he said. "I want a pretty woman."

Now then he ran back down over there. "I will go and see her!" He [Old Marten], however, paid no attention, for now he was lying down, that Old Marten. But he was watching even from there.

Now (Weasel) was lying around in her lap this way. And she said, "Would you let me do something to you?" She was carrying something, something this long, very smooth, well made. And she said, "Take this in your mouth!" she said, doing it to Weasel. "Take this in your mouth," she said. "I'll put it in your mouth for you," she said. Now he lay on her lap, as she sat there. And she said, "Take this in your mouth! This is nice," she said, "this is something nice," she said. Now then she made him open his mouth wide, wide. "Open much wider!" she said. Then he opened his mouth very very wide. Now then she shoved it in, that woman. Now she shoved it through (him), and fished out his heart. Now she fished out his heart, doing thus, to Weasel. "Now they are doing it there," said old Marten. Now he was watching as they did thus.

Now then having taken that heart, she now ran back toward Crater Lake (*gi-was*), that woman. She was from there, from Crater Lake. . . . And she, having arrived back, there were a great many beings there where it is so flat on the other side of Crater Lake. "The Ball Court" it is called. . . . It is very, very flat there on the other side of Crater Lake. And many lived there, various things. And they did not like Kamukamts. The "Lε-w," who lived there at Crater Lake. The Lε-w, as he is named, he lived there. He lived in the water.

Then having run back there, the woman said, "This is Old Marten's heart! This heart is Old Marten's!" And they said, "Ye-e-e-es!" And they spread out (on the Ball Court), everything—deer, those, everything that lived there.

And they said, "Yes, we will play ball with that heart of his!" And it being thus, they threw it back and forth. Just as they (play) ball, they threw it back and forth, running here and there. Everything, deer, antelope . . . they did thus for a long time.

Now then that Old Marten, he came now. He arrived after a long while, leaning on his staff with difficulty, that Old Marten. Then he arrived leaning on his staff and fooled them. Yes, he came supporting himself much. "He [Old Marten] made me this way too there!" He had pitch on his face—pitch, yes, all over.

And he said, "He made me this way too," he said. "I am his doing! . . . He does all of us wrong, and he kills us," he said. "I also want to catch it [his heart] once. I want to catch the heart just once. Yes, I want to catch it. So throw it to me!" he said.

Now then they threw it to him. Then he caught it. Now then he ran off, just when he caught it. Now he came running back this way, towards Yamsi, from whence he had gone. Now he came running back. And they ran off (after him). Now they came chasing him. And he changed into (various) things. Again a stump stood in the way, he having become a stump. Yes, again having become something else, he stood in the way. Again they did not know what.

And further on that Dove, sitting up high, spoke. He was together (with) Old Marten. He said, "o · · · l, o · · · l," Dove said. And those running along said, "He has gone very far, he speaks from afar," they said. Dove spoke thus—even though he spoke sitting up high right there. Now then they quit, it being thus.

Now then Old Marten took it [Weasel's heart] home, and now there, he pushed it back into little Weasel. "I told you so," he said. "Now do you know?" he asked. . . . .

Now then having put (Weasel's heart) back inside (of him), he said, "We will attack them," he said. "We will attack them! There towards Crater Lake." Now Old Marten got ready, being angry now. Now then having climbed down there (into the Crater), they killed the Lɛ-w . . . and those who were with him (the Lɛ-w) did not know it. Having killed him, now they tore up all his body into pieces. They tore up the Lɛ-w's body, all. And having done thus, they threw it down, being there on the cliff.

And (Old Marten) said, "This is Marten's thigh! This is Marten's leg! Now he threw it down. And they, having risen up out of the water, gobbled it up. Now it turned white there (with foam, bones, and the creatures themselves) . . . bones they gobbled up of that Le-w, who lived at Crater Lake. And finally he said, "This is Marten's heart!" [really the Le-w's] he said, "This is Marten's heart!" he said. He threw it saying "This is Marten's heart!" . . . And they did not miss, when [he] threw it down. . . .

The Story of Swa-ya

KLAMATH

ONCE THAT little Swa-ya's mother and father lived somewhere. And Frog baby-sat for them there. The little boy there was very pretty, looked very nice. And every day she caused [the baby] to float back [on the river], that Frog. And she put him to sleep that way, floating [him] in the little river. Continually floating him downstream, she pulled him back again, then floated him again. Then someone said, to his mother, "Do you let her do that?" And [his mother] said, "Yes, she's good. She'll keep my baby from crying, and she puts it to sleep that way." The every day she floated [him] out a little farther. Then she pulled [him] back again. Now then she stole [him], having floated [him] out. And she jumped into the water together [with him] and went.

Now then she arrived there, there where she lived—whether on a mountain, perhaps on the lake, or wherever she was living. And her relatives met her, being glad [to see her], there where she lived. And they said, "Ohhh, where did you [get] this?" —"There I [got] it—somewhere."

Then they put something down for a bed. Having put something down, [according to] what she said to do, they said, "Ahhh, that's no good! Now we will take you there [back]." And only little frogs jumped off, when they shook out the blanket. Only little frogs, her little girls only. Three times perhaps they tried to do it that way. And they said, "You stole this [baby]!" It always happened that way.

Now then he grew up. He became very big, a man. And she said, "Don't you ever do evil to these, [your] sisters." And he said, "Yes, I [will never do anything to] them." And then someone told him, "You are a stolen [child]." Then he cried and cried. "Why are you crying?" He didn't eat now, he cried, always, [because] of what someone said.

Now then that Frog, because she was going somewhere, said, "You be good to them! Don't make them cry!" And he said, "Yes." And he made bracelets for all of them. And earrings. And they sat by the fire. Then he killed them all. Then he left, that Swa-ya now. He killed his sisters and left, and they lay in the fire all curled up.

And then Old Frog returned. And she cried and cried. "How you have played with them!" she said. Nobody pitied her, when she cried. "You stole him!"

Now then he returned. Somebody or other told him where to go. And Louse lay in wait for him on a rock. And Swa-ya said, "What are you doing, staying here?" —"Why, I'm lying in wait for Swa-ya." —"Don't do it that way. Here, let me show you how to lie in wait for Swa-ya." Then he squashed [Louse] with his thumb.

And again somebody or other came. And he stepped on him also. And he went on. And then somebody or other met him— perhaps Kamukamts? And he said, "They are looking for you there, your mother and father. And do not shoot any antelope, because that is your mother, having a spotted teat, on one side."

And he went on and on. And many things [i.e., creatures] met him on the way, lying in wait for him. But he always killed them, whoever they were—Flea, Ant, Louse, whoever. But [there were] many.

And he was very, very gloomy. And he camped in the Dragonflies' place. They did not let him go to sleep. They made so much noise, because they were bachelors. . . . Then little Swa-ya said, "These [people] are disturbing me very much!" Then he made some of them [into] women, those Dragonflies. And . . . thus, there have come to be many, many dragonflies, because some became women.

Now then those Dragonflies were very, very stupid. And he left the next morning. And one of those Dragonflies caught up with him and said, "Now my wife is pregnant. How should we do?" And he said, "You certainly make me tired!" And he said, "You will do thus." He told them, he prescribed something or other for them. Just like you go to an Indian doctor and ask him what to do. "My wife's pregnant." And he told them what clothes to get, or moss, or whatever they used at that time—rabbitskins or something. He advised them whatever to get.

Now then he went on. Then he saw an antelope. And then he forgot. Those Dragonflies had quite confused him. Then he shot that Antelope. And he killed his own mother. Then because of that he was sad. "If I could kill my mother, then I could kill anybody at all!" he said. . . .

However, he then came to the Pelicans' place, they [being] five brothers, five. And they were blind, all blind. And then they were roasting their fish. . . . Then in order to tease them, he took one fish from each one. They were roasting five fish [each], those Pelicans. And he took one away from each there. And those Pelicans ate only four each. . . . And [since] they could not see, he hid from them. And sitting in a corner, he ate them all. . . . And then one—perhaps the eldest, or perhaps the youngest—said, "I have swallowed only four! And [another] said, "I also [had] only four!" Again one [said], "I also [had] only four! Why, we roasted five apiece! Let us make wind!" Then they flapped their wings. Then a very dusty wind blew there. Then [Swa-ya] said, "I did that to you-u-u! I ate your fish! I took one away from each of you-u-u-u!" Then they said, "Listen! Who's that?" —"I am the one! Little Swa-ya!" Then they said, "Oh, Grandfather's Brother! . . . He did that to us." —"I'll go get some more [fish] for you." Then they were happy. And he went and fished for them. (And everything was all right. Now that's as far as I know this one, too.)

Little Porcupine and Coyote

KLAMATH

Now I will start. They say that little Porcupine once could not cross a river. And he went crying and crying along the bank. Then a buck buffalo walked down to the bank. He said, "What's the matter with you? What are you crying so much for?" And he said, "I'm crying because I can't get across. I want to get on the other side, to see a sick person—my relative."

Then he [the buffalo] said, "Crawl up on here, on (my) back." —"Ahhh, no," Porcupine said, "you would spill me off into the water." —"Not at all! Sit here between my horns!" Then he said, "No, you'll spill me off into the water." And the buffalo said, "Catch hold of (my) tail, and I'll drag you across!" And he said, "No, I'd get wet." Then he said, "Ohhh, grab hold here, on my neck!" —"No. Shaking your head, you'd throw me into the water." —"Ohh, crawl up my [asshole]." —"Yes, yes, yes, yes! Only thus can I go across." So he crawled inside, behind.

Then he waded across, that elk, rather, that buffalo. And he said, "I don't feel well." And he [Porcupine] ate all of his liver. And (his) kidneys. He ate it all. Then as the buffalo barely got to the other side, he [Porcupine] swallowed his heart. Then he fell down. Then, crawling back out, Porcupine said, "How should I have done? Shaking (his head), he would have thrown me off into the water right away. And so hungry, we (Porcupine and his family) are so hungry. We are very, very hungry. It was for that that I wanted to kill this one. Even though he did carry me across here."

Then he said, while going to and fro along the bank, he said, "I wish I had something to make a knife-handle with! I wish I had something to skin this buck buffalo with!" As he said thus, that little Coyote heard (him). "Ohhh, whatever is that? What's doing that?" —"I wish I had something to make a knife-handle with!" —"Ahh, that's no good," he [Coyote] said. "I wish I had something to skin this buffalo with!" —"Ohh, that's good!" he [Coyote] said. Then he ran up and sat down again. Then Porcupine said, "I wish I had something to make a knife-handle with!" —"Ah, but that's no good," he [Coyote] said. And he just sat. Then again he said, that little Porcupine, "I wish I had something to skin this buffalo with!" —"But that is good!" he [Coyote] said. And again he ran a little closer. "I wish I had something to make a knife-handle with!" —"Ahhh, but that's no good," he [Coyote] said, and he sat without moving.

Now then that little Coyote came near. And he said, "How are you?" And said, "What's that you're doing, old fellow?" —"Nothing at all." —"I misunderstood you to say, 'Skin a buck buffalo.' " —"Yes, he's lying over there." —"This is my knife. Skin (it) with this!" —"No, you will want to take it away from

me." —"But I won't take it away from you. I'll help you at it."
—So he [Porcupine] said, "Yes."

Then, when they had skinned it all, Coyote said, "I wonder if
you'd give me a piece of this?" —"No," he [Porcupine] said,
"I can't give you (any). You never do good to me. Always you
make it bad for me." Then Coyote said, "But I won't make it
bad for you, if you could give me (some). My children are
many, and my wife, and we are hungry. And shall I jump with
you for this?" —"No. You can beat me." Then Coyote said,
"Shall we race? Then we'll see whose this will be." —"No," he
[Porcupine] said. "You can beat me in this also."

Then he [Coyote] beat up on little Porcupine. He beat and
beat and beat on him, and he lay on the ground, little Porcupine,
like one dead. Then he left his hat behind. "If this one should
move, then call me, and I'll return, and beat him." Now Coyote
went off to bring back his children. He went and went and
went, and then little Porcupine moved.

Then the hat, sitting by the fire, said, "He's moving! He's
mo-o-oving!" Then he [Coyote] returned and beat, beat, beat,
and beat (little Porcupine). Again he lay prostrate, like one
dead. And again he (Coyote) went off to bring them back. Then
little Porcupine moved again. Now that hat, lying by the fire—
that hat said, "He's moving! He's mo-o-oving!" Then, having
returned again, Coyote beat and struck, beat and struck (him).
Then again he left him dead—thinking him dead. And little
Porcupine played possum. He thought, "What can I do?" And
thus, "I'll lie longer this time." So then he lay and lay. That
little Coyote had been gone a long time. Now then he moved.
Now then that hat called and called and called, "This one's
moving! This one's mo-o-o-ving!" Then little Porcupine poked
him into the fire . . . that hat. Then he lay on edge, all curled
up in the fire.

Then he [Porcupine] took it all up into a tree, that meat.
Having cut it all up—only the backbone he did not break. With
the head left on the end, he took it up; very very high—on what
sort of a tree I don't know. However, it was a big tree indeed.

Now then little Coyote came back (with his children): "Ohhh,
now we'll eat. Now we'll eat. Yakyakyakyakyak! Now we'll
eat! Now we'll eat!" Then he tracked around the fire. Then he
saw that hat thus, sitting in the fire. Then he said, "What should
I do? Where has he gone? Ohhh!" Then, being hungry, they
yapped all around, those little Coyotes.

Then he said, "Where are you? Where are you?" Then he looked up in the tree. "Ohh, did you take it way up there? Could you give me (some)? We're very poor! We are hungry! Give (some) to me!" —"No. Not to you." —"Just give me one shoulder even!" —"No!" —"Give me a piece of rib!" —"No!" —"Please give me a haunch!" —"No!" —"We are very, very hungry. Even just give me a bone from the back!" —"Yes, yes," he [Porcupine] said then. "You all stand in a line!" Thus, "You all will stand in a line, thus, and I'll throw this (backbone) down!"

Indeed, with their mouths open to catch it, they were looking up. Now then he threw it down. And he killed them all. Just the youngest one, the littlest, he escaped. (Porcupine) didn't kill him, but killed some. This having happened in that way, now coyotes have become very many. Because they didn't all die, just that one remaining, now they have become numerous again. Yes. That's as far as (it goes) now.

Coyote in Love with a Star

KLAMATH

IN THOSE DAYS the Coyote was a spirit Coyote; he was a friend of the Man: they were cousins and talked together. The Coyote loved the night: all night long he would sit and watch the stars. There was one large star, more beautiful than the moon or the sun. He was in love with the star and would talk to her, night after night, and all night long. But the star would not answer him; she walked across the sky, looking at him, but saying nothing.

The Coyote grew more and more crazy for that star. He noticed that always, as she walked through the sky, she passed very close to a certain mountain peak, so close it would be easy to touch her. The Coyote traveled as fast as he could, a long, long way; till, very tired, he stood on this mountain, at the place the star always touched. He would not sleep for fear of missing her, so he sat and waited.

In the evening he saw her coming; she was very beautiful. He could see now that she and the other stars were dancing; they moved through the sky dancing. The Coyote waited; his heart was nearly bursting through his skin, but he kept quiet. The star danced nearer and nearer; at last she was on the mountain. He reached up as high as he could, but he could not quite touch her; then he begged her to reach her hand down to him. She did so, and took his paws into her hand.

Slowly she danced with him, up from the mountains; far up into the sky, over the earth. The Coyote got very dizzy; his heart was afraid. They went higher into the sky, among all the stars. It was bitter cold and silent. None of the stars spoke. The Coyote looked down, and fear made his heart very cold. He begged the stars to take him back to the earth. When they were at the very top of the sky, the star let go of the Coyote. He was one whole moon falling, and when he struck the earth, he knocked a great hole in it. His blood turned to water and made a lake. This is Crater Lake, in Klamath country. When the Coyotes talk to the stars at night, they are scolding the star that killed their father.

Chiloquin the Hero

KLAMATH

CHILOQUIN WAS a short man, deep-chested, powerful, and exceptionally hardy. It is related that he overtook a party camped in the deep snows atop the Cascades. Not being properly equipped, he lay beside a fire covered only with a single blanket. In the morning he was covered with frost but apparently had not suffered.

Somewhere in the north, possibly Warm Springs, was a man who owned a big slave who was very much a bully. While the slave was absent Chiloquin traded three horses for the master's best horse. When the slave returned he inquired for the horse and sent a man to demand it. That man went twice but each time Chiloquin sat quietly sewing and did not reply. Then the slave himself went out and demanded its return but Chiloquin paid no attention. When the slave went to untie the horse,

Chiloquin tripped him. The slave struck at him with his hatchet but missed. Then Chiloquin wounded him and he retreated.

Chauchau, a northerner, wanting Chiloquin's daughter, offered horses and other valuables. The latter refused. He came to Chiloquin at night and fought with him till daybreak. Chiloquin clung to Chauchau's hair despite the beating he was receiving. Chauchau came again the next night and again they fought. This performance kept up through the whole winter. When spring came, Chauchau acknowledged his defeat: "Yes, Chiloquin, you are fierce," and they were again friends.

Again in the north some northern shamans went into a sweat-lodge. They wanted a shaman among their Klamath visitors to accompany them. None was present so the Klamath insisted on Chiloquin joining them. One after the other each northern shaman sprinkled water on the hot rocks as he sang his song, hoping to force the others out. Some, overcome by heat and steam, had to be dragged out. Once outside they wondered what had become of Chiloquin; he was nowhere to be seen. They thought he must have died. After a long time he began to talk, throwing water on the rocks. When he was quite ready he came out and walked to his own people. He had bested the shamans. . . .

Two Klamath Monsters

SKA'MDI (an eddy in Williamson River)

A man and a boy were going to Klamath Marsh afoot. The boy was six or seven. The man wanted to try swimming in Ska'mdi. He told the boy, "If those things bite and kill me, you go home." The man had lost his wife; the boy alone was left. "I do not want to stay here; I want to die," the man said. The boy cried to him not to swim there. He walked back from the river bank, ran and plunged in. Big animals reached up and bit him. They came up twice; then he appeared no more. The boy saw it and wept. He started home; it took all night for him to reach Bezükse', below Chiloquin. At [Ska'mdi] the water boils

and cannot move down the river. No one can swim there;
something always bites and kills them.

A Paiute woman was cutting willows. She left her little baby
nearby while she worked. A goga′nə came along and, devouring
her baby, substituted himself in the cradle board. When the
mother came back she thought it was her own. She picked it
up and began to nurse it. The baby would not stop suckling.
She pinched its mouth but it wouldn't stop, it only smiled. When
she got home she heated an iron and put it against the baby's
mouth, but still it just smiled. They could not get the baby
away from her. Then they built a big fire. They cut her breast
off, but the woman immediately died. They threw the baby into
the fire, but at once it jumped out and ran away. This happened
after the whites arrived in this country.

Grizzly Bear and Black Bear

TAKELMA

A HOUSE THERE WAS, Grizzly Bear, Black Bear, Grizzly Bear's
two children, and Black Bear's two children. Every day they
used to pick hazel nuts, and were wont to return; "sisters" they
called each other. Then, 'tis said, a long time elapsed. "Let us
hunt for your lice," said Grizzly Bear, to Black Bear she said
it. Whenever the evening came, they always brought home
burden baskets full of hazel nuts, every day they did that in the
mountains. "For your lice let us hunt," said Grizzly Bear, and
for her [Black Bear's] lice she always hunted.

Then, 'tis said, a long time elapsed. "Let us hunt for your lice,"
(said Grizzly Bear). Now, 'tis said, she bit Black Bear's head a
little (while) hunting for her lice. "You've bit me!" —"I did not
know that I was biting you," said Grizzly Bear. Then, it is said,
when the evening came they returned home, each other's neighbors they were. Now they used to pick hazel nuts. Then again,
'tis said, Grizzly Bear said, "Let us hunt for your lice." Now

again she bit her a little. "You've bit me, haven't you?" said Black Bear. Now for a long time she did that to her. Then again they returned home, and burden baskets full of hazel nuts they brought home. "I did not know that I was biting you, sister," said Grizzly Bear. Then, 'tis said, Black Bear knew that Grizzly Bear was intending to kill her. Then, 'tis said, when they returned home in the evening, "Now when the next day comes, then let us again pick hazel nuts," Grizzly Bear said to her. "Sister," she called her.

Now then, 'tis said, Black Bear stood up an acorn pestle; she knew that (Grizzly Bear) was intending to kill her. Then to her daughters she said, "Should this acorn pestle fall, then she will have killed me. You should watch that. Should it fall, then she will have killed me," said Black Bear, to her daughters that she said. "In that case, to those children of Grizzly Bear next door, you shall say, 'Let us bathe!' and then you shall drown them," said Black Bear to her daughters. Then, 'tis said, they watched this acorn pestle. "If it should fall, in that case you shall say to them. 'Let us play in the water!' " she said, "and then you shall bury them in the fireplace," said Black Bear to her daughters. "When they are done, you will take them out, and you will split them open," said Black Bear to them.

Now then, 'tis said, noon came, and the acorn pestle fell. They went next door to Grizzly Bear's children. "Let us all bathe, let us play in the water!" said the daughters of Black Bear. "Yes!" they said. Then, 'tis said, they bathed in the water. Now they drowned them in the water, the two daughters of Grizzly Bear died. Then into the house of Grizzly Bear they took her children; now they roasted them in the ashes, down under the ground they threw them into the fire. Then, it is said, they were done, and the daughters of Black Bear took them out. . . . Then they ripped them open. In the afternoon, just then they did so, they roasted the children of Grizzly Bear.

Now formerly, their mother had told them, "You will lift up the rock acorn-mortar, [under] there you will go," said Black Bear; [she said that] to her daughters. Then into their own house returned the children of Black Bear. Then the rock acorn-mortar they lifted up, and went off; in there they passed, off they went [in a tunnel]. Now Black Bear's children ran away, Grizzly Bear's children they had killed. Then off they went.

When evening came Grizzly Bear returned. Now her children were not there; she listened. "Where L-are you?" In the water there was laughter (as of) little girls, "He he he he! He he he he!" A burden basket full of hazel nuts she carried on her back. Not yet had she entered the house. After a little while she went inside. Now then (they lay there) all done, spread out, ripped open. Now then, 'tis said, she ate their livers. Now just then (she said), "S-come back, S-come back!" as she rushed out to where there was laughter (as of) little children; now there she came. "S-come back, S-come back!" Now into the water she went. Then, 'tis said, where there was laughter, there she went; there she arrived, but they were not there. Just down river: "He he he!" Now again there she ran: "S-come back, S-come back!" There she arrived, but they were not there. Now again up river there was laughter (as of two little children). Now again up river she ran. "S-come back, S-come back!" Now again there she arrived, but they were not there. Now then just down river there was laughter again; again there she ran. "Come back!" said Grizzly Bear. Now again just up river there was laughter once more; she was plumb tired out. Right there she then found it out, she stood still. "What L-is the matter?" she kept shouting. Now she was tired; to every place had she run.

Now she went home into her own house. "L-so it is L-my children? So that was their livers that I ate?" she said. Next door she went. Then everything she turned over; the earth she asked, everything she asked, "Where did my children go?" Some time elapsed, and then she lifted up the rock acorn-mortar, last of all she discovered their footprints right there. Now then, 'tis said, she pursued them. "O L-my liver! O L-my liver!" now thus she cried. She pursued them, and "O L-my liver; O L-my liver!" she said. Somewhere or other they had arrived, and now Black Bear's children were on the other side of the water. Indeed Crane had thrown his leg across the river and made a canoe of it, and the little girls passed over on it.

Grizzly Bear arrived at the house of old woman Excrement, and went inside. "Where are the L-orphans?" said Grizzly Bear. "I swing about the shells in my ears, I coil my basket tight," said a certain Excrement woman, I know not what sort of woman. "I swing about the shells in my ears," said the old woman, she answered not Grizzly Bear. "Where are the L-orphans? Did you not hear what I said to you?" said Grizzly Bear. After a little while the old woman became angry . . . , towards the fireplace she turned around, her awl she seized. "Wherefore do you ask me?"

Now Grizzly Bear, for her part, jumped out of the house,

then ran to the water. Now she called for a canoe, "Paddle a canoe over here!" she said. Now Crane, indeed, (said) "Eehhh!" and he stretched his own leg across, his own leg he gave her. Now she walked on top of it. And she scratched his leg with her claws, . . . in the middle of the water. "Eehhh!" (exclaimed Crane). Now Crane turned his leg to one side, and Grizzly Bear died, Crane threw her into the water. But Black Bear's children had escaped by just passing over Crane's leg.

The Theft of Fire

SHASTA

LONG AGO, in the beginning, people had only stones for fire. In the beginning every one had only that sort of fire-stone. "Do you hear? There is fire over there. Where Pain lives there is fire." So Coyote went, and came to the house where Pain lived. The children were at home; but all the old people were away, driving game with fire. They had told their children, "If any one comes, it will be Coyote." So they went to drive game by setting fires.

Coyote went into the house. "Oh you poor children! Are you all alone here?" said he. "Yes, we are all alone. They told us they were all going hunting. If any one comes, it will be Coyote. I think you are Coyote," they said. "I am not Coyote," he said. "Look! Way back there, far off in the mountains, is Coyote's country. There are none near here." Coyote stretched his feet out toward the fire, with his long blanket in which he had run away. "No, you smell like Coyote," said the children. "No, there are none about here," he said.

Now, his blanket began to burn, he was ready to run. He called to Chicken-Hawk, "You stand there! I will run there with the fire. I will give it to you, and then you run on. Eagle, do you stand there! Grouse, do you stand there! Quail, do you stand there!" Turtle alone did not know about it. He was walking along by the river.

Now, Coyote ran out of the house; he stole Pain's fire. He seized it, and ran with it. Pain's children ran after him. Coyote gave the fire to Chicken-Hawk, and he ran on. Now Chicken-Hawk gave it to Eagle, and he ran on. Eagle gave it to Grouse, and he ran on. He gave it to Quail, and he ran far away with it. Turtle was there walking about. The Pains were following, crying, "Coyote has stolen fire!" Now, Turtle was walking about; he knew nothing, he was singing. "I'll give you the fire," said Quail. "Here! Take it!" Just then the Pains got there. Turtle put the fire under his armpit, and jumped into the water. Pain shot at him, shot him in the rear. "Oh, oh, oh! That is going to be a tail," said Turtle, and dove deep down into the river.

All the Pains stood together. By and by they gave it up, and went away. Coyote came up, and asked, "Where is the fire?" —"Turtle dove with it," they said. "Curse it! Why did you dive with it?" Coyote said. He was very angry. After a while Turtle crawled out of the water on the other side. Coyote saw him. "Where is the fire?" he called out. Turtle did not answer. "I say to you, where did you put the fire?" said Coyote. "Curse it! Why did you jump into the water?" After a while Turtle threw the fire all about. "You keep quiet! I will throw the fire about," said Turtle. "O children, poor children!" said Coyote; he said all kinds of things, he was glad. Now, everybody came and got fire. Now we have got fire. Coyote was the first to get it, at Pain's that way. That is all. That is one story.

Genesis

JOSHUA-TUTUTNI

IN THE BEGINNING there was no land. There was nothing but the sky, some fog, and water. The water was still; there were no breakers. A sweat-house stood on the water, and in it there lived two men—The Giver and his companion. The Giver's companion had tobacco. He usually stayed outside watching, while The Giver remained in the sweat-house.

One day it seemed to the watcher as if daylight were coming. He went inside and told The Giver that he saw something strange coming. Soon there appeared something that looked like land, and on it two trees were growing. The man kept on looking, and soon was able to distinguish that the object that was approaching, was white land. Then the ocean began to move, bringing the land nearer. Its eastern portion was dark. The western part kept on moving until it struck the sweat-house, where it stopped. It began to stretch to the north and to the south. The land was white like snow. There was no grass on it. It expanded like the waves of the ocean. Then the fog began to disappear, and the watcher could look far away.

He went into the sweat-house, and asked, "Giver, are you ready?" and The Giver said, "Is the land solid?" —"Not quite," replied the man. Then The Giver took some tobacco and began to smoke. He blew the smoke on the land, and the land became motionless. Only two trees were growing at that time, redwood to the south, and ash to the north. Five times The Giver smoked, while discussing with his companion various means of creating the world and the people. Then night came, and after that daylight appeared again. Four days The Giver worked; and trees began to bud, and fell like drops of water upon the ground. Grass came up, and leaves appeared on the trees. The Giver walked around the piece of land that had stopped near his sweat-house, commanding the ocean to withdraw and to be calm.

Then The Giver made five cakes of mud. Of the first cake he made a stone, and dropped it into the water, telling it to make a noise and to expand, as soon as it hit the bottom. After a long while he heard a faint noise, and knew then that the water was very deep. He waited some time before dropping the second cake. This time he heard the noise sooner, and knew that the land was coming nearer to the surface. After he had dropped the third cake, the land reached almost to the surface of the water. So he went into the sweat-house and opened a new sack of tobacco. Soon his companion shouted from outside, "It looks as if breakers are coming!" The Giver was glad, because he knew now that the land was coming up from the bottom of the ocean. After the sixth wave the water receded, and The Giver scattered tobacco all over. Sand appeared. More breakers came in, receding farther and farther and farther westward. Thus the land and the world were created. To the west, to the north, and to the south there was tide-water; to the east the land was dry. The new land was soft, and looked like sand. The Giver stepped

on it, and said, "I am going to see if the great land has come";
and as he stepped, the land grew hard.

Then The Giver looked at the sand, and saw a man's tracks.
They seemed to have come from the north, disappearing in the
water on the south. He wondered what that could mean, and
was very much worried. He went back to his first piece of land,
and told the water to overflow the land he had created out of
the five cakes of mud. Some time afterward he ordered the
water to recede, and looked again. This time he saw the tracks
coming from the west, and returning to the water on the north
side. He was puzzled, and ordered the water to cover up his new
land once more. Five times he repeated this process. At last he
became discouraged, and said, "This is going to make trouble in
the future!" and since then there has always been trouble in the
world.

Then The Giver began to wonder how he could make people.
First he took some grass, mixed it with mud, and rubbed it in his
hands. Then he ordered a house to appear, gave the two mud
figures to his companion, and told him to put them into the
house. After four days two dogs—a male and a bitch—appeared.
They watched the dogs, and twelve days later the bitch gave
birth to pups. The Giver then made food for the dogs. All
kinds of dogs were born in that litter of pups. They were all
howling. After a while The Giver went to work again. He took
some white sand from the new land, and made two figures in
the same way as before. He gave the figures to his companion,
and ordered a house for them. Then he warned the dogs not to
go to the new house, as it was intended for the new people.
After thirteen days The Giver heard a great hissing; and a big
snake came out of the house, followed by a female snake and
many small snakes. The Giver felt bad when he saw this, and
went to his companion, telling him that this trouble was due to
the tracks that had first appeared in the world. Soon the land
became full of snakes, which, not having seen The Giver,
wondered how everything had come about. The world was
inhabited by dogs and snakes only.

One day The Giver wished three baskets to appear, gave
them to his companion, and told him to fill them partly with
fresh water and partly with salt water. Then he put ten of the
biggest snakes into the baskets, crushed them, and threw them
into the ocean. Two bad snakes got away from him; and all

snake-like animals that live today come from these snakes. The Giver said to these two snakes, "You two will live and surround the world like a belt, so that it won't break!" Then he crushed five bad dogs in the same way, made a great ditch with his finger, and threw the dogs into the ditch. These dogs became water-monsters. All animals that raise their heads above the water and smell, and then disappear quickly under the water, came from these five dogs.

Pretty soon The Giver began to think again, "How can I make people? I have failed twice!" Now, for the first time his companion spoke. He said, "Let me smoke tonight, and see if people will not come out of the smoke." For three days he smoked, at the end of which a house appeared with smoke coming out of it. The man told The Giver, "There is a house!" After a while a beautiful woman came out of the house, carrying a water-basket. Then The Giver was glad, and said, "Now we shall have no more trouble in creating people." The woman did not see The Giver and his companion, as they were watching her. After nine days the woman became sad, and wondered who her father and relatives were. She had plenty of food.

One day The Giver said to his companion, "Stay here and take this woman for your wife! You shall have children and be the father of all the people. I am leaving this world. Everything on it shall belong to you." And the man answered, "It is well; but, perchance, I too may have troubles." Then The Giver asked him, "How are you going to be troubled?" So the man said, "Do you make this woman sleep, so that I can go to her without her seeing me." The woman found life in the house very easy. Whenever she wished for anything, it appeared at once. About noon she felt sleepy for the first time. When night came, she prepared her bed and lay down. As soon as she was sound asleep, the man went in to her. She was not aware of this, but dreamed that a handsome man was with her. This was an entirely new dream to her. At daybreak she woke up and looked into the blanket. No one was there, although she was sure that someone had been with her. She wished to know who had been with her that night. So next evening she prepared her bed again, hoping that the same thing would happen; but no one came to her. She did the same every night without any one coming near her.

Soon the woman became pregnant. The Giver and his companion were still on the land, watching her; but she could not see them, because they were invisible to her. After a while the child was born. It was a boy. He grew very fast. The young woman made a cradle for him. After six months the boy could talk. The woman still wanted to know who the father of her child was. So one day she wrapped the child in blankets, and said, "I will neglect the boy and let him cry, and, perchance, his father may come. I will go and look at the country."

She started south, carrying the baby on her back. She traveled for ten years, seeing no one and never looking at the child. After a long time she could hear only a faint sound coming from behind. Nothing remained of the boy but skin and bones. Finally she stopped at Salomä [a camas prairie far up the Coquille River] and here for the first time she took the child from her back and looked at it. Its eyes were sunken and hollow; the boy was a mere skeleton. The woman felt bad and began to cry. She took the boy out of the cradle and went to the river to bathe. After she had put on her clothes, she felt of the child's heart. It was still beating!

The boy urinated, and was dirty all over. His body was covered with maggots, and he had acquired various diseases. The woman took him to the water and washed his body. She had no milk with which to feed him; so she sang a medicine song, and milk came to her. She gave the breast to the child, but it was too weak to suck: hence she had to feed it gradually. As the days went by the boy grew stronger. After three days his eyes were better. Then they went back to their house, where they found plenty of food. The boy grew soon into a strong and handsome young man, and was helping his mother with her work. One day he asked her, "Mother, where is your husband?" and she replied, "I only dreamed of my husband." Then she told him all that had happened before he was born; and the boy said, "Oh! Maybe my father may turn up some day."

Then The Giver said to his companion, "The woman is home now." That night the woman longed for her husband. She had been dreaming all the time that he was a handsome man, and that her boy looked just like him. At dusk it seemed to her as if someone were coming. Her heart began to beat. Soon she heard footsteps. The door opened, and her boy exclaimed, "Oh, my father has come!" She looked and saw the man in her dreams. At first she was ashamed and bashful. The man told her all that had happened before, and claimed her as his wife.

One day The Giver told the man that all the world had been made for him. Then he instructed him how to act at all times and under all conditions. He also admonished him to have more children, and the man had sixteen children. The first one was a boy, then came a girl, then another boy, and so on. Half of his children went to live north of the Rogue River, while the other half settled down south of the river. The Giver told the man that hereafter he would obtain everything by wishing. Then he straightened out the world, made it flat, and placed the waters. He also created all sorts of animals, and cautioned the man not to cut down more trees or kill more animals than he needed. And after all this had been done, he bade him farewell and went up to the sky, "You and your wife and your children shall speak different languages. You shall be the progenitors of all the different tribes."

Part Six

THE GREAT BASIN

Bands of the
Northern Paiute

Northern Paiute basket *Courtesy of Thomas Burke Memorial
Washington State Museum, cat. #2-770*

Northern Paiute water bottle *Courtesy of Thomas Burke Memorial Washington State Museum, cat. #2-3910*

Great Basin petroglyphs (from Cressman, *Petroglyphs of Oregon*), *Courtesy of University of Oregon Books*

THIS WAS the largest Indian homeland in the Oregon country, an immense high desert country covering thousands of desolate square miles in northern Nevada and California as well as south-western Oregon. Here, under the most marginal ecological circumstances in the Northwest, the Northern Paiutes, a Shoshonean people, wandered in small bands, generally known to each other by some dietary specialty—"the Groundhog Eaters" (Warner Valley), "the Hunibui (biscuit-root) Eaters" (John Day), "the Pine-Nut Eaters" (Paisley), "the Berry Eaters" (east of Steens Mountains), "the Wada (seed) Eaters" (Burns, Malheur Lake), "the Deer Eaters" (Crooked River), and so on.

We have only the vaguest knowledge of these people and their movements before the white settlement of Oregon, but it seems clear that their way of life—tribally unstructured, highly mobile, unmaterialistic—was as different as can be imagined from that of, say, the Wasco Indians, or the Coos; and the imagination simply boggles in trying to connect the Paiute way (as it may have been followed for eleven thousand years or more, according to archaeological studies [1]) and our own culture today.

There has been a great deal of controversy among ethnographers about the prehistorical relations between the Northern Paiutes and Indians living further north and about

Great Basin petroglyphs (from Cressman, *Petroglyphs of Oregon*), *Courtesy of University of Oregon Books*

Great Basin petroglyph, from southern Deschutes County *Courtesy of Oregon Historical Society*

*their relationship to the so-called "Snakes" of Idaho and east
central Oregon. According to one theory, the Snakes were a
distinct but related group that moved across the Snake River
into Oregon, mingled with the Northern Paiutes, and, possessing
horses and therefore mobility, after 1750 swept north clear to the
Columbia River, displacing some "Salish" tribes permanently into
Washington and in general initiating a century of aggression and
territorial expansion throughout eastern Oregon.[2]*

*According to a generally convincing counter theory advanced
by Verne Ray and others,[3] first of all there was no distinct group
of "Snake" Indians, the term being used loosely (and
prejudicially) to label Northern Paiutes and their Shoshonean
relatives in eastern Oregon and western Idaho. Second, far from
being territorial aggressors in the eighteenth century, the
Northern Paiutes were driven south from ancestral lands as far
north as the Warm Springs and John Day countries by Columbia
River Sahaptians like the Tenino, who then claimed but did not
extensively occupy most of Central Oregon until, ironically, they
were placed on the Warm Springs Reservation there in 1856.
Then the Northern Paiutes, especially the "Walpapi" band led
by a warrior named "Paulina," struck back at their old Indian
and their new white adversaries, riding into Indian settlements
and white farms and freight convoys as far north as the
Columbia, and carrying off horses, cattle, and women and
children. In particular, the Warm Springs Reservation along the
Deschutes River—once Paiute territory according to Ray's
theory—became a favorite target; the "Snakes," under Paulina's
leadership, often timed their attacks to coincide with the absence
of the Warm Springs menfolk on hunting and fishing expeditions.
Legends about these raids are still told at Warm Springs.*

*The white response, organized during the Civil War, was
brutally simple: extermination. The unpublished "Field Journals"
of Lt. William McKay (a medical doctor who was himself part
Indian) make it vividly clear that army detachments like
McKay's, aided by Indian scouts from Warm Springs and elsewhere, went through the upper reaches of the Great Basin
country hunting Paiutes and other Shoshoneans down like deer,
killing for the sake of what in the Viet Nam era became known
as "body-count." The marauding bands of Paulina, We-wea, and
others were eventually broken up—but it is a fact that the
Oregon Shoshoneans were never permanently reservationized,
despite efforts in the 1870s to contain them on the immense*

Malheur Reservation.[4] *Some are now part of the Confederated Warm Springs Tribes. Other remnants of bands—lacking tribal identity and therefore largely deprived of government aids and benefits—live around Burns and Lakeview, and at Fort Bidwell at the head of Surprise Valley across the California line.*

The Paiutes' world was and is bleak, open, inhumanly spacious at first encounter. And their stories evoke this great emptiness unforgettably—a blank space, with here a sagebrush, there a rock (both capable of talking), and over there on the horizon, a butte. Time is a spring that has gone dry. Then someone appears, traveling through, Coyote perhaps, and he happens to meet another wanderer, and. . . . As the myths of the Coastal Indians express their deep imaginative preoccupation with the ocean, so these Paiute stories seem to be premised on the fact of sheer desert space—the ecological imagination in them seems somehow wilder, more manic than in the other repertories, as if driven to fill up endless and nearly featureless vistas with outrageous characters and explosive events. It is a cartoon-like literature, really, with lots of "white space" and little shading—but hardly primitive, in the usual condescending sense. Like the other Oregon regional mythologies in this collection, it is a viable Indian way of imagining the local reality, a way of making "Home" into good stories, ones to live by.

Great Basin petroglyphs (from Cressman, *Petroglyphs of Oregon*), *Courtesy of University of Oregon Books*

The Tracks of the Creator

IT IS SAID that the Indian Creator, Gray Wolf [Nümüna], burnt
everything in the old world; everything was burnt to ashes.
Then Gray Wolf talked with the Sun. "There should be a flood,"
Gray Wolf said, and the mountains were covered with water,
there were no mountains to be seen, it is said, no land. Then
the Indian Creator, Gray Wolf, went with his woman far across
the water.

After a time, it is said, the water began to dry up; the mountains appeared, there were banks and shores again. Then the Sun
said to Gray Wolf, "You should make children." "Yes," said
Gray Wolf, and he created pine trees, juniper trees, aspen trees,
cottonwood trees, willows, springs, deer, otter, beaver, trout,
buffalo, horses, mountain sheep, bears.

When Creation was finished, Gray Wolf's children began to
do wrong; they fought amongst themselves with bows and
arrows. Their father, Gray Wolf, became angry, and kicked
them all out. He decided to go south: he said, "My children
are not going to see me again!" Then his woman cried, "But my
children are here!" But they went down to the water anyway,
it is said, and walked away over its surface.

Gray Wolf and his woman came to a tall mountain, with a
pine-covered summit. He said, "I am going in there; afterwards
my children will see my tracks going in. Here I have come and
left my tracks; Indians will see them, and so will white men."
So it was.

How the Animals Found Their Places

In the old time Coyote was boss.
Coyote said, "Bear, you better stay in the mountains."
Deer said, "I want to go live in the mountains too!"
Sucker said, "I want some water."
Duck said he wanted water too.

Swan said, "Look at me, I am growing pretty now;
see, I am white all over."
Bear pounded the ground.
"Ground," he said, "who is talking about me?"
Ground said, "Indian talks pretty mean,"
so Bear went out and bit him.
"I want to stay here in the rocks,"
said Mountain Sheep.
"I like to feel the ground," Rock said,
I like to stay here in one place and not move."
Sagebrush said he felt the same way.
This is Coyote's story.

The Purging of Malheur Cave

IN THE OLD TIME, after the Creator had made the world, all kinds
of bad things, water-imps, Indian-crushers, cannibals, lived in
Malheur Cave. So he, the people's father, said to those things,
"You are evil creatures! You would destroy the people when
they came! You must go to another place, in a different country,
to the earth-hole near Sucker Lake [Pyramid Lake, Nevada]."
So he sent all the bad things from Malheur Cave over yonder a
long way, in the sunrise direction, to the bad hole he had dug
for them. . . .

The Water Cave [Malheur Cave] was once the water-imps'
country, then, it was said by our forefathers. Many of them say
they saw such creatures in the cave, and they did not lie. You
can still see rocks piled up by the water-imps there.

The Creation of the Indians

A LONG TIME AGO there used to be the first Indian here. I don't
know just what he was. Then something came and covered these

mountains with water to kill those Indians. The Sagehen was the only kind of bird saved from the water. He saved fire on a tall mountain. He covered it with his breast; he had it under his breast; he lay on it. Then that Sagehen, he made a fire stick of sagebrush. It was about three inches long and had a hole in one end. He tied on a handle of willow. He made a fire hearth about a foot long. He put sagebrush bark outside and underneath for tinder. He put a little sand in the hole. Then pretty soon it began to smoke; the smoke fell on the bark; he picked it up and blew; and then he had fire. He had to cover the fire all the time so it wouldn't go out.

Some kind of man happened along after the water dried. He was called Nümüzo'ho [Cannibal: *nümü*, people, Paiute; *zoho*, pound]. He was a big man who ate other men. He had a big kettle or rock, and in it he ground all the Indians that he killed. He ground them just like sausage; he put in a whole Indian and mashed him.

In those days they had a big tule camp. There were lots of Indians playing the hand game, but there was just one woman who had a camp off by herself. She was not with the others. Then that woman heard someone calling. He was saying, "*Wi, mohu, mohu, mohu.*" That meant there was someone coming from the south eating all the Indians. It was that Cannibal himself making that sound. The woman ran over to the gamblers and told them what she heard. She had some kind of a hole where she kept her seeds for winter. She hid there and covered herself with a basket tray. She covered herself in that hole.

Nümüzo'ho was still making that song when he got to the gamblers. When he came to the door, he said, "*Pss, pss, pss.*" They all looked up. Then the Cannibal said, "Shut your eyes dry." They all sat still without closing their eyes. The Cannibal just looked and went away. He killed them just by looking at them, but he didn't eat them. One woman was sitting there with her baby asleep on the ground at her back. That Cannibal didn't see that baby. He went away. And then that baby woke up and was crawling over those dead Indians. And that woman was safe in her hole. She came out and got the baby, and those two were saved.

There was a big mountain southeast from Fallon [Nevada], and one man was living on that mountain. That woman thought of him and thought that she should marry him. She packed that little baby on her back and set out toward Mission Valley. She went in search of roots; she was hungry. She came towards that valley.

Then another one of those Cannibals found her, and he asked, "Why are you here alone?" She had fear. She had left her baby at her fireplace. She told the Cannibal that she left a man at her camp with the baby and that he had better go over and talk with him. That Cannibal went over and found the baby alone and ate that baby.

Then he came back to the woman. She pulled out sagebrush and got in the hole. The Cannibal looked for her; he thought she was buried where she had dug roots. He looked for her in the dirt with his hands. It was late in the evening, and he said, "I shall come back tomorrow and find her."

In those days Beaver was an Indian. That woman came to Beaver; she stayed one night with her. Beaver gave the woman fish to eat, because that is what beavers eat. She told that woman, "You had better eat right away and then hide yourself." Those Cannibals lived with Beaver; that's why she fed the woman before the Cannibals came home. When those Cannibals were coming home, they found the woman's track. Then they asked Beaver about her, Beaver told them that the woman had put on Cannibals' shoes to deceive them and that she was still out in the sagebrush. But she was really hiding right there, and she was wearing her own shoes.

Every night when those Cannibals came back they brought Indians for food. Beaver never ate with them; she didn't eat what they did. Early in the morning they started out again to hunt. They carried fire in the tips of their fingers. When all those Cannibals had gone away, Beaver told the woman, "I am going to throw you way over a big mountain. I am going to throw you with a long stick. I shall throw you where they can't find you."

Beaver had a sister, Gopher. When she threw the woman over the mountain, that woman stayed one night with the sister. Gopher asked her to stay one day. She fixed lots of food for her to pack on her trip. She gave her some roots; she gave her many. Then that woman went on her way to find the man she was going to marry.

When she left, Gopher said to her, "There's a head lying on the road. Pass by it. Don't bother it. On the other side of that head is a winnowing basket. It's on the road too, that basket. Don't touch it." But when the woman came to the head, she kicked it; she rolled it around. She didn't believe what Gopher had told her. When she came to the basket, she took a stick and turned it over. Then both the head and the basket started to follow her.

Rat was the brother of Beaver and Gopher. He had a house on the woman's road. Rat could hear the head. It went "*hu*" every time it hit the ground. Rat knew what was coming; he knew that head was following the woman. That basket was going in front of the head. "*Tsai'a tsai'a*," that's the basket's noise.

When Rat heard them coming, he painted his house. This Rat was really the woman's uncle. That's why he painted his house; he wanted to save her in there. She stayed one night with him. When that basket came along ahead of that skull, it hit against Rat's house. That house was painted hard, and that basket broke into little pieces. When that skull which was coming behind hit the man's house, it broke into pieces—just like a cup. That was the last of those two things. Rat gathered up the basket and the skull and took them back where they belonged. The woman stayed there all night and left the next morning. Her uncle told her, "That's all of those bad things on the road."

The next day she came to the man's house, on the mountain. When she reached there, she sat down outside. That man had some food, and he threw some outside. The woman was hungry, and he took some of that food to eat. Then the man asked her to come in. He said, "What kind of a tribe do you belong to? Don't eat that food out there; there is nothing good there. Come in and eat with me." So the woman went inside. She sat down by the door; she didn't go [all the] way in. That man had mountain sheep meat, and he cooked it and gave her some to eat. Then she went outside to get the food she had packed. She was going to give him some.

That night she slept by the door, right where she had been sitting. Every night she moved a little closer to that man. I don't know how many nights before she reached him. Then they lay together and were married. . . .

[The myth has a variety of endings, all of them providing for the begetting of children, who grow up, quarrel, and, having been cast out and dispersed by the father, become the Indian tribes. The following version is particularly haunting in its treatment of conflict, separation, and reconciliation at the beginning of human experience.]

Pretty soon they had one boy. The next time they had a girl.

Then they had another boy and then another girl. They had four of them. They were always playing somewhere outside. One boy and one girl and the other boy and the other girl played together. They were pretty rough. The boys fought with each other, and the girls fought too. The girls cried a lot.

The father said, "Don't fight. You fight too much. You make me angry." The father sat down. He had a girl and a boy on each side of him. He had a short stick, and he pricked them on the legs until he made the blood come out. Then he kicked them away from him. He sent them in opposite directions. "Go somewhere and fight," he told them. Each pair went in a different direction. Once in awhile they built a fire and then moved on again.

The next morning the man told his wife, "Stay here. I want to go away. Follow me when you die." This is what he told her. Then he went away, and the woman followed. Pretty soon he came to the ocean. He got up on it just like it was ice. That woman came along and tried and tried, but she couldn't get up. She just cried around there close to the water. The man kept on going for a long time. Pretty soon he was out of sight.

Then that woman died. Pretty soon she found that man. They stayed together again. He had water there and they bathed. Pretty soon their children died too, and they came over there. That's how the Indians started.

Vagina Dentata

COYOTE WAS CAMPED ALONE. He had a rye grass house behind his camp. A nice looking girl went by early in the afternoon. She asked Coyote to have intercourse with her. After she asked him that, she went on; she didn't stop. When she was a little way off, Coyote got up and followed her. His net caught him on the leg. He went back and put away the net and started after her again. Then that net caught him again on the leg, and he fell down. Then it caught him once more. He fell down every time. The woman was almost over the hill while Coyote was still falling down. When she got to the other side of the mountain, the net no longer caught him.

Coyote followed. That girl could fly. The sagebrush on the trail she followed was still moving. She went right on; she didn't stop. The sun was almost down; then it went down. Coyote couldn't catch up with her. He went home.

Then he fixed a long net for his hair. He made long hair out of that net. He used it for hair. In the middle of the night he finished his hair. Then he braided it in little braids. He made beads out of that net, and he put them in his hair. He put abalone shell in his mouth so that it would shine nicely when he opened his mouth. When he was home, he opened his mouth, and green shone all over the house.

Coyote couldn't sleep. He thought of that girl all the time. Then the sun came up. Coyote covered all his things. He must have had lots of things. He left early in the morning after he had covered everything.

Coyote followed the same route as the day before; he tracked that girl. He went over the same hill. He saw smoke. He could see where she had slept the night. He could see where she had stopped. He visited that place where she had been. Then he went on. He could see her tracks. It was pretty fresh. "That is yesterday's track; it looks pretty fresh," he thought. He went over another hill.

He sat up on the hill looking around. He could see an island in the middle of a lake. He tried to cross to the island. He put his trousers on top of his head and tried to cross. He got all wet. He didn't cross; he went back. Then he lay down there and went to sleep. He dreamed of a road going toward that island. Then he woke up. He looked, and there was a road going to that island.

Coyote got to the island. He sat over there with his mother-in-law. He wanted to possess her; he thought she was a girl. He said, "I wonder how that girl looks. I wonder if she is this nice." He thought that to himself. The old woman said, "She is not here. She is out hunting." The old woman knew what Coyote was thinking. Then he found out that she was the old woman.

Coyote sat there very still. The girl was out hunting swans. When she got home, her mother said, "Hurry and cook something. A stranger has come, and I haven't given him anything." Then the girl went outside. She brought in those swans. She cooked lots of swans.

When it was time to eat, Coyote went outside. He brought his dog in the house. They started to eat. The girl and her mother threw the bones under them. They had toothed vaginas, those women. When the dog heard the crunching of the bones, it growled. Coyote put just a little food in his mouth every time. When the fire died down, he put in a great deal more.

Coyote could see lots of quivers hanging on the wall. They belonged to the men these women had killed. Coyote put his dog outside. The old woman and her daughter closed the house so that there were no holes left open. It was nearly bedtime. Coyote went outside. Then the mother said to the daughter. "You watch him closely. When he tries to have intercourse, bite his penis." Then Coyote lay down with the girl. He whispered when he lay with her. He gaped all the time because he had that shell in his mouth, and it shone well. The old woman had a weapon of some sort by her side. She was going to kill Coyote if the girl missed him.

Coyote asked for something to make a hole through the door. He had long fingernails. He was going to use them on that girl. He tried her, and she bit him. Then Coyote went through the hole he had made. He went outside the tent and down to the edge of the water. He was looking for some stones. He picked up a rock which they used to rub arrows. He broke off some rose twigs that had plenty of thorns.

Then Coyote went back in the house. He wasn't afraid now. He was going to try again. He lay beside the girl and inserted the stone. She broke all her teeth on it. Then he picked up the rose twig. He said, "I have never seen anything that could kill men like this." He rubbed the girl with those rose twigs. Then he took that other rock that they used to rub arrows. He took that rock and rubbed out all the teeth that were left. Then he got up and went over the girl's mother. He used his stone on her; then he picked up the rose twig; then he took the other stone and used it on her. He did just the same thing to her. She lost all her teeth also. So Coyote finished them. When he was through, he slept with the girl.

Coyote and his wife went hunting. He packed some of the quivers that were hanging in the house. He tried to kill some swans, but he couldn't do it. All day long he hunted. They hunted every day. . . .

Coyote's mother-in-law was making a water-jug. This jug was next to the place where Coyote and his wife slept. After a while

Coyote wanted to go. "We ought to go over to my place," he said. Soon after this the water jug began to roll around. Coyote could hear noises coming from inside it. The girl asked her mother if she could go with Coyote. "Yes, you can go," she told her daughter. Then she told her what to do when she went to her husband's home.

She told her daughter not to open that jug until they were home. But Coyote couldn't wait. "I don't see why a person who is traveling shouldn't have some children to love," he said. His wife told him, "Mother says not." Every time they stopped Coyote wanted to open the jug. He wanted his children. That woman wouldn't open it. One day she asked him to go after water because he bothered too much about the jug. He came back with the water. When he came back, he opened the jug. There was lots of noise inside. All the children came out and ran to the west. Their mother cried and followed them. The youngest child had a great big round belly. He was rolling around there after the others and their mother had left.

Then Coyote said to this child, "May you be strong in all things." He went home. He didn't know where his children and his wife were. He thought that if he hadn't opened that jug on the way he would have had his children at home. Then they would have been raised right.

Coyote and His Daughter

COYOTE MADE a big storm come. He asked his daughter to fix the roof of the house. While she was there, Coyote looked up at his daughter. He saw that she was well-formed; she was larger than her mother. Then Coyote wanted to possess her.

He got a toothache. He was nearly dead. "When I die, I want you to marry a good man who can do things for you," he told his daughter. "When I die, don't bury me. Just gather some sagebrush and lay me out on top and burn me. When you leave, don't look back," he said. Then he died.

They did as he told them. They started off, and his son had his arms on his head. He looked back over his shoulder. He saw his father fall the other way. He said to his sister, "It looks to me like our father fell the other way." Then they came to the place they were going. They camped there. After a few days there came this man whom Coyote wanted his daughter to marry. He married her.

One day he asked Coyote's son, "Let's go where your father used to take you to hunt rats." They found a rat under the rock. The boy was on one side poking under the rock, and Coyote was on the other side! The boy looked under the rock at the rat. He wondered why his brother-in-law made a noise as though he were using his teeth. Then he looked at the man's teeth. He saw his teeth; he saw that he had a rotten tooth. When he saw that tooth, he saw that the man looked like his father.

That boy went home. He cried when he saw that. He came and told his mother and sister, "He has teeth just like father. It is he all right."

Then the mother said to her daughter, "When he comes home, hunt for nits on his head." So she did; she laid his head on her lap. He tried to hide his mouth and ears. But when that girl looked she found that he was her father. Then her mother got after him with a stick; she was going to hit him. "This is your father; he doesn't know what he is doing," she told her daughter. She tried to hit him but she missed. Coyote ran off.

After a while he came home, a pretty old man. He came back and found his daughter had a little child. That was his child, a girl. She called Coyote, "My grandfather." Then Coyote wanted to hold the baby. He said, "You don't take good care of my little granddaughter. That's why she has bowel trouble." That's the end of this story.

Coyote Learns to Hunt

IN THOSE DAYS there was lots to eat, but they destroyed it. They used to get game easily, but Coyote and Wolf made it hard to get food. Wolf went hunting. He was going to hunt groundhogs. He went and stood under a rock cliff. He said, "Rocks, come after me," and all the groundhogs came down to him. Then he killed what he thought would be enough for a meal and went home.

Coyote was his brother. He was home, and asked him, "How do you kill so many like that?" Then Wolf told him how he did it. Coyote thought he would try. He did what his brother had told him, and got many groundhogs. Then he ate them, and afterwards he stood there and said the same thing again. Then all the rocks rolled down after him. That's how Coyote spoiled easy hunting.

They went to another place. They were going to hunt rabbits. Wolf went out first. He piled sagebrush roots, as many as he wanted, maybe three piles. He did this as he went along. Then he looked back, and there were rabbits piled there. He went home, and his brother asked him, "How do you always get lots of rabbits to eat? How do you catch them so easily?" Wolf told him once more, and Coyote thought he would try it. He did what his brother had told him, and when he looked back there were the rabbits. After he had eaten them, he tried it a second time. When he looked back, he saw only sagebrush.

Then he went home and asked Wolf, "How do you always have lots of birds to eat?" —"I go along under the willows, and I shake them. Then all the birds fall down. I pick them up and go home." Coyote thought he would try this. He did the same thing; he shook the trees, and many birds fell. He ate them and shook the trees again. This time all the leaves fell down.

When Coyote went home, he asked his brother, "How do you always dig lots of roots to eat? How do you always have lots of *ha-pi'*?" Wolf said, "I go along and see a pile of mole dirt. I kick it open as I go along. When I look back, Mole comes out with a basket of *ha-pi'* in her hands. She has pretty beads around her wrists. She gives me the basket, and I come home." Coyote asked him again, "How do you find *ha-pi'*?" Wolf told him once more, and Coyote thought he would try it. He kicked open a pile of dirt as he passed by. He looked back and saw Mole come out with her basket full. He thought, "I'm going to reach across the basket and get her bracelet." He came to her and grabbed her wrist. She went underground, pulling him with her. He kept hold, and she went on down in the ground. Finally, only Coyote's tail was left above ground. He was helpless, so he let her go.

When he reached home, he asked his brother, "What do you do to get all this *ya-pa'* [yampah]?" —"There is a woman who always gives me *ya-pa'*. These women are always digging it. But if they give you any you must be careful not to spill it, or they will chase you." So Coyote went to get some. When he reached there, he saw the women from a distance. "I guess I'll make love to them," he thought. Those women knew what he was thinking, and they didn't give him any *ya-pa'*. Instead they bunched together and sat down. They thought they would give him some kind of louse. They gathered those lice and gave them to him in a basket. Coyote thought, "Well, if they're going to give me that, I'll throw it at them and help myself to their *ya-pa'*."

When they gave it to him, he threw it back and took their *ya-pa'*. Then he ran home, all those women chasing him. He knew that they would follow. Wolf followed Coyote because he knew what was going to happen. He met Coyote just as he was almost caught by those women. They were making a terrible noise as they came after him. Wolf said to Coyote, "Throw that basket back." He did, and those women took their basket and went home.

Coyote and Wolf Go Hunting

COYOTE AND WOLF were brothers. They told their mother to cook *wa'-da* [seeds] for their lunch. She was cooking it. She covered herself, and she told them not to look at her as she was cooking it. She said, "*Sa'wapoñ, sa'wapoñ, sa'wapoñ*." She told them not to look at her; if they did, the food might burn. She ground that food for them on the *ma-ta'* (metate) and put it in a buckskin bag for their lunch.

Rat was smoking a groundhog in his hole. That Coyote said, "Let me go over there; he might give me one. We could cook and eat it." Wolf told Coyote not to bother Rat. "He might put you in the hole and smoke you," he said. But Coyote went anyway. Rat didn't see him come. He stooped over and tried to get out the groundhog. When he leaned over, his testes hung down. Coyote took a long piece of rye-grass and stuck Rat with it. He stuck him again and again. Rat dodged each time. He made a hole in the ground and sat down over it. Then Coyote stuck him again. This time Rat looked back; he tried to see what was hurting him. He said to Coyote, "Oh, my grandchild, you are always so silly."

He told Coyote to go inside and get the groundhog, for he could not reach it. So Coyote went in, and Rat closed him in there and left him. Wolf wondered why his brother didn't come back. He came looking for him. Coyote was smoked to death, but he had the groundhog in his arms all right. Wolf said, "*Tupi'ku kwana*," and he broke the rock over the hole into little pieces. He kicked it aside. He found his brother dead. He took him out. Coyote had a groundhog in his arms. [Coyote revives.]

They saw fawn tracks. Coyote said, "Let me track one. I might kill one for supper and breakfast." Wolf said, "You better let them alone; they might follow us with fire." Wolf went on and left Coyote. Coyote took that little fawn all right. The fire followed him. When it had nearly caught him, he threw down the fawn. Then the fire stopped. Then Coyote ran back and grabbed the fawn again. The fire followed him once more. He grabbed the fawn and ran. He jumped on his brother. He had that fawn in his arms. The fire was blazing behind him, and it caught Wolf and singed his hair. The Wolf, he grabbed the fawn and threw it away. Then the fire stopped.

They went on again and saw an elk. Coyote said, "There's the great big animal that can look over the mountain." He kept telling his brother this, but Wolf went right on. He said, "My brother, you stay right here and take care of our lunch. If you eat any, I shall bring that deer to life after I've killed it." Then Wolf shot the [deer]. Coyote watched him kill it. He ran to him. Wolf told him to go after the lunch.

Coyote felt happy. He broke a hole in the lunch and ate some. Wolf said, "Did you eat any?" —"No, I came under some brush. That's what tore the hole." —"I think you ate some. Yes, you have eaten some." Wolf tickled Coyote, and he laughed. "I know you have eaten some; I see it in your teeth." He was going to make that deer alive again. He asked Coyote, "Are you going to follow even if he goes in deep water?" —Coyote said, "Yes, I'll follow him. I'll turn into a spider and go on top of the water." And Wolf revived that deer. He ran away and Coyote ran after him. He was near him. Coyote was left in the desert where there was no water. He was so thirsty.

All kinds of birds were playing a game. Lizard and some Flies were outside. They weren't playing. Lizard and the Flies kept saying, "*Didu'kwi nini, dudu' skaonai.*" They said, "Something is coming way off." The gamblers were inside. "We better see what they mean by that," they said. One went out to see what they were saying. Weasel came out, and he began to say the same thing, "*Didu' kwi nini, dudu' skaonai.*"

Then they thought, "Wolf and Coyote went hunting. Maybe they scared a deer this way." They said to Dove, "Go and watch. If he comes by, kill him." But Dove said, "No, I'm afraid of everything. If anything comes near me, I want to fly away." So they got Rattlesnake, and asked him to go. Rattlesnake didn't want to do it. He made teeth of rosebush thorns and tried to bite someone. He didn't kill him. So he made teeth of burning coals.

Rattlesnake lay under the sagebrush. The deer didn't see him. He went right over him, and the Snake struck and killed him. Then the people who had been gambling came there to butcher that deer. Rattlesnake said he was going to take the ribs and backbone because he had killed the animal. They tried to push him away with a stick, but he came back. They took everything away from him, and threw him to one side with a stick. The chief talked to them. "Maybe Coyote and Wolf will be coming," he said. They dried the meat and put it away.

Wolf went back to his mother's home. He went to bed. His mother asked, "Where is your brother?" —"He was so silly. He ate the lunch we had. I killed a deer, and when he ate the lunch I revived the deer. He followed him. Perhaps he is dying for lack of water."

So Wolf sent Horned Toad to follow the deer tracks. He carried water, and away he went. He found Coyote lying under the brush; his mouth was wide open. Horned Toad put water in his mouth. Coyote did not know where the water came from. Horned Toad was on the other side of the brush. He put water in Coyote's mouth every few minutes. When Coyote was feeling better, he jumped up and shot in the air with his arrows. Horned Toad got under the sagebrush, and Coyote didn't see him. Then Coyote was all right, but Horned Toad stayed there under the brush for good.

Coyote followed the deer tracks again. He came along. He knew that those people had killed his deer. He went to their camp and gathered up all the meat they had. He packed it and went home to his mother.

They [the gambling people] said, "Has anybody power enough to make deep snow so Coyote will freeze to death?" And Porcupine said, "I'll do that." Then he said, "*Hoñi'tchu, hoñi'tchu, poboi'ta, boi'ta.* May a deep snow fall." The snow fell, and Coyote could hardly walk. The snow half-covered the pine trees.

Coyote took his *muka'nu* [firedrill] and hunted for a rock. Then he drilled fire so that he could heat the rock. He made it red hot and threw it toward home. He told the snow to dry. It began to melt and dry.

Wolf had told his brother not to sit on a rock. "If you sit on a rock, it will grow with you," he told him. Coyote was sitting on top of a rock. It grew way up in the air, like a rim rock. Coyote's pack was on the ground. Weasel was Coyote's wife. She took the pack and gave it to his mother. She saved the fat and made it into balls. These she saved for Coyote. He was way up in the air on top of that rock. Weasel came under the rock every morning and cried and cried.

She told Eagle to bring down her husband. Eagle flew into the air. He took a little rock in his claws. He practiced to see how heavy a rock he could carry. Then he flew way in the air. Coyote thought to himself, "Well, maybe he is going to take me down." He lay on one side where Eagle could catch hold of him. Finally Eagle took him in his claws. He circled round and round in the air, coming lower and lower.

Coyote's wife was packing wood. Eagle put Coyote where she would find him. Weasel came along, and there she found her husband under the sagebrush. She was packing wood on her back, and she put him on top of it and packed him home.

Then she took that grease. She put it on the end of a stick and warmed it. When it melted, she put it in Coyote's mouth. He liked it. Then he became fleshy and stout again.

Coyote the Eye-Juggler

COYOTE WAS walking along. He heard someone laughing. "Come in," they said. Wild Cat and some others were sitting there. I think Skunk was there too. Coyote asked them, "What shall I do?" —"Take out your eyes. Throw them in the air. Then hold your head back, and they will fall in again."

Coyote tried to take out his eyes. He took them both out and threw them up, but not very far. He held back his head, and the eyes fell right in the sockets. Everybody laughed.

Then Wild Cat tried it again. He threw his eyes way up in the air, and they came back. Everybody laughed and told Coyote to try it again. "Throw them way up in the air this time," they said. He did it. One had a stick in his hand. When Coyote's eyes were coming down, he knocked them to one side. Then everybody ran away. They took Coyote's eyes with them.

Coyote couldn't see a thing. He was all alone. He tried to follow but he couldn't find the way. He ran into the Sagebrushes, and he scolded them. They said, "We never move. You come right over us." Then he ran into the Rocks. "You're in my way all the time!" he told them. But the Rocks said, "We never move. You just run over us."

Coyote heard some Birds singing. He went over there and called them. The Birds came to him. "Will you give me your little eye so that I can see?" They gave him a little one so that he could see where he was going.

Coyote traveled until he came to a camp. An old woman was there and Coyote asked her, "Where is everybody?" She told him, "I have three daughters. They're out there dancing over Coyote's eyes." —"What do you do when your girls come back?" —"I tell them to get me water. That's the first thing I say," the old lady told him. Then Coyote asked, "How do you cook for them?" —"I cook *wa'-da* for them."

Then Coyote took a rock. He hit the old woman on the head and hid her away. He took off her clothes and put them on. Then he lay down where she had been. The girls came back, and Coyote asked them for water the first thing. One ran to get water. Soon the girls said to him, "Everybody wants you over there, grandmother. They're going to dance over Coyote's eyes." —"How am I to go?" —"We can pack you on the back." One picked up Coyote and packed him. When she was tired, another packed him. The girls were pretty tired. Then Coyote said, "Let me go. I'll go myself." And then he went on alone. The girls were over a hill, and Coyote ran to gain time. When anyone was looking, he leaned on his stick and walked like an old woman.

Then he reached the place where they were dancing. "Let me have that Coyote's eye for a while. I want to dance with it," he said. They gave the eyes to him. He held them in his hand and danced. "I feel like flying away," he said. Then he ran, taking the eyes with him.

They all ran after him, but nobody could catch him. Fox tried to take the eyes from him. Coyote told him, "These are my own eyes," so Fox let him go.

Coyote put his eyes in a spring to soak. They were pretty dry. He soaked them and put them in their sockets. Then Coyote was all right again.

The Theft of Pine Nuts

COYOTE WAS CAMPED somewhere. He smelled something to the north. Then he kept on going. Soon he found a camp. A little boy had pine nuts in his hand. He came out, and Coyote said, "My nephew, let me have some." But that boy went back and said to his mother, "That stranger asked me for pine nuts. He said, 'Nephew, let me have some.'"

Then one man said, "Take pine nuts and mix them with water; make it pretty thin. He's not the right kind of a man." So they did, and gave some to Coyote. They gave him a cup full of it. Coyote began to drink it, but it wouldn't stay in his mouth. He tried to hold it in his hands, but it came right out of his skin. He tried to hold it in his hands, but it came right out.

Then Coyote went home. Wolf was his brother. They were living together. He told his brother, "That's what I saw." He told everybody. Then Coyote said, "Don't call me Coyote. Call me Tall Fellow. Say 'This Tall Fellow finds everything.'" But they didn't mind him; they called him Coyote just the same.

Pretty soon everybody set out. They traveled a whole day. All kinds of game went, everybody. When they reached there, they started to gamble. They played the stick game all night. Those people had hidden the pine nuts. Coyote wanted to take them away; he told Mouse to look for the nuts. He looked all night, but he didn't find anything until nearly daylight. He tried to scratch out the nuts. Everybody saw him. All but the people who owned the nuts saw him. Then Woodpecker said, "I'll get it. As soon as I get it, everybody must run." Then he took the nuts out quickly, and they all ran.

The people chased after them. They killed Wolf first. He and Coyote were the bosses. Then they killed all the others except Coyote. He wasn't killed because he was way ahead. Chipmunk with the red on the side didn't get tired. He put his brother on his back and carried him. Frog was with them. He gave out. But the people didn't kill him; they didn't bother him at all. Wolf got up after he had been killed. He came along and made everyone alive again. They all got up, every one of them. Frog was way behind.

Pretty soon they found ice ahead of them. It was high. They couldn't climb over. Then Coyote tried to get through, but he couldn't make it. He hit it again and again with his nose. It gave him a pretty short nose. Some of those Black Crows were at one side. Coyote said, "I can never break through this." Those Indians had some obsidian. They put it in the fire and made it hot. Crow took this in his mouth and flew high into the air. Everybody looked up and watched. Then he went so high that they couldn't see him. He was out of sight. Coyote said, "I see him way up there," but he couldn't see him. Coyote was only talking. Pretty soon Crow came down fast. He hit that ice. It became loose. Coyote jumped through quickly. He was the first one through. Then everyone else came through.

That Frog was still coming. He saw their old fire. He put his hand in the ashes to see how long ago they had been there. Some grass was just coming up. He picked out a stick, and it burned his hand. "It's just a little while ago," he said, "because that stick burned my hand." Then Frog went on. He saw a sunflower [*aki*]. "A big girl is looking at me," he thought. Pretty soon he gave up. He found a spring. "I might as well stay here," he said. He jumped into the water and stayed right there.

The others went on home. They mixed the pine nuts with water. They cooked them. They wanted to raise some. So Wolf and Coyote put pine nuts in their mouths and spat them out, way over the mountains. Coyote cheated and ate most of his. Wolf raised good pine nuts, but Coyote raised juniper trees.

Nümüzo'ho Plays Ball

NÜMÜZO'HO AND THE PEOPLE had been quarreling. The birds made a game so that the others would lose. "We never say anything even if you eat us," they told Nümüzo'ho.

There were some little grey Birds who had two boys. These

boys were angry, and the big one shot the little one with his bow and arrow. The mother said, "Why do you treat him that way? We are nearly gone now. Everybody is killing us. There are just the three of us left." At last the big brother killed his little brother. He packed him home. The father and mother were crying in the sagebrush. They took the feathers from that little bird, and they made a ball of his feathers. They buried him under the rock.

Those two Birds told all the Birds and Animals that they wanted a big council. The Cannibals were camped alone, away from the others. They stayed in the sun even if it [was] very hot. These two Birds had them gather too. They told them, "We are going to play ball clear around the mountain. The losers are going to be roasted." They fixed a big hole with a fire in it. This was to cook those who came in last.

They started from this pit. They put the ball near there. They were going to kick it. Nümüzo'ho played against the Crows. The others stayed behind to keep the fire going. The Birds hired Gopher (*pimi mabida'* = "backward palms") to make an underground tunnel so that the Cannibals' ball would hit against its roof and bounce backward. They told Owl to flap his wings to make it light at night for the Birds, and they had Woodpecker do the same thing. Owl winked his eye, and Woodpecker flapped his wings.

They wanted to get rid of Nümüzo'ho because he was destroying them. Magpie was the leader. He went over the mountain. They took turns. Coyote and Wild Cat took turns kicking the ball.

Nümüzo'ho scolded Gopher because he made the tunnel in front of him. "What kind of animal is this that makes all this trouble for us? He makes our balls bounce back every time." The others were already over the mountain, but they were not. They had no light, and when the ball bounced back they lost it. They fell down and skinned their knees and elbows.

The Birds were winning. Coyote was watching for them to reach the goal. Coyote felt happy. He yelled and jumped around. He kicked the ball ahead when they came to the roasting pit.

Black Crow (*a'da*) was glad his people were winning. He knew they were winning because he saw the daylight coming. That's how he knew. Black Crow yelled and jumped around the fire. He made Nümüzo'ho angry. "You black-legged thing, you laugh. You would make anybody angry." He took a stick and hit Black Crow. He broke both his legs. But Black Crow was happy. "I don't care if my legs are broken; I feel pretty good just the same. Bring me a stick so I can tie it to my legs." He told his people, "My legs are all right. I can jump and hop around just the same."

The Cannibals came in last. They didn't kick their ball. They just came along. They knew they were beaten. They were hot and tired. They had sore shoulders and knees and toes where they had fallen down.

Nümüzo'ho was so big and stout. Eagle and Owl and Badger were going to throw him in the fire. Eagle and Owl grabbed him by the head, and Badger pushed him in the roasting pit. They pressed him down with his breast right into the fire. Then they threw his wife and children into the fire to roast.

Nümüzo'ho kicked around in that pit. They covered him with earth. When he was cooked, they took him out; when those Cannibals were tender, they took them out. They cleaned their teeth. They took out the meat they had been eating. Coyote cleaned their teeth. He made people alive again from the meat he took from their teeth.

Nümüzo'ho in the Mortar

COYOTE WAS GOING ALONG. He saw Nümüzo'ho on a rim rock. Nümüzo'ho stood there and called to anyone who happened to come along. When they were close to him, he pushed them over the cliff. He told them there were mountain sheep below. He killed those people every time.

Coyote knew what Nümüzo'ho was doing. He came up but didn't go very close to the edge. Nümüzo'ho tried to get him closer. "Come on, there's a mountain sheep way down here," he said. But Coyote watched him closely. As he came near the rim, Nümüzo'ho put out his hands to shove him over. Coyote dodged, and Nümüzo'ho went right over the cliff.

That's how Coyote killed the first Cannibal. Then he went along and found another one. He found a shady place, and he changed the willows into old dry ones. Then Coyote made himself look sick. He lay down under that shade. He made the camp look as though it had been left a long time before.

This Nümüzo'ho came up and asked, "How long have you been here? How long ago did they leave you?" And Coyote said, "I have been here a long time. See the dry sagebrush. See how old the camp is." Nümüzo'ho said, "Well, anyway, let's play some games. Let's play a hand game." —"No, I don't want to play that game. It hurts my knees to kneel so long." Then Nümüzo'ho asked Coyote to play hoop and pole, but Coyote told him, "No, I don't want to play that. It hurts my legs to keep running back and forth."

Nümüzo'ho was packing his mortar on his back. He put it down and said, "Let's hit each other with rocks." Then this Coyote thought how he would kill him. He crawled out. He was nothing but skin and bones. He said, "I am weak," and fell back. Then he went outside and sat down. He asked his *siwa'* (intestinal worms), "I wonder what I am going to do." His *siwa'* answered, "When you get in the mortar, put just your skin in the center. Put your flesh and bones around the edge."

When Coyote came back, Nümüzo'ho asked him, "What have you been talking about all this time?" Coyote answered, "That's the way I always sound when I defecate. I'm pretty weak and sick."

Coyote climbed in the mortar first. Nümüzo'ho thought he would kill him. Coyote did what his *siwa'* had told him. When he was hit, Coyote barked and jumped out. The stone just hit his skin. As soon as Nümüzo'ho saw he had missed, he called, "Two times," but Coyote said, "No, we already said just once."

Nümüzo'ho was pretty big. When it was his turn, he filled the mortar plumb full. When Nümüzo'ho climbed in, Coyote tried to raise the rock. He was so weak he could hardly lift it from the ground. Coyote called out to Nümüzo'ho, "I didn't look at you. Turn the other way." He made Cannibal look the other way. As he turned his head, Coyote picked up the stone and killed him with it. He kept on pounding him with it. "You carry this mortar all the time. You kill my brothers and my sisters and my relatives," he was saying. He kept on pounding and talking.

Coyote and Bear

COYOTE WAS LIVING with his wife and son. Coyote went rabbit hunting. His wife and little boy were hunting ants. They found an ant nest, and Coyote's wife was gathering those ants. She sent her little boy to find more nests. Bear was watching him as he hunted for those nests. Bear was in an ant nest. He was cleaning it. When the ants got on his paw, he licked them off. The little boy came to the spot where Bear was standing, and that Bear killed the little boy.

Coyote's wife went home. When Coyote came home, he found his wife sitting there crying. He brought one rabbit with him. She told her husband that Bear had eaten their little boy. Then Coyote told her that he would go and hunt that Bear.

They left home. They went in different directions. Coyote was hunting that Bear. He was looking for him on the hillside. He knew where Bear went for chokecherries. There was a spring there with lots of willows. Bear went for a drink and went under those willows. He lay down for a nap, that Bear did. Coyote tracked him there. He found him asleep.

When Coyote saw him, he called out, "Who is that sleeping there? Is it my aunt (*pa-wa'*: father's sister)?" He called for Bear to come; he wanted to talk with him. Bear heard him, but he didn't move. Coyote called, "Come on, my aunt." Then Bear went out to see him. They sat down in the shade of the Willows.

Then Coyote said to Bear, "What are you hunting? Why are you lying down under these willows?" Then Bear told Coyote he was looking for service berries and chokecherries. Then Coyote said, "Did you ever do any mischief?" —"No, I don't think I ever did any mischief." —"Sometimes people forget what they have done." Then the Bear said, "Yes, I remember, I did kill one little child about a year ago."

Coyote tried to trick that Bear. He told him, "You'll find lots of service berries on that hill. When you pass the thick places, it may look as though someone is going to shoot you. That is all right. Just go right on." That's what Coyote told the Bear. Then Bear said, "Yes, I'm going over there." Coyote said, "I am going this way through the meadows. I want to catch some mice to eat." As soon as Bear was over the hill, Coyote ran into the thick brush. Bear thought someone was going to shoot at him with a bow and arrow, but he went right on because of what Coyote had told him. Then Coyote killed that Bear.

He made a fire to roast him in the ground. He roasted him and was resting. The cottonwood trees around there were split. When the wind blew, they opened and shut. Coyote thought he would play with them. He put his hand in the split. The wind stopped blowing, and he was held fast. Some Black Crows came along. They scratched the earth off the meat and ate every bit of it. Coyote was hanging on that tree, and those Crows ate all his meat. After they had left, the wind started to blow again, the tree opened, and Coyote got free.

He ran and picked up the bones; he gathered all of them. Then he broke them and ate the marrow. He had killed a big Bear, and that is all he got. He ate those bones and piled them all together. "I'm a pretty stout person. Even if you kill me, I'll come back to life. I'll get up in two years even if green grass grows through my bones," Coyote told that pile of bones.

Coyote Shoots the Night

WOLF KNEW about the Night. He had it hanging inside his house, that Wolf. He told his brother not to fool with the Night. He said to Coyote, "You let it alone. Everybody will starve if you bother the Night." That's what he told Coyote.

Coyote took a blade of grass and shot it from his hands. He shot that Night with grass. Then he broke the Night. It stayed Night. It was Night a long time. No daylight came at all. It was Night all the time.

Coyote was drilling fire. He lighted that bark and went to look for rabbits. When he heard a rabbit, he hit him with that light. Every time the fire struck the ear of the rabbit. Then Coyote chased the rabbit wherever he saw the light on its ears. He killed many rabbits. He had rabbits to eat; everybody else was starving. Those who hunted in the daytime were getting hungry. It was Night all the time.

Then the Indians gathered and talked about the Night. None of the doctors could make the sun come up. They just couldn't do it. They asked Mallard Duck (*guda'*). They asked him to do it. He asked for white shell beads. He said he would do it for that price. They gave him just enough beads to go around his neck. Those beads show on his neck now. They put those beads around his neck.

He said, "If there is going to be day, I'll have to sing." About the time for daylight, he began [to sing]. Daylight was coming; the sun was nearly up. Then the sun came up. Then Duck told them how long the day would be. "It's going to be long," he said. Then the day was as before.

Cottontail Shoots the Sun

THAT COTTONTAIL [RABBIT] wanted to go after the Sun. He made many arrows because he wanted to go after the Sun. Cottontail was on his way. A Chipmunk stood on top of a rock and yelled, "Who is that?" Then those Chipmunks made fun of Cottontail's tail. He became angry and ran after them. He kept on going until he was just out of sight over the hill. Then he looked back. Those Chipmunks were standing on the rock—the mother and all her little ones. He shot at them. They were frightened and said, "*Tisu'ku, tisu'ku, tisu'ku.*" They ran in their hole. Cottontail let them go, and he traveled to the east.

There were some Lice in the sandy ground where the Red Ants live. They were talking. They said, "That Cottontail is from the south. He is going to kill everybody. If he kills me, I'm going to do this," and that Louse yelled and jumped around and fell to the ground. He jumped up because he hadn't noticed Cottontail. That Cottontail was coming along. He had a rope of sagebrush bark over his shoulder for packing his quiver. His shoulder was sore. He said to that Louse, "Try again." He took some grass roots and told that Louse to try again. He said, "I wonder how you people happen to know anything about me. You are always talking about me." Then he hit that Louse with the grass roots and killed him.

He kept on going. . . . Cottontail came to the place where the

North Winds were camped. They had a wickiup. Cottontail took a long hollow pole and placed it by the door. He tied a rock over the doorway of that wickiup. When he had hung the rock there, he painted his eye with red paint. He was sitting right in the middle of the room. When he heard those Winds coming, he didn't look up until they were all inside. Then he looked up and frightened them. They ran out. They bumped their heads on that rock as they ran.

They gave that Cottontail one poor cottontail rabbit. They told him to eat it. They cooked the rabbits in hot ashes. When they took them out of the pit, they gave him a poor one. He said to himself, "Let all the grease come into my cottontail; let all the grease come into my cottontail." When they were ready to eat, they said, "Oh, where is all the grease?" That Cottontail had got the best of them.

He was the last one to take out his rabbit. It was full of grease. When they saw that, they all jumped on him. Cottontail slipped out; he left just his tail under the Winds, and they thought they had him. He sat outside and ate his cottontail and laughed at them. He ate all of that rabbit. Then he put one little log on the fire after the Winds had gone to sleep. Then their rye grass house caught on fire. They all yelled inside the house; they were burning. That's how Cottontail got rid of the North Winds. If it weren't for him, it would be awfully cold.

Then Cottontail went on. He burned all the grass he saw. He wanted to see what wouldn't burn. He found a green bush called *wazo'bü* that wouldn't burn. "If the world should catch fire, I'll get under this," he thought.

When Cottontail came to the Sun, it was just daybreak. The Sun was just coming up. Cottontail shot an arrow. It went just halfway and burned. He shot until he had just one arrow left. He shot the Sun with that. When the Sun fell, he ran to it, split it open, and took out its gall. He threw that into the air. "The Sun shall go this way so that it won't be dark before I kill enough cottontails for my meals," he said.

Then the fire started to burn. Cottontail ran into Badger's hole. Hot ashes fell on his neck, and he ran for another place. He burned his paws. Finally he got into the bush that wouldn't burn. That's how he saved his life.

Cottontail killed the Sun. He took his gall and threw it into the air. That's how we got long days.

Humming Bird's Space Flight

Humming Bird wanted to see beyond the sun, way up in the heavens. He took lots of *atsa'* [mustard] seeds and filled his trousers full. He was going to eat just one seed a day. He started flying upward. He ate just one seed a day, but he turned back because he ran out of food. He didn't see anything.

When he came back, everybody was anxious to know what he had seen. He told them he had seen nothing.

The Thunder Badger

Thunder Badger lives up in the sky,
he is striped like any badger.
When the earth dries up it makes him angry,
He wants the earth to be moist.
Then he puts his head down and digs like a badger,
then the clouds come up in a flurry,
then the loud earth-cursing comes, the thunder,
then the rain comes down all over.

How to Control the Weather

"The mother of Tadagai could make the snow melt. She cried like a stallion, took a firebrand of sagebrush, and pointed it toward the south, saying, 'Come on, rain; come on, rain!' She did not dance. The wind blew, the rain came, and the snow began to melt. . . .

"You must not boil cottontail because it brings snow; you must fry or roast it. Once some old men were going to boil cottontail and they told me to stand outside. In my hand I had a bullroarer made from a dried juniper limb. It was about two inches wide and six inches long. It was not notched. Two or three black marks ran cross wise on the face. A stick, like a handle, was tied to the end of its thong.

"I blew the water, in which the cottontail was boiling, to the south, saying, 'Come, rain and wind.' It was winter, a long time ago, before any white men were here; I was a small boy, born in the middle of summer when it was hot. That was why they had me do this to counteract their boiling cottontail. There is no way to keep snow from coming. Porcupine brings snow. You roast the meat and when you have eaten it, you mash the bones. Then it will snow."

A Hunter's First Kill

"A MAN TOLD his son, 'Do not eat the first deer you kill. Butcher it and hang it up. Then let me know. I will go with you to bring back the meat.'

"Once I killed a deer up above Lake City [California]. My father came and asked me, "What kind of tree would you like? Service?' I said, 'yes, that is stout; maybe it will make me strong.' Then we cut green service to make a ring. I pulled over the stem and my father cut it, saying, 'I cut you.' Then he sliced thin meat from inside the deer's ribs and twisted it around that service ring.

"Then my father said, 'Take off your shirt, your moccasins. Take the beads from your neck.' I took off my clothes. My father said, 'Step in this ring. Do it carefully; be sure not to touch it.' I did that, and he lifted the ring up over my head and then let it down, and I stepped out. Then he put it over my head and pulled it down. I stood still. 'Step over,' he said. Every time my father did this he called all kinds of game—goose, swan, mountain sheep, bear, elk, and otter.

"This is called *natsa'-tiha'niu* ['skinning an animal'], and afterwards a person will always be lucky. My father said, 'You can eat this meat tomorrow.' I wanted some that day, but I waited."

White Men Are Snakes

"ALMOST EVERYTHING was Coyote's way. The Indian planted the apple. When he planted it, he said for all the Indians to come and eat. When he told them that, all the people came.

"The white man was a rattlesnake then, and he was on that tree. The white people have eyes just like the rattlesnake. When the Indians tried to come to eat the apples, that snake tried to bite them. That's why the white people took everything away from the Indian; because they were snakes. If that snake hadn't been on the tree, everything would have belonged to the Indian. Just because they were snakes and came here, the white people took everything away. They asked these Indians where they had come from. That's why they took everything and told the Indians to go way out in the mountains and live."

The True Beginning of the Earth

"ONE TIME this was all water but just one little island. That is what we are living on now. Old Man Chocktoot was living on top of this mountain. He was living right on top of this mountain. In all directions the land was lower than this mountain. It was burning under the earth. Nümüzo'ho was under there, and he kept on eating people.

"The Star (pa'-tuzuba) was coming. When that Star came, it went up into the sky and stayed there. When that Star went up, he said, 'That is too bad; I pity my people. We left them without anything to eat; they are going to starve.' This Star gave us deer, and antelope, and elk, and all kinds of game.

"They had Sun for a god. When the Sun came up, he told his people, 'Don't worry, come to me; I'll help you. Don't worry; be happy all your life. You will come to me.'

"The Sun and the Stars came with the Water. They had the Water for a home. The Indian doctor saw them coming. He let his people know that they were coming. There were many of them. The little streams of spring water are the places from which silver money comes. It comes from the Sun shining on the water.

"The first white man came to this land and saw that silver, but he lost himself and didn't get to it. Finally white people found this place, and they came this way looking for the silver. Those white men brought cattle, sheep, pigs, and horses. Before they came, there were no horses in this land.

"The Sun told his people, 'Deer belong to you. They are for you to eat.' These white men don't know who put the deer and other animals in this land. I think it is all right for me to kill deer, but the white men say they will arrest me. Whenever I see cattle or sheep, I know they don't belong to me; I wouldn't kill them. I feel like going out and killing deer, but I am afraid. I am getting too old. Maybe white people don't know about the beginning of this earth."

Notes

Parenthetical listings following the titles of individual stories refer to the standard motif-index system (Stith Thompson, ed., *Motif-Index to Folk-Literature*).

INTRODUCTION

1. Melville Jacobs, "The Fate of Indian Oral Literatures in Oregon," *Northwest Review*, 3 (Summer 1962): 90.

2. Ibid., p. 97.

3. Robert Frost, "The Gift Outright," in *The Poetry of Robert Frost* (1969), p. 348. Perhaps this claim is too sweeping, in the light of recent publications in Oregon folklore like Stephen Dow Beckham's *Tall Tales from Rogue River* (1974).

4. William Stafford, "The Well Rising," in *The Rescued Year* (1966), p. 31. See also the "Wind World" section in *Someday, Maybe* (1974).

5. See Jacobs' *The People Are Coming Soon* (1960) *and The Content and Style of an Oral Literature* (1959), both works based on his monumental study of the Clackamas Chinook language and literature; and Hymes's model of sensitive structuralist interpretation, "The 'Wife' Who 'Goes Out' Like a Man: Reinterpretation of a Clackamas Chinook Myth" in *Social Science Information*, 7, no. 3 (1968): 173–99. Also useful, if much less specific, are introductory essays by T. P. Coffin, *Indian Tales of North America* (1961); and by Stith Thompson, *Tales of the North American Indians* (1929).

6. Ruth Underhill, ed., *The Autobiography of a Papago Woman* (1936), p. 23.

7. Mircea Eliade, *Myth and Reality* (1963), pp. 18–19, 141–42. A useful brief survey of schools of interpretation is Percy Cohen's "Theories of Myth," in *Man*, 1969, pp. 337–53.

8. The Klikitat narrator Joe Hunt explained to Melville Jacobs that his people recognized "a former world" when all living things were persons, which was followed by a "Great Change," resulting in the present world. Myths from the former world, including the events of the Transformation, are *wat'i't'ac;* stories from the latter days are *txa'nat*, "happenings" or "customs." Hunt also gave Jacobs examples of Klikitat *cu'kwat*—"knowledge, learning, teaching," often in the form of reflections on the meaning of myths and stories. In fact most Northwest tribes had some such division according to "kind." See Melville Jacobs, *Northwest Sahaptin Texts* (1929), 2:244.

9. MS letter, dated Nov. 20, 1929, in the collection of the American Philosophical Society Library, and printed with the permission of the Library. Phinney's field work—mostly with his mother!—resulted in a superb collection of tales, *Nez Perce Texts* (1934).

10. Jacobs, *Content and Style*, p. 7, and *The People Are Coming Soon*, pp. ix–x. See also Phinney, *Nez Perce Texts*, p. viii.

11. For a different view of the relationship of myth and ritual in Northwest Indian life, see Dell Hymes, "Two Types of Linguistic Relativity," in *Sociolinguistics*, ed. William Bright (1966), pp. 114–57.

12. Eliade, *Myth and Reality*, p. 19.

13. Jacobs, *Content and Style*, p. 73.

14. The work of Jerome Rothenberg and Dennis Tedlock (co-editors of *Alcheringa: A Journal of Tribal Poetics*) points in this direction. Tedlock's brilliant translation of Zuni narratives, *Finding the Center* (1972), is keyed to performance and is cast as poetry—and I believe that most of the items in the present volume would be best rendered as verse, if we could re-transcribe them from performance. But that would be impossible in the Northwest today.

15. See Dell Hymes's essay on "Breakthrough into Performance" in *Folklore: Performance and Communication*, ed. Dan Ben-Amos and Kenneth Goldstein (1975).

16. Stith Thompson, ed., *Motif-Index to Folk-Literature* (1929).

17. The subject of Indian assimilation of European stories has been oddly neglected: such study might shed light on the fundamental principles or "rules" by which native narratives were generated. See Stith Thompson's early study, *European Tales among the North American Indians* (1919), and for examples see his *Tales of the North American Indians* (1929).

18. In Edward Sapir's *Takelma Texts* (1909), there are several stories about Daldal ("dragonfly"), who is a "straight," virtuous transformer and hero—and is doubled with a younger brother who is wholly a trickster, always into mischief which Daldal must straighten out. Thus the contradictions inherent in Coyote are resolved in a kind of literary miosis; in many Indian mythologies, of course, one or more sets of twins are prominent actors, representing the fundamental duality of human life.

19. *The Future of an Illusion*, trans. W. D. Robson-Scott (1961), p. 18.

20. See "The Structural Study of Myth," in *Structural Anthropology* (1967), especially pp. 250 ff.

21. Adapted from Leslie Spier and Edward Sapir, *Wishram Ethnography* (1930), pp. 258–59.

PART ONE. NORTHEASTERN OREGON

1. *Original Journals of the Lewis and Clark Expedition*, ed. Reuben Gold Thwaites (1904–5), 5:18.

2. See Merrill D. Beal, *"I Will Fight No More Forever": Chief Joseph and the Nez Perce War* (1963). For general ethnographic information on the Nez Perce and their tribal relatives, see Herbert J. Spinden, *The Nez Perce Indians*, Memoirs of the American Anthropological Association, vol. 2, pt. 3 (1908); Francis Haines, *The Nez*

Perce: Tribesmen of the Columbia Plateau (1955); Robert Ruby and John A. Brown, *The Cayuse Indians: Imperial Tribesmen of Old Oregon* (1972); Edward S. Curtis, *The North American Indian,* 8 (1911): 3–78, 157–71; Alvin Josephy, *The Nez Perce Indians and the Opening of the Northwest* (1965).

COYOTE AND THE SWALLOWING MONSTER (*A1611; F911.6; K82.4*)

Archie Phinney, *Nez Perce Texts* (1934), pp. 26–29. Phinney was himself a Nez Perce Indian: the source of his superb collection was his own mother, Wayi'latpu, who lived on the Fort Lapwai Reservation in Idaho. His brief introduction to *Nez Perce Texts* remains one of the most sensitive appreciations of Western Indian myth, especially in treating questions of sacredness and humor. An amusing if heavy-handed early attempt at "total translation" of an Indian reciting this story is by Dr. O. T. West, in H. S. Lyman, "Items from the Nez Perce," *Oregon Historical Quarterly,* 2 (1901): 289 ff.

SMOHALLA'S GHOST DANCE COSMOGONY (*A1200 ff.; A1600 ff.; K952*)

As transcribed by Major J. W. MacMurray in 1884, in James Mooney's *The Ghost Dance Religion and the Sioux Outbreak of 1890* (1892–93), pp. 720–21. Smohalla's people, the Wanapum, were closely related to the Nez Perce. Like the Ghost Dance religion itself, Smohalla's creation story is a remarkable synthesis of several Western mythologies. After his symbolic "death" in the Columbia River at the hands of a rival chief, Moses, Smohalla undertook an arduous expedition through Indian communities all over the West—hence the broad appeal of the chiliastic doctrines he went on to preach. Like his Paiute counterpart, Wovoka, by all accounts the Wanapum shaman was a highly intelligent and compelling man, arriving too late in history to redeem his people's cause.

DREAM PROPHECY SONG

In Edward S. Curtis, *The North American Indian,* 8 (1911): 76. The song in fact prophesies the coming of "a new race with wonderful implements."

HOW THE CAYUSE GOT FIRE (*A1415*)

C. E. S. Wood, *A Book of Indian Tales* (1929), pp. 75–80. As a young man Wood served in various Indian-fighting army detachments all over the West; he was an eye-witness to the flight and capture of the Nez Perce, and in the long remainder of his career as a lawyer, poet, and editor, he was an active champion of Indian rights. His transcriptions of Indian tales are by no means scholarly, as compared with most of the others in this collection, but neither are they merely fanciful or sentimentalized. Compare other "Prometheus" myths in this book, that of the Shasta, for example, "The Theft of Fire" in Part 5.

COTTONTAIL BOY AND SNOWSHOE RABBIT ($A2430$ ff.)

Phinney, *Nez Perce Texts*, p. 3. Cf. the Paiute habitat myth, pp. 231–32; as in "The City Mouse and the Country Mouse," home is where you're snug! What is especially appealing here in ecological terms is how the two friends can exult in their very different habitations, and feel pity for each other, and yet still remain friends. I have substituted "happy contentment" for "happy *gustatory* contentment."

COTTONTAIL BOY STEALS THUNDERER'S WIFE ($A284$; $L101$ ff.)

Phinney, *Nez Perce Texts*, pp. 190–91. Cf. the genial Thunderer in Coos mythology ("The Man Who Lived with Thunderer" in Part 4); cf. other instances in this collection of young boys who experience, to their friends' amazement and their foes' ruin, a miraculous accession of spirit power—a favorite Indian theme.

COYOTE BECOMES A BUFFALO" ($D410$ ff.; $D560$)

Phinney, *Nez Perce Texts*, pp. 9–10.

TURTLE OUTSWIMS WHITE BULL ($K1969$)

Phinney, *Nez Perce Texts*, pp. 124–25. I have added the sound of Bull's running from Phinney's literal text of the story.

COYOTE AND FOX MARRY HUSBANDS ($K1321$ ff.)

Adapted from Herbert Spinden, "Nez Perce Tales," in *Folk Tales of Salish and Sahaptin Tribes*, ed. Franz Boas (1917), p. 184. Instances of transvestite behavior did occur in some Northwest tribes—occasioned, at least formally, by visions of women during a spirit quest.

THE UMATILLA BIRDMAN ($F1021.3$)

A. W. Nelson, *Those Who Came First* (1934), p. 61. Nelson's texts are nonscholarly, but this rare Umatilla story of perseverance rewarded is ungarbled and worthy of inclusion.

HOW FISH-HAWK RAIDED THE SIOUX

Editor's working from unpublished literal "Cayuse Interlinear Texts" transcribed by Morris Swadesh in 1930 on the Umatilla Reservation; in the American Philosophical Society Library, and used by permission. Narrated by Gilbert Minthorn. This stirring hero-narrative, like an episode in an epic in both content and style, was told in Umatilla Sahaptian; the Cayuse language that these heroes spoke did not survive to celebrate their feat.

LAPTISSA'N AND THE SEVEN-HEADED MONSTER (*G346; G361.4; G510*)

Spinden, "Nez Perce Tales," pp. 200–1. A very fragmented example of the Indians' assimilation of Canadian trappers' stories about the Provençal folk-hero, "Le Petit Jean." See Introduction, p. xxix, and "Ptchiza' and the Seven-headed Snake," the much fuller Kalapuya version, adapted to a Willamette Valley setting, in Part 3. For the original text, see G. Massignon, *Folktales of France* (1968), pp. 34–39.

CRY-BECAUSE-HE-HAD-NO-WIFE (*D1208; F530 ff.; H1236.4*)

Spinden, "Myths of the Nez Perce Indians," *Journal of American Folklore* 21 (1908): 156–57. This tale, too, has a European quality to it, and may be an adaptation.

RED WILLOW (*B130 ff.; N271; S110 ff.*)

Phinney, *Nez Perce Texts*, pp. 175–76. Cf., as another story of stark and mysterious horror, the Clackamas Chinook "Seal and Her Younger Brother Lived There," in Part 3. I have substituted *stinking* for the obtrusively academic *fetid*. Phinney notes parenthetically that as the youth sings his song, he clutches a lock of the dead girl's hair.

MORNING SONG

Re-working by the editor in *Love in an Earthquake* (1973), p. 27, from Spinden, "Nez Perce Tales," p. 201.

HOW ENGA-GWACU JIM MET THE GREAT FATHER

In R. Lowie, "The Northern Shoshone," *Anthropological Papers of the American Museum of Natural History*, 2 (1909): 301–2. Cf. "How a Chinook Man Went to the Land of the Dead," in Part 4. "Issue-day" was the day when the Agency dispensed provisions.

COYOTE AND THE SHADOW PEOPLE (*A1335; E482; F81.1*)

Phinney, *Nez Perce Texts*, pp. 283–85. Compare the Wishram Orpheus myth, "Coyote and Eagle Go to the Land of the Dead," in Part 3. One might quarrel with the Latinate tendencies in Phinney's wording in this story and several others, but overall, given his special authority as a native Nez Perce scholar and translator (a model let us hope for Indian scholars to come), the *accuracy* of the translation is probably not to be questioned.

CHIEF JOSEPH SPEAKS IN WASHINGTON, D.C.

In *North American Review*, 128 (1879): 415–33. Encouraged by well-wishers to come to the Capitol and plead his people's cause (the Nez Perce were still enduring a miserable exile in Indian Territory), Joseph delivered this celebrated speech to Congressmen and officials in 1879. I have excerpted passages not usually quoted which touch on the Nez Perce devotion to their land and to the memory of parents buried there: but the speech, a noble and lucid and largely unsuccessful appeal, should be read in its entirety.

PART TWO. THE COLUMBIA

1. Luther Cressman, *The Sandal and the Cave* (1962), p. 2.
2. Leslie Spier and Edward Sapir, *Wishram Ethnography*, p. 210. For additional ethnographic information, see Edward S. Curtis, *The North American Indian*, vol. 8 (New York, 1911); and on language and ritual see Dell Hymes, "Two Types of Linguistic Relativity," in *Sociolinguistics*, ed. William Bright (1966), pp. 114–57. For a vivid glimpse of life on the Warm Springs Reservation (as well as the Klamath) in 1884, see *The Memoirs of Jeremiah Curtin* (1940), pp. 351–80.
3. The relation between the Columbian tribes and the Northern Paiutes and other Shoshoneans has been extensively debated, on one side by James Teit, Joel Berreman, and others claiming that the tribal distribution prevailing on the Columbia in the nineteenth century was the result of a century of Paiute and "Snake" encroachments from the south; and on the other side by Verne Ray and others claiming that, on the contrary, it was the Tenino and other Columbian groups who were the aggressors, pushing the Paiutes south out of ancestral territory in Central Oregon. The latter theory seems more tenable—see the introductory section to Part 6; and Ray et al., "Tribal Distribution in Eastern Oregon and Adjacent Regions," *American Anthropologist*, 40 (1939): 384–415.

COYOTE AT THE MOUTH OF THE COLUMBIA RIVER (*G520*)

Edward S. Curtis, *The North American Indians*, 8:107. This story and the next five are episodes in a loose cycle of tales—central in the mythology of many Northwest tribes—which follows Coyote as he goes east up the Columbia, getting into mischief and, almost in spite of himself, ordering the land and the circumstances of life for the people who "are coming soon." Cf. the saga of the Nehalem Tillamook Transformer, South Wind, in Part 4.

COYOTE FREES THE FISH (*A1421; A1457 ff.*)

Curtis, *The North American Indians*, 8:107–9. The first salmon run coincides on the river with the arrival of the swallows.

COYOTE AND THE MOUTHLESS MAN (*A1660 ff.; F513.0.3*)

Edward Sapir, *Wishram Texts* (1909), pp. 19–24. Narrated by Louis Simpson, and wonderfully calculated as a narrative for dramatic effects, gestures, and so on.
A number of the myths recorded by Sapir are also included in Curtis, in usually more stylized and readable form. There is no reason to doubt the basic accuracy of Curtis' transcriptions, although Sapir's are verbally far more exact. For the myths included here, I have tried in each case to choose the version that had the greatest narrative clarity and richness of significant detail.

COYOTE AND THE FIRST PREGNANCY (*A1351–2; T166.2*)

Curtis, *The North American Indians*, 8:112–13. Cf. Sapir, *Wishram Texts*, pp. 25–27.

COYOTE'S CARELESSNESS (*D55.2.5; K1300 ff.; J1117.2*)

J. Ramsey, "Three Wasco–Warm Springs Stories," *Western Folklore*, 31 (April 1972): 119. Told by Mrs. Alice Florendo. Cf. Coyote's disguise in "Coyote Frees the Fish."

TSAGIGLA'LAL (*A974*)

Curtis, *The North American Indians*, 8:145–46. The story is unusual in that it "accounts" for the existence and meaning of a petroglyph—perhaps the most elaborate and impressive rock design in the Northwest, and still to be seen, staring across the Columbia above the site of "Wishram," at the head of the Five-Mile Rapids, on the Washington side. Seeing Tsagigla'lal for the first or the hundredth time, one easily understands how she served the Wishram people (for how long?) as a kind of visible super-ego.

CHIEF MARK CONSIDERS MONOGAMY

Reported by A. B. Meacham, *Wigwam and Warpath* (1875), pp. 174–75. Meacham, Superintendent of Indian Affairs in Oregon, and Capt. Smith, first and long-time Superintendent at Warm Springs, were pressing for abolition of polygamy; ultimately a compromise was reached—there would be no *new* polygamous marriages.

A WASCO WOMAN DECEIVES HER HUSBAND (*A974; K1510 ff.; T232*)

Jeremiah Curtin, "Wasco Tales and Myths," in Sapir, *Wishram Texts*, pp. 242–44. Recorded on the Warm Springs Reservation in 1885, probably from Charlie Pitt.

Like "Tsagigla'lal," this very naturalistic story (which turns into myth as if by afterthought) is notable for its references to Indian rock-art.

THE DESERTED BOY (*S350 ff.*)

Sapir, *Wishram Texts*, pp. 139–45. Narrated by Louis Simpson. See also Curtin's Wasco version, pp. 260–63. The boy is vindictive, certainly, but he has been terribly wronged by his people. The Merman (Itch'ə'xian) was Guardian of the fish. See comment on the story by Dell Hymes in the journal *Poetics*, vol. 5, no. 2 (June 1976).

LITTLE RACCOON AND HIS GRANDMOTHER (*A2413*)

Ramsey, "Three Wasco–Warm Springs Stories," pp. 117–19. Told by Mrs. Alice Florendo.

When told to children, at least, the story would have served to emphasize certain moral points—the folly of spoiling children, the dire consequences of being finicky, the inescapability of ill-fame, and the need to attend to one's elders with promptness and good will.

WREN KILLS ELK (*A1520; T617.1*)

Verne Ray, *Lower Chinook Ethnographic Notes* (1938), pp. 146–48. This amusing tale would have been current on both sides of the lower reaches of the Columbia, and is continuous in language and substance with the other selections in this section. Given the extraordinary and loving detail, it may have been a children's learning story—but presumably adult hunters would have relished it, too, the way fishermen relish Hemingway's ritualistic fishing yarn, "Big Two-hearted River." For other texts from the St. Helens–Rainier region, see Boas, *Kathlamet Texts* (1901).

THE ELK, THE HUNTER, AND HIS GREEDY FATHER (*C37; J2751*)

Curtin, "Wasco Tales and Myths," pp. 257–59.

THE BIG-FOOTED MAN AND HIS SON (*S22; S354; F531.1.3*)

Curtin, "Wasco Tales and Myths," pp. 248–52. Narrator: probably Charlie Pitt.

The Oedipal overtones, even to the possibly phallic emphasis on "feet," are striking. See Melville Jacobs' explication of such details in the Clackamas Chinook version, in *The Content and Style of an Oral Literature*, pp. 108–16.

WISHRAM CANOE SONG

Curtis, *The North American Indian*, 8:185–86. Sung while canoeing; some of the singers drum on the gunwales.

THE BATTLE OF THE WINDS (*A1127*)

Adapted from Curtin, *Myths of the Modocs* (1912), p. 384. Curtin spent the winter of 1884–85 at Warm Springs and Simnasho, before going on to his Modoc studies. This story was probably narrated by Donald McKay, formerly a hero of the Modoc War, star of several snake-oil shows, and protagonist of a dime novel, *Daring Donald McKay*.

THE SUN-BOX (*A721*)

"Reconstructed" by the editor from Lucien N. Lewis, "Sunlight Legends of the Warm Springs Indians," in *Southern Workman*, 38 (Dec. 1909): 685–86. Lewis, alas, chose to present his stories in the mode of *Hiawatha*: "I shall tell you of their legends,/Of their legends and traditions,/Of their songs of love and wooing,/Of their tales of war and bloodshed,/I shall tell them as I heard them. . . ." Cf. "Theft of Light" myths among the Tsimshian and other Northwest Coast tribes.

THE WISHRAM CALENDAR

Adapted from Curtis, *The North American Indian*, 8:203.

THE GIRL ON THE ICE (*D2143.6; V17.4*)

Curtin, "Wasco Tales and Myths," pp. 244–46. Told by Charlie Pitt.

THE BOY WHO WENT TO LIVE WITH THE SEALS (*D127.1; G263.1.2*)

Curtin, "Wasco Tales and Myths," pp. 259–60. There were, in fact, seals in the middle Columbia in the nineteenth century.

A BOY AND HIS SISTER ESCAPE FROM AN AT'AT'A'HLIA (*G441; G550; R231*)

Curtin, "Wasco Tales and Myths," pp. 274–76. Cf. the stupidly playful monsters in Nehalem Tillamook, Paiute, and Modoc folklore. The monster's misunderstanding of the boy's complaint is probably based on a pun in Wasco.

ARROW-POINT MAKER AND TOBACCO-HUNTER (*G30; G51.1; F561.4*)

Curtin, "Wasco Tales and Myths," pp. 246–48.

Two Brothers Become Sun and Moon (*A710; A740*)

Curtin, "Wasco Tales and Myths," pp. 308–11. Loosely organized and probably a fusion of several stories, this tale begins with a revealing picture of the story-telling and baby-sitting duties of old Wasco men, goes on to explain casually the existence of fine camas-root beds near Prineville in Central Oregon (in Wasco, *tak'si*), and concludes with what must be one of the most casual of all Sun-Moon cosmogonies. Cf. the Paiute "Cottontail Shoots the Sun," in Part 6.

Coyote and Eagle Go to the Land of the Dead (*A1335; E481.8.2; F81.1; H1035*)

Curtis, *The North American Indian*, 8:127–29. There are several versions; see Sapir, *Wishram Texts*, pp. 107–17. In this unforgettable story, the mythic imagination, taking nothing for granted, penetrates to the heart of man's experience, and offers an unblinking view of human nature, and some consolation for the tragic way things are. Coyote wouldn't be so ruinously impatient, if he didn't love and miss his wife so much—he is, like Orpheus, like his brother Coyote in the Nez Perce version of the story in Part 1, "too human" to do otherwise, in the full tragic sense of the phrase. The *structure* of the myth is unusually rich in parallelisms and foreshadowings.

Song for Gathering Bones for Burial

Curtis, *The North American Indian*, 8:100.

The "Stick" Indians (*C40 ff.; F402.1.1*)

Ramsey, "Three Wasco–Warm Springs Stories," p. 119. What is striking, of course, is the continuation of such animistic beliefs into modern times—"the age of matches." If the work *stick* really is a corruption of a Sahaptian word for *spirit*, then perhaps our colloquial expression "out in the sticks" derives from that word, rather than from the Chinook Jargon term *stick* for forest, wood, etc., as is generally thought. See a Nez Perce account of "Stick Indians" in *Indian Legends from the Northern Rockies*, ed. Ella E. Clark (1966), pp. 50–51; and a note on the st'iyaha' or "whistlers" of the Upper Cowlitz, in Melville Jacobs, *Northwest Sahaptin Texts*, 1:206.

PART THREE. THE WILLAMETTE VALLEY

1. Trustworthy ethnographic information on the Indians of the Valley is scanty: but see Jacobs, *The Content and Style of an Oral Literature* (1959), and *Kalapuya Texts* (1945); H. Mackey, *The Kalapuyans* (1974); and the vivid glimpses from the 1840s by Father Blanchet and other Jesuits in *Notices and Voyages of the Famed*

Quebec Mission to the Pacific Northwest, trans. Carl Landerholm (1956).

2. See Joel Berreman, *Tribal Distribution in Oregon* (1937), p. 20.

3. Personal communication to the editor.

4. Verne Ray et al., "Tribal Distribution in Eastern Oregon and Adjacent Regions," *American Anthropologist,* 40 (1938): 395 ff. The identification of the Teninos as the aggressors directly contradicts Joel Berreman's thesis that the Molalas were harried across the Cascades by "Snake" Indians.

5. There was *no* tolerance among Valley settlers, of course, during the Indian uprisings in Southern Oregon in 1855. After a young Tenino Indian named Sam Anaxshat had successfully led Lt. Henry Abbot and his surveying party over the Cascade crest from the Deschutes River to the outskirts of Oregon City in October of that year, the Indian guide immediately turned back, not daring to go on with Abbot into Oregon City, because of anti-Indian feelings there and elsewhere in the Valley. *Reports of Explorations and Surveys* (generally known as the Pacific Railroad Surveys), vol. 6 (Washington, D.C., 1857), pp. 96 ff.

6. Rev. Samuel Parker, *Journal of an Exploring Tour beyond the Rocky Mountains* (1838), p. 235. In her collaboration with Melville Jacobs, *Clackamas Chinook Texts,* 2 (1959): 563, Mrs. Victoria Howard remembered with glee how her mother-in-law coped with such clerics—"When the person-who-continually-prayed first came to Oregon City, he told them, 'You should pray all the time, the above chief will see you then. But if you do not believe it, then you will have tails and you will remain just like the animals you are, like the various animals that run about in the forests.' Now my husband's mother would say, 'Dear oh dear! Probably it would be something different and really funny when we play woman's shinny. We would whip each other with our tails!' "

CoYOTE BUILDS WILLAMETTE FALLS AND THE MAGIC FISH TRAP (*A1457 ff.; F986*)

Adapted by the editor from H. S. Lyman, "Reminiscences of Louis Labonte," in *Oregon Historical Quarterly,* 1 (1900): 183–84. The narrator, Labonte, was born in Oregon to a French-Canadian and his Indian wife, and knew the valley tribes intimately. Lyman deserves credit as one of the first Oregonians to attempt to take the state's mythological literature seriously.

THE SKOOKUM'S TONGUE (*F544.2.1; G120*)

Adapted from Lyman, "Reminiscences of Louis Labonte," pp. 184–85. *Skookum* is a Chinook Jargon word meaning, variously, "very powerful," "monstrous," "monster."

THE SKOOKUM AND THE WONDERFUL BOY (*D.176; E61, H1381.2; P233.2*)

Adapted from Lyman, "Reminiscences of Louis Labonte," pp. 185–87.

Badger and Coyote Were Neighbors (*E30; V60 ff.*)

Melville Jacobs, *The Content and Style of an Oral Literature* (1959), pp. 27–29. Narrated by Mrs. Victoria Howard. In this remarkable study, Jacobs presents the fullest interpretive commentary yet made on a western Indian literature; his elucidations of selected stories like this one and "Grizzly Woman Killed People" are indispensable for the serious reader. Compare "Badger and Coyote Were Neighbors" and its Orpheus-motif with the Wasco "Coyote and Eagle Visit the Island of the Dead" and the Nez Perce "Coyote and the Shadow People."

I have, in some passages in this and subsequent stories, followed ambiguous pronouns with bracketed specific nouns or proper names, and have incorporated Jacobs' parenthetical restatements of lines, based on his knowledge of the literature, for the sake of clarity. By ignoring the material in parentheses and brackets, the reader can attempt to engage the highly elliptical style of these stories in performance.

Seal and Her Younger Brother Lived There (*K1910; S118.2*)

Narrated by Mrs. Howard, and given in Melville Jacobs, *Clackamas Chinook Texts*, 2 (1959):340–41. The present text is a new verse translation by Dell Hymes, based on his study of Chinookan narrative style, and printed here for the first time by permission. See Hymes's exemplary structuralist interpretation of the story, "The 'Wife' Who 'Goes Out' Like a Man: Reinterpretation of a Clackamas Chinook Myth," in *Social Science Information*, 7, no. 3 (1968): 176–79. Hymes reveals how in narrative structure, dialogue, and imagery the story dramatizes the conflict between the socially normative behavior of Seal, and the empirically alert behavior of her young daughter.

Note that this chilling and mysterious little story is embedded in the Coos narrative, "Revenge against the Sky People," in Part 4. In the longer version, the homicidal and sexually ambiguous "wife" becomes a heroic younger brother who disguises himself as the wife of his older brother's murderer, amongst the Sky People! See my study, "The Wife Who Goes Out like a Man, Comes Back as a Hero: The Art of Two Oregon Indian Narratives," *PMLA*, vol. 92, no. 1 (Jan. 1977).

She Deceived Herself with Milt (*D376; D521*)

Jacobs, *Clackamas Chinook Texts*, 2:348–50, 560. Narrated by Mrs. Howard. The story begins with a kind of sexual wish-fulfillment, it seems—the lonely widow gets a husband made out of the reproductive fluid of a male salmon. And at the end her attack with milt on the second wife underscores the sexual tensions in the story. As in "Seal and Her Younger Brother," a female perspective seems to prevail.

A GIRLS' GAME

Melville Jacobs, *Texts in Chinook Jargon* (1936), p. 12. Narrated by Mrs. Howard in Jargon.

THE KALAPUYA WAY

Melville Jacobs, *Kalapuya Texts* (1945): "The Good Old Days," p. 26; "People Spoke to the New Moon," p. 34; "Mosquito and Thunder," p. 32; "A Shaman Dreamed the Earth Became Black like Ploughed Land," p. 69; "Making Bows and Arrows," pp. 30–31; "Blind People Made Arrow Points," p. 31; "The Heart Journeys to the Land of the Dead," p. 73; "Dreams about the Dead People," p. 73. Narrated by John B. Hudson. (The texts are based on nineteenth-century work by Albert Gatschet and Leo Frachtenberg.)

THE FOUR CREATIONS (*A1111; A1420*)

Jacobs, *Kalapuya Texts*, pp. 173–78; edited, with the help of Louis Kennoyer, from original text by Albert Gatschet, from "Wapato Dave." These four myth-generations all seem to be set in the Myth Age proper, before the advent of a Transformer like Coyote. The archetypical "Birth-of-the-Hero" circumstances of the heroic boy's origins and growth are noteworthy.

KALAPUYA CEREMONIAL SONG

Probably recorded by Gatschet; in American Philosophical Library collection—reproduced by permission.

AMHULUK, THE MONSTER OF WAPATO LAKE (*G308*)

Adapted from Albert Gatschet, "Oregonian Folklore," *Journal of American Folklore*, 4 (1891): 141–42. The weird mountain pool is apparently Wapato Lake, southwest of Forest Grove, in the foothills of the Coast Range. Amhuluk is another Valley *skookum*.

PTCHIZA' AND THE SEVEN-HEADED SNAKE (*D1072.1; H335.3.1; L161*)

Jacobs, *Kalapuya Texts*, pp. 312–21; originally narrated to Leo Frachtenberg by William Hartless in the Mary's River Kalapuya dialect in 1914. An instance of the assimilation by Oregon Indians, probably from French-Canadian employees of the Hudson's Bay Company, of Provençal folk-tales centering on the exploits of "Le Petit Jean," Little Jack. See Introduction, and a Nez Perce version, "Laptissa'n and the Seven-headed Monster," in Part 1. For a text of the Provençal original, see G. Massignon, *Folktales of France* (1968), pp. 34–39.

COYOTE'S SWALLOWING MATCH WITH GRIZZLY BEAR (*A1611; K82.4*)

Harold Mackey and Thomas Brundage, "A Molale Indian Myth of Coyote," *Northwest Folklore*, 3, no. 2 (Winter 1968): 10–11, from notes made by Gatschet in 1877. A rare text from and about the Molala.

THE INDIANS HEAR A TREATY SPEECH IN 1855

Jacobs, *Kalapuya Texts*, p. 167. The treaty, arranged by Joel Palmer, Oregon's first Superintendent of Indian Affairs, was signed at Dayton in 1855. The text is remarkable for preserving the *Indian* understanding of what the whites offered.

JO HUTCHINS' SPEECH, 1869

A. B. Meacham, *Wigwam and Warpath* (1875), pp. 117–19. Meacham's remarkable book is full of texts of Indian orations, evidently authentic, taken down verbatim by him or his clerks, during the course of his travels as Superintendent.

PART FOUR. THE COAST

1. Ethnographic information on the Oregon coastal Indians is meager, but see the introductory commentary in Franz Boas, *Chinook Texts* (1892); Leo Frachtenberg, *Alsea Texts and Myths* (1920); Wallis Nash, *Oregon: There and Back in 1877* (1878); Melville Jacobs, *Coos Ethnologic and Narrative Texts* (1939); and H. G. Barnett, "Culture Element Distribution VII: Oregon Coast," *Anthropological Record*, 1, no. 3 (1937); 155–203. For stories about unrecorded early White–Coast Indian encounters, see C. A. Carey, *General History of Oregon* (1971), pp. 46–48.
2. John Swanton, *The Indian Tribes of North America* (1952), p. 472.

SOUTH WIND MARRIES OCEAN'S DAUGHTER (*A1120; B81 ff.*)

Nehalem Tillamook Tales, recorded by Elizabeth Derr Jacobs, edited by Melville Jacobs (1959), pp. 92–93. Narrated by Mrs. Clara Pearson. South Wind, or "Everlasting Man," is the Nehalem equivalent to Coyote.

THE EXPLOITS OF SOUTH WIND (*D55.2.5; D695; K1391; etc.*)

Jacobs, *Nehalem Tillamook Tales*, pp. 198–99. This synopsis was prepared by Elizabeth Jacobs. The full, original text of the cycle is given in Mrs. Jacobs' book; the synopsis form here seems to touch on just about every narrative motif employed in Oregon Indian mythology, especially those associated with the Trickster. Compare Paul Radin's synopsis of the Winnebago Trickster cycle in *The Trickster* (1956).

COYOTE IN THE CEDAR TREE (*A2322 ff.; E781.1; F1035*)

Katherine Berry Judson, *Myths and Legends of the Pacific Northwest* (1910), pp. 74–76. The motif of Coyote dismantling himself is widespread in the West.

COYOTE INVENTS THE FISHING RITUALS (*A1520; 229.4*)

Franz Boas, *Chinook Texts* (1894), pp. 101–5. Narrated by Charles Cultee. A better illustration of how Indian myth can serve to expound tribal rituals entertainingly would be hard to imagine. I have inserted some bracketed English spellings of place names.

HOW COYOTE KILLED THE GIANTESS AND HERDED THE SALMON (*A1520; G441; G550*)

Boas, *Chinook Texts*, pp. 110–12. Narrated by Charles Cultee. For Crane to escape from Coyote's club by using a trick that Coyote himself had taught him is a comic irony typical of Indian humor. The reference to good weather at the end is apparently a closing formula.

THE MAN WHO LIVED WITH THUNDERER (*A284.2; F531 ff.*)

Franz Boas, "Traditions of the Tillamook Indians," *Journal of American Folklore*, 11, no. 40 (Jan.–March 1898): 23–27. Even more than most Indian texts, this has the wild but unsmiling exaggeration of the Tall Tale. Generally, Thunderer or Thunderbird is portrayed as he is here: as a terribly powerful but usually benign spirit. Cf. the Nez Perce "Cottontail Boy Steals Thunderer's Wife," in Part 1. In several coastal myths Crow once had Thunderer's voice, but they traded. —The boy is scolded at the end because the dead should never be named directly.

Once or twice the narrator forgets and refers to the man's *wife:* I have added the correction, *wives*, in brackets.

THUNDERSTORM EXORCISM (*D2140 ff.*)

Working in verse by the editor in *Love in an Earthquake* (1973), pp. 26–7, following Leo J. Frachtenberg, *Alsea Texts and Myths* (1920), p. 231.

How the Coos People Discovered Fire (*A1111; A1415*)

Text by Leo J. Frachtenberg in *Handbook of American Indian Languages*, ed. Franz Boas (1922) pp. 427–29. Bracketed material is mine, derived from Frachtenberg's notes.

The myth lacks the Promethean heroics of other versions, the Cayuse and Shasta stories for example, but the Coos chief must be given his due as a steely gambler! Note how, at the end, willow becomes a good fire-holder. (I have incorporated Frachtenberg's suggestion that the two chiefs hold "gambling sticks" rather than "shinny clubs," as the narrator recalled it.)

The Chetco (*A1130; B555; G512.11; R246*)

Rewritten from Silas B. Smith, "Customs of the Northwest Coast Indians," *Oregon Historical Quarterly*, 2 (1901): 262–65. The weather lore set forth in myth here is still observed along the Coast—the *chetco*'s roar is not the diffused roar of the surf, but a distinctive sound that seems to come from a particular point farther out. The Leg-Bridge motif is common all over the West; usually it is Crane who offers a leg.

Wild Woman Ate Children (*G10 ff.*)

Elizabeth Jacobs, *Nehalem Tillamook Tales*, pp. 158–61. Narrated by Mrs. Clara Pearson. Compare the equally frightening German "Strüwelpeter" cautionary tales for children.

The Woman Who Married a Merman (*B82.1; D170*)

Harry St. Clair, "Traditions of the Coos Indians of Oregon," ed. Leo J. Frachtenberg, *Journal of American Folklore*, 22 (1909): 27–32. Narrated by Jim Buchanan. The kindness exchanged between the two worlds is remarkable.

Coyote and the Two Frog-Women (*S176*)

Rewritten by the editor from literal wording by Leo J. Frachtenberg, "Myths of the Alsea Indians of Northwestern Oregon," *International Journal of American Linguistics*, 1 (1917–20): 72–74. Narrated by Thomas Jackson. Coyote is evidently incensed by the presumptuousness of the two women. The transcriber saw fit to narrate the sexual consequences of Coyote's prank (in the fifth paragraph) in Latin, which I have rendered in English.

The Magic Hazel Twig (*D110; D430*)

Frachtenberg, *Alsea Texts and Myths*, pp. 237–39. Narrated by "Alsea George." In other Alsea stories Mo'luptsini'sla is identified as Coyote.

Xi'lgo and the Brother and Sister Who Married Each Other (*D152.2; P203; T415.5*)

Franz Boas, "Traditions of the Tillamook Indians," pp. 34–38. (Bracketed phrases added by Boas.) In *Nehalem Tillamook Tales*, pp. 45–58, Jacobs gives a very long, wonderfully detailed version, in which Xi'lgo is identified as "Wild Woman," and the old man who tells the children stories is her estranged husband, High Class Crane. High Class Crane's stories, in Jacobs' version, are disguisedly sexual in content, and arouse his wife's desire when she hears about them from the children.

Several morals might have been drawn from the tale in either version: children should be leery when outdoors, lest mothering old creatures like Xi'lgo carry them off; sexual hanky-panky between adults may influence children who observe it; incest invariably leads to disaster, for the participants if not for their offspring.

May M. Edel has studied versions of this and other Tillamook stories as recorded by herself and Mrs. Jacobs (from one narrator, Mrs. Clara Pearson) and by Boas, and she concludes that the Tillamook mythological repertory was remarkably *stable*—tellers did not innovate or depart much from the tradition. See "Stability in Tillamook Folklore," in *Journal of American Folklore*, 57 (1944): 116–27.

The White Wife of Mouse

Melville Jacobs, *Coos Myth Texts* (1940), pp. 165–66. Told by Mrs. Annie Miner Peterson. Mouse's song was recorded by Jacobs on an Ediphone record, but has not been transcribed, regrettably.

The Girl Who Married a Ghost (*A522.2.1; E474; E481; E485.1; T113*)

Boas, *Chinook Texts*, pp. 167–71. Narrated by Charles Cultee. Blue Jay sometimes replaces Coyote as Trickster, especially in coastal stories, where Coyote is really out of his ecological element, anyway. (Bracketed phrases are my explanations. To avoid confusion, I have rendered Boas' own interpolations in parentheses. Boas' interpolations, like those of Melville Jacobs in his Clackamas texts, derive from details implied or understood in performance but not actually stated.)

How a Chinook Went to the Land of the Dead and Came Back (*F80*)

Boas, "Doctrine of Souls among the Chinook Indians," *Journal of American Folklore*, 6, no. 20 (Jan.–March 1893): 42. The story was given to Boas as the real-life experience of his informant's grandfather, who "died" during an epidemic. Compare the Bannock story, "How Enga-gwacu Jim Met the Great Father," in Part 1—both texts have the vivid plausibility of a bad dream or a chemical vision.

THE JOURNEY ACROSS THE OCEAN (*F110 ff.*)

Boas, "Traditions of the Tillamook Indians," pp. 27–30. Bracketed interpolations are mine.

If the new kind of wood the hero finds across the sea, "like reed but tall as a tree," isn't bamboo, what is it? Pieces of bamboo sometimes wash up on the Oregon Coast, presumably from Japan—but how did the Tillamooks know that it grows to be tree-sized? Can the tale be based on some sort of historical encounter, or is it the result of imaginative projection from Oregon's Coast to "a land in the sunset"?

THE REVENGE AGAINST THE SKY PEOPLE (*F537; G30; K1910; K1941; K1311.0.2*)

Frachtenberg, *Coos Texts* (1913), pp. 149–57. Narrated by Jim Buchanan.

Versions of this hair-raising story were current among the Chinooks, the Alsea, and the Tillamooks. In the very detailed Alsea and Nehalem Tillamook versions, there are two avengers working as a team; they are "dog-children." Without its revenge-premise, the story appears in Clackamas Chinook as a tale of mysterious homicide and value-conflict: see "Seal and Her Younger Brother Lived There," in Part 3. (I have inserted some clarifying words and phrases, in brackets. Parenthetical readings are Frachtenberg's.)

THE FIRST SHIP COMES TO CLATSOP COUNTRY

Boas, *Chinook Texts*, pp. 278–79. (Parentheses are the transcriber's; brackets are mine.) This "historical" text haunts with questions—were the unfortunate captives befurred Russians? What happened to the rest of the crew? When did they sail into the Columbia mouth? Did they mean to establish trade, as the cargo described suggests? What was the basis of "the tale we have heard" about other ships? Like the Eskimos, the Chinookans and other Oregon Indians seem to have maintained an oral history of considerable detail within their mythological repertory; in this case, "history" is unforgettably mingled with an old woman's private grief.

PART FIVE. SOUTHWEST OREGON

1. Verne Ray, *Primitive Pragmatists: The Modoc Indians of Northern California* (1963), p. xiii.

2. Leslie Spier, *Klamath Ethnography* (1930). See also Theodore Stern, *The Klamath Tribe* (1965). Stephen Dow Beckham has chronicled the Contact era fate of the Takelma and other "Rogue" groups in *Requiem for a People* (1971).

3. See Vine Deloria's excoriation of the Termination policy as it was applied to the Klamaths and the Menominees of Wisconsin, in *Custer Died for Your Sins* (1970).

4. Spier, *Klamath Ethnography*, p. 100. Crow's metamorphosis of various beings into rocks is accounted for fragmentarily in Albert S. Gatschet, *The Klamath Indians* (1891), 2:131–32: "When the Klamath Lake people danced at the dancing place, there were many people there. Kamukamts was there. Then Crow laughed at them as they danced, and the people dancing there became rocks."

5. Mircea Eliade, *Myth and Reality* (1963), p. 18. For lucid commentary on Klamath mythology as oral literature, including what is probably the most thorough and helpful discussion of the Indian art of story-telling yet written, see Theodore Stern, "Some Sources of Variability in Klamath Mythology," *Journal of American Folklore*, 69 (1956): 1–9, 135–46, 377–96. See also Professor Stern's "The Trickster in Klamath Mythology," in *Western Folklore*, 12, no. 3 (July 1953): 158–74.

CREATION OF THE KLAMATH COUNTRY (*A810; A960; A1610*)

Edward S. Curtis, *The North American Indian*, 13 (1924): 210. Kamukamts (I have regularized a variety of spellings) is the Klamath and Modoc "Creator"—the idea of Creation as a genial competition is unusual and pleasant, as is the high priority given here to games.

MODOC PRAYERS

Verne Ray, *Primitive Pragmatists: The Modoc Indians of Northern California* (1963), pp. 27–29. Narrator: Peter Sconchin. Tibetans also pray to sacred rock piles, and of course add votive rocks. The "Prayer to a Slain Animal" seems to involve a kind of magic psychology— playing on the animals' curiosity, to bring them within range of the hunter. The last prayer seems to be highly personal, with some Christian elements, as in most Northwest Indian religious forms today. (I have supplied the "titles" of the individual prayers; bracketed phrases are the transcriber's.)

THE RAINMAKER (*A1018.3; T425*)

Jeremiah Curtin, *Myths of the Modocs* (1912), pp. 118–21. (Brackets in this and subsequent stories from Curtin are mine.)

THE WILDCAT BROTHERS (*A2423.1.3; D150 ff.; F827.4; S165.5*)

Curtin, *Myths of the Modocs*, pp. 268–71. Versions of this vivid tale of frustrated incestuous desire are widespread in the Northern California mythologies. See Theodora Kroeber's superb retelling in *The*

Inland Whale (1971). In Curtin's translation the evil sister becomes "a large spotted sea-bird": clearly a loon is meant.

FROST AND THUNDER (*A284.2; A289.1; H1116*)

Curtin, *Myths of the Modocs*, pp. 145–47.

THUNDER AND EAGLE BOY (*A284.2; D152.2; D281.3; G341.1*)

Curtin, *Myths of the Modocs*, pp. 153–58. This story, unusually rich in ethnographic detail (the importance of fire drills, ritual painting, wrestling, etc.), is worth close study for the detailed characterization of Thunder as an odious, mocking bully, and such narrative subtleties as the pairing of Eagle Boy as Hero with the anti-heroic Skunk.

CHIEF ALLEN DAVID OF THE KLAMATHS AND CAPT. JACK OF THE MODOCS, 1869

In A. B. Meacham, *Wigwam and Warpath* (1875), pp. 331–33. The treaty, which returned the Modocs to the Klamath Reservation, was short-lived; in four years the Modoc War broke out.

THE KLAMATH CALENDAR

Rewritten by the editor from literal texts in Albert S. Gatschet, *The Klamath Indians*, 2 (1890); 75–76. The Klamath year had twelve and one-half months; it began after the return from *wokas-harvest* (August?). Cf. "The Wishram Calendar" in Part 2.

THE CRATER LAKE MYTH (*E786; G308; S139.6*)

M. A. R. Barker, *Klamath Texts* (1963), pp. 70–75. Narrator: Robert David. Barker's translations, done for linguistic purposes, are especially literalistic in syntax and narrative order; I have inserted some words in brackets (changing Barker's own brackets to parentheses to avoid confusion) and have omitted a few repetitious or digressive phrases (indicated by ellipses) for clarity's sake.

Barker indicates that Mr. David inadvertently left out some episodes from Old Marten's first trip to the lake, and then, catching himself, wove them back into his narration of the second trip: no doubt such adroit juggling of details was common in "classical" recitations of Indian stories. That Lɛ-w and his kind "did not like Kamukamts" indicates that they were indeed "unnatural," evil. According to Peter Sconchin's Modoc wife, Evaline, "Dove is the chief mourner: he cries as a person. Once while Dove was engrossed in playing a game he was told that his grandmother had died and he must mourn. He replied that there would be plenty of time to mourn later, and continued playing. He has been mourning ever since" (Ray, *Primitive Pragmatists*, p. 25).

THE STORY OF SWA-YA (*B535.0.6; R10 ff.; S366*)

Barker, *Klamath Texts*, pp. 50–55. Narrated by Mrs. Patsy Ohles. Note the mimetic distortions in Swa-ya's speech at the end, for dramatic effect. (Words in brackets are Barker's.)

LITTLE PORCUPINE AND COYOTE (*D1067.1; K952.1*)

Barker, *Klamath Texts*, pp. 16–23. Narrated by Mrs. Patsy Ohles. If Mrs. Ohles really meant to say *buffalo* (once she slips and speaks of the meat as *elk*), then the story is quite old—buffalo had vanished from the Oregon country by the middle of the nineteenth century, at least. Several Paiute versions of this story are given by Isabel Kelly, in "Northern Paiute Tales," *Journal of American Folklore*, 51 (1938): 406 ff. Words in brackets are mine; I have changed Barker's brackets to parentheses to avoid confusion.

COYOTE IN LOVE WITH A STAR (*A762 ff.; A920.14; F15*)

C. E. S. Wood, *A Book of Indian Tales* (1929), pp. 97–99. Like Wood's collection as a whole, this story is stylized and rather "literary" in the retelling, but he seems to have gotten it first-hand from a Klamath friend named "Debe," and it is worth including. According to Modoc tradition, "When it appears that many coyotes are howling at night, it is just one" (Ray, *Primitive Pragmatists*, p. 25).

CHILOQUIN THE HERO (*F610 ff.*)

Leslie Spier, *Klamath Ethnography* (1930), pp. 37–38. The family name is preserved in the village of Chiloquin, just east of Klamath Agency; this particular hero was a nineteenth-century chief. In Spier's phonetic spelling the name is Tcǐʼlokǐn.

TWO KLAMATH MONSTERS (*F420 ff.; G312; G371.1*)

Spier, *Klamath Ethnography*, pp. 100, 105–6. Ska'mdi is a big eddy in Williamson River, north of Chiloquin.

GRIZZLY BEAR AND BLACK BEAR (*B555; N271; R246; S112*)

Edward Sapir, *Takelma Texts* (1909), pp. 117–23. Narrator: Mrs. Frances Johnson. The Paiutes have a parallel story, "Bear and the Fawns," in Kelly, "Northern Paiute Tales," pp. 431–32. Sapir's translations from Takelman are strange reading, what with the frequent inversions of syntax, the literary-sounding " 'tis said," and so on; but I have refrained from reworking the texts because Sapir, a great pioneer linguist and mythologist, clearly was trying to render something of the literary style of the Takelma originals. Grizzly Bear's distorted language after her children are killed ("S-come back!" "O L-my liver!") represents a special "Grizzly Bear" dialect.

THE THEFT OF FIRE (*A1415 ff.*)

Roland Dixon, "Shasta Myths," *Journal of American Folklore*, 23 (1911): 13–14. The detail of Fire being kept by the Pain people is memorable; the basic motif of the myth—the relay-race through which fire is stolen, ending up in the care of some lowly animal—is widespread in Western mythologies. See, for example, "How the Cayuse Got Fire," in Part 1.

GENESIS (*A560; A810; A950; A1240; A1330; A1820; A1831; A2145; H1381.2.1*)

Leo J. Frachtenberg and Livingston Farrand, "Shasta and Athapascan Myths from Oregon," *Journal of American Folklore*, 28 (1915): 224–28. Narrated by Charlie Depoe. The native name for the chief figure in this story is "Xowa'läshi"; I have incorporated Farrand's apt and lovely translation, "The Giver." The cosmogony in this haunting myth is unusually detailed and subtle, suggesting the creation stories of Southwestern Indians. How much of primal human experience is given form here, from The Giver's wry response to the beautiful woman's appearance—"Now we shall have no more trouble in creating people"—through her awakening to love—"This was an entirely new dream to her"—to the ultimate coming home of the first husband and father. (Note how all the creatures, even, as Farrand suggests, the howling dogs, are in search of a progenitor.) The mysterious human tracks that The Giver is unable to erase might suggest the influence of Christian theodicy, but I doubt it; the detail "works" in its own context. When the neglected baby's diseases are washed off by the repentant mother, Farrand explains in a note, they form the basis of all human illnesses to come.

PART SIX. THE GREAT BASIN

1. Luther Cressman, *The Sandal and the Cave* (1962), and Stephen F. Bedwell, *Fort Rock Basin: Prehistory and Environment* (1973).
2. Joel Berreman, *Tribal Distribution in Oregon* (1937).
3. Verne Ray et al., "Tribal Distribution in Eastern Oregon and Adjacent Regions," *American Anthropologist*, 40 (1939): 384–415. See also Erminie Wheeler-Voegelin's study, "The Northern Paiute of Central Oregon," in *Ethnohistory*, 2, no. 2 (Spring 1955): 95–132; 2, no. 4 (Fall 1955): 241–72; 3, no. 1 (Winter 1956): 1–10.
4. The classic account of the Paiutes' ordeals on the Malheur Reservation before the outbreak of the Bannock War is Sarah Winne-

mucca Hopkins' first-hand narrative in *Life among the Piutes* (1883). This absorbing book, written with the help of Mrs. Horace Mann while the heroic Sarah was in New York City and Washington, D.C., on behalf of her people, is also rich in ethnographic descriptions. The best modern studies of Paiute culture have also been written by women: Isabel Kelly, "Ethnography of the Surprise Valley Paiutes," *University of California Publications in American Archaeology and Ethnology*, 31 (1932): 67–209; Margaret Wheat, *Survival Arts of the Primitive Paiutes* (1967); and Beatrice B. Whiting, *Paiute Sorcery* (1950).

The Tracks of the Creator (*A560; A901; A1010; A1330*)

Rewritten from literal text by W. L. Marsden, "The Northern Paiute Language of Oregon," *University of California Publications in American Archaeology and Ethnology*, 20 (1923): 185–86. For many years, until his death in 1913, Dr. Marsden was a physician in Burns, Oregon, in the heart of Paiute country. Presumably the Wolf's tracks correspond to some natural feature. In this and subsequent texts, all bracketed materials are my additions.

How the Animals Found Their Places (*A2430*)

Verse adaptation by Jarold Ramsey in *Love in an Earthquake* (1973), p. 21, from Isabel Kelly, "Northern Paiute Tales," *Journal of American Folklore*, 51 (1938): 375. Narrated by Charlie Washo.

The Purging of Malheur Cave (*F455; G510 ff.*)

Adapted from Marsden, "Northern Paiute Language," p. 187. The cave, southeast of Burns, is now the site of meetings of various lodges and fraternal orders!

The Creation of the Indians (*A1270; A1600 ff.; E261.1; E481.6.2; G10 ff.; T298*)

Kelly, "Tales," pp. 365–68. Narrated by Billy Steve, who is described by Kelly as a master story-teller.
Note the detailed account of fire-making in the opening paragraph, giving the operation a mythic significance, and the incorporation of the Rolling Skull motif in the woman's journey. The pricking of the children's legs must refer to a practice of ritual scarification at puberty. The alternate ending was narrated by Bige Archie (Kelly, "Tales," p. 370); compare it to the eviction of the First Children in "The Tracks of the Creator." In *Life among the Piutes*, Sarah Winnemucca recalls that her grandfather Truckee urged his people to welcome the whites as returning descendants of one of these dispersed original human couples!

Vagina Dentata (*A1313.3.1; F547.1.1*)

Kelly, "Tales," pp. 372–75. Narrated by Billy Steve. The toothed vagina motif is widespread in Western Indian mythology. The final episode here, the premature birth of Coyote's children from a water jug (shades of *Brave New World!*) is probably a subsequent episode in the overall Coyote cycle. Having facilitated intercourse, Coyote goes on, typically, to ruin this painless alternative to childbirth.

Coyote and His Daughter (*H50 ff.; T411.1*)

Kelly, "Tales," pp. 404–5. Narrated by Billy Steve. As a Trickster, Coyote is the trier-out of self-serving possibilities, even incest.

Coyote Learns to Hunt (*J2411 ff.; J2751*)

Kelly, "Tales," pp. 385–86. Narrated by Daisy Brown. Coyote's flagrant disregard for what we now call ecology is notable here: in a mythic time when game is abundant, and the hunt is magically easy, his greed and lack of foresight spoil everything. Contrast the reverent ritual of sympathetic magic in "A Hunter's First Kill"; except for Coyote, it might have been otherwise!

Coyote and Wolf Go Hunting (*B542.1.1; D2143.6; J2751; N314*)

Kelly, "Tales," pp. 391–93. Narrated by Nannie Ochiho, who was a daughter-in-law of the Paiute chief Ochoco (a contemporary of Paulina), whose name is perpetuated in Central Oregon in a National Forest, a range of hills, a creek, and so on. Coyote is at his irresponsible worst in these stories, as Wolf's "kid brother." The incidence of magic and ritual language is striking here, in contrast to Coyote's *ad hoc* exploits. In the fifth and sixth paragraphs, there seems to be a confusion of deer and elks.

Coyote the Eye-Juggler (*J2423; K333.3*)

Kelly, "Tales," pp. 418–19. Narrated by Bige Archie. Like others in this series, the story seems to call for a manic, wildly mimic performance by the narrator.

The Theft of Pine Nuts (*F759.5 H1116.3; R220 ff.*)

Kelly, "Tales," pp. 401–3. Narrated by Bige Archie. Here, as in the hunting stories, Coyote is bumptious, a sort of mythic adolescent who wants to be called "Tall Fellow," and who is usually "just talking." (Note how Frog's stupidity parallels and mocks Coyote's clownishness.) The detail of the Ice Wall is strange—if, as seems likely, Indians were in southeast Oregon at the end of the last period of heavy glaciation, could a tribal memory of the glaciers account for this detail?

Nümüzo'ho Plays Ball (G10 ff.; K850 ff.)

Kelly, "Tales," pp. 409–10. Narrated by Nannie Ochiho. What in the Paiute experience, what *fears*, did these giant, ravenous, rather stupid cannibals represent? A note in Kelly's collection reports that "Nümüzo'ho is the one who made all the manos, metates, and mortars. When the earth was burning, he jumped into the lake. That's why they find all these kinds of things on all the lake shores" ("Tales," p. 436). The burning refers either to the primal conflagration caused by Wolf, or the world-blaze set off by Cottontail when he shoots the Sun.

Nümüzo'ho in the Mortar (G10 ff.; G321; G676; K850 ff.)

Kelly, "Tales," pp. 410–11. Narrated by Daisy Brown. Compare Coyote's cunning here with his shenanigans in the hunting stories— the tale ends on a note of rare, if gruesome, moral triumph for him; rarely is he so personally involved.

Coyote and Bear (H1228)

Kelly, "Tales," pp. 420–21. Narrated by Nannie Ochiho. Typically, after his cunning (and dramatic) deceptions of Bear, Coyote fools away his prize of bear-meat, and is left with only the bones—and big talk.

Coyote Shoots the Night (A1170 ff.)

Kelly, "Tales," p. 420. Narrated by Billy Steve. Again, Wolf is irresponsible Coyote's knowledgeable elder brother.

Cottontail Shoots the Sun (A1031.4; A1038)

Kelly, "Tales," pp. 425–26. Narrated by Nannie Ochiho. Cottontail, brash, bent on violence, most unrabbitlike, partakes of aspects of the Trickster, it seems; the world conflagration he causes, with a "dead" Sun and "hot ashes," makes one wonder if, incredibly, the Indians had a kind of mythological memory of the violent eruption of Mt. Mazama, which formed Crater Lake, and buried sandals and other artifacts under volcanic ash and pumice in Fort Rock Cave, seven thousand years ago.

Humming Bird's Space Flight (F60 ff.)

Kelly, "Tales," p. 436. Narrated by Daisy Brown. The sense of vertical space in this droll little tale is remarkable; Humming Bird obviously went a long way up into the cosmos, but still didn't get anywhere—a Paiute shaggy dog story.

THE THUNDER BADGER (*A1130*)

Verse-working by Jarold Ramsey, in *Love in an Earthquake*, p. 26, from Marsden, "Northern Paiute Language," p. 185.

HOW TO CONTROL THE WEATHER (*D1548*)

Isabel Kelly, "Ethnography of the Surprise Valley Paiutes" (1932), p. 201. Narrated by "Piudy." Note that in "Coyote and Wolf Go Hunting," Porcupine serves as the bringer of snow.

A HUNTER'S FIRST KILL (*C229.4*)

Kelly, "Ethnography," p. 80, reported by Joshua Brown, a former shaman. It is tempting to speculate that the elaborate stylized "hoop dances," popular with young Indian dancers throughout the Northwest still, derive from some such "first-kill" ritual. See discussion in Beatrice Blyth Whiting, *Paiute Sorcery* (1950), p. 106.

WHITE MEN ARE SNAKES (*A1331.1; A1614.9*)

Kelly, "Tales," p. 437. Narrated by "Piudy." A clear—and devastating—instance of adaptation of Christian teachings for Indian purposes. Note the sharp irony implicit in white newcomers asking the Indians "where they had come from," and in transferring the name "Snake" from Indians to whites. Another example of Paiute eloquence is the following speech given by Egan, a sub-chief at Malheur who was later killed in the Bannock War, against a rapacious Indian agent named Reinhard: "Did the government tell you to come here and drive us off this reservation? Did the Big Father say, go and kill us all off, so you can have our land? Did he tell you to pull our children's ears off, and put handcuffs on them, and carry a pistol to shoot us with? We want to know how the government came by this land. Is the government mightier than our Spirit-Father, or is he our Spirit-Father? Oh, what have we done that he is to take all from us that he has given us? His white children have come and taken all our mountains, and all our valleys, and all our rivers; and now, because he has given us this little place without our asking him for it, he sends you here to tell us to go away. Do you see that high mountain away off there? There is nothing but rocks there. Is that where the Big Father wants me to go? If you scattered your seed and it should fall there, it would not grow, for it is all rocks there. Oh, what am I saying? I know you will come and say, Here, Indians, go away– I want these rocks to make me a beautiful home with . . ." (Hopkins, *Life among the Piutes*, pp. 133–34).

THE TRUE BEGINNING OF THE EARTH (*A250; A800; A1420*)

Kelly, "Tales," pp. 437–38. Narrated by Doctor Sam Wata, a shaman. Old Man Chocktoot was a celebrated chief of the Silver Lake

Paiutes. The myth seems to be a personalized rather than a "tribal" account; all the more poignant for that, surely. The contrast between the lovely little myth of the Sun "coining silver" on the surface of creeks and the coming of white silver-miners is remarkable; so is the narrator's utterly logical explanation of the illogical and tyrannical ways of the white men. Those who don't know about the true beginning of the Paiute world they have invaded, as set forth in the myths, are certain to be misguided—an instance of the primacy of myth in the Indian world-view.

Bibliography

Barker, M. A. R. *Klamath Texts*. University of California Publications in Linguistics, vol. 30, 1963.

Barnett, H. G. "Culture Element Distributions VII: Oregon Coast." *Anthropological Records*, 1, no. 3 (1937): 155–203.

Beal, Merrill D. *"I Will Fight No More Forever": Chief Joseph and the Nez Perce War*. Seattle: University of Washington Press, 1963.

Beckham, Stephen Dow. *Requiem for a People: The Rogue Indians and the Frontiersman*. Norman: University of Oklahoma Press, 1971.

———. *Tall Tales from Rogue River*. Bloomington: Indiana University Press, 1974.

Bedwell, Stephen F. *Fort Rock Basin: Prehistory and Environment*. Eugene: University of Oregon Books, 1973.

Berreman, Joel. *Tribal Distribution in Oregon*. Memoirs of the American Anthropological Association, no. 47, 1937.

Boas, Franz. *Chinook Texts*. U.S. Bureau of American Ethnology, Bulletin no. 20, 1894.

———. "Doctrine of Souls among the Chinook Indians." *Journal of American Folklore*, 6, no. 20 (Jan.–March 1893): 37–43.

———. *Kathlamet Texts*. U.S. Bureau of American Ethnology, Bulletin no. 26, 1901.

———. "Traditions of the Tillamook Indians." *Journal of American Folklore*, 11, no. 40 (Jan.–March 1898): 23–28, 137–50.

Carey, C. A. *General History of Oregon*. Portland: Binfords and Mort, 1971.

Clark, Ella E. *Indian Legends from the Northern Rockies*. Norman: University of Oklahoma Press, 1966.

———. *Indian Legends of the Pacific Northwest*. Berkeley and Los Angeles: University of California Press, 1953.

Coffin, Tristram P. *Indian Tales of North America*. Philadelphia: American Folklore Society, 1961.

Cohen, Percy. "Theories of Myth." *Man*, 1969, pp. 337–53.

Cooke, S. F. "The Epidemic of 1830–3 in California and Oregon." *University of California Publications in American Archaeology and Ethnology*, 56 (1955): 307–25.

Corning, Howard McKinley. *Dictionary of Oregon History*. Portland: Binfords and Mort, 1956.

Cressman, Luther. *Petroglyphs of Oregon*. Eugene: University of Oregon Publications in Anthropology, 1937.

———. *The Sandal and the Cave*. Portland: Champoeg Press, 1962.

Curtin, Jeremiah. *The Memoirs of Jeremiah Curtin*. Wisconsin Biography Series, vol. 2. Madison, 1940.

———. *Myths of the Modocs*. Boston: Little Brown, 1912.

Curtis, Edward S. *The North American Indian.* Vol. 8: New York, 1911; vol. 13: New York, 1924.
de Anguelo, Jaime. "Atfalati Dance-Song in Parts." *American Anthropologist,* 31 (1929): 496–98.
Deloria, Vine. *Custer Died for Your Sins.* New York: Avon Books, 1970.
Dixon, Roland. "Shasta Myths." *Journal of American Folklore,* 23 (1911): 1–34.
Dorsey, J. Owen. "The Indians of Siletz Reservation, Oregon." *American Anthropologist,* 2 (Jan. 1889): 55–60.
Drucker, Philip. "Contributions to Alsea Ethnography." *University of California Publications in American Archaeology and Ethnology,* 35, no. 7 (1936): 81–102.
———. "The Tolowa and Their Southwest Oregon Kin." *University of California Publications in American Archaeology and Ethnology,* 36, no. 4 (1937): 221–99.
Edel, May M. "Stability in Tillamook Folklore." *Journal of American Folklore,* 57 (1944): 116–27.
———. "The Tillamook Language." *International Journal of American Linguistics,* 10, no. 1 (1939): 1–57.
Eliade, Mircea. *Myth and Reality.* New York: Harper and Row, 1963.
Fiedler, Leslie. *The Return of the Vanishing American.* New York: Stein and Day, 1968.
Frachtenberg, Leo J. *Alsea Texts and Myths.* U.S. Bureau of American Ethnology, Bulletin no. 67, 1920.
———. *Coos Texts.* Columbia University Contributions to Anthropology, vol. 1 (1913).
———. "Coos." In *Handbook of American Indian Languages,* ed. Franz Boas. U.S. Bureau of American Ethnology, Bulletin no. 40, pt. 2, 1922. Pp. 422–29.
———. *Lower Umpqua Texts.* Columbia University Contributions to Anthropology, vol. 3, 1914.
———. "Myths of the Alsea Indians of Northwest Oregon." *International Journal of American Linguistics,* 1 (1917–20): 64–75.
———, and Livingston Farrand. "Shasta and Athapascan Myths from Oregon." *Journal of American Folklore,* 28 (1915): 207–42.
Freeman, John F. *A Guide to Manuscripts Relating to the North American Indian in the Library of the American Philosophical Society.* Philadelphia: American Philosophical Society, 1966.
Frémont, J. C. *Report of the Exploring Expedition to the Rocky Mountains in the Year 1842, and to Oregon and North Carolina in the Years 1843–44.* Washington, D.C., 1845.
Freud, Sigmund. *The Future of an Illusion,* trans. W. D. Robson-Scott. New York: Doubleday, 1961.
Frost, Robert. *The Poetry of Robert Frost.* Ed. Edward C. Lathem. New York: Holt, Rinehart and Winston, 1969.
Gatschet, Albert S. "Kalapuya Ceremonial Song." MS in collection of American Philosophical Society Library, Philadelphia.
———. *The Klamath Indians.* 2 vols. Contributions to North American Ethnology. Washington, D.C., 1891.

————. "Oregonian Folklore." *Journal of American Folklore,* 4 (1891): 139–43.

Gibbs, George. "Account of Indian Mythology in Oregon and Washington Territory" (1865). Ed. Ella E. Clark. *Oregon Historical Quarterly,* 57 (1956): 133 ff.

Haines, Francis. *The Nez Perce: Tribesmen of the Columbia Plateau.* Norman: University of Oklahoma Press, 1955.

Hopkins, Sarah Winnemucca. *Life among the Piutes.* New York: G. P. Putnam's Sons, 1883.

Howe, Carrol B. *Ancient Tribes of the Klamath Country.* Portland: Binfords and Mort, 1968.

Hultkrantz, Äke. *The North American Indian Orpheus Tradition.* Stockholm: Ethnological Museum of Sweden, Monograph Series no. 2, 1957.

Hymes, Dell. "Breakthrough into Performance." In *Folklore: Performance and Communication,* ed. Dan Ben-Amos and Kenneth Goldstein. The Hague and Paris: Mouton, 1975. Pp. 11–74.

————. "Louis Simpson's 'The Deserted Boy.' " *Poetics,* 5, no. 2 (June 1976): 119–58.

————. "Folklore's Nature and the Sun's Myth." *Journal of American Folklore,* 88 (Dec. 1975): 345 ff.

————. "Two Types of Linguistic Relativity." In *Sociolinguistics,* ed. William Bright. The Hague: Mouton, 1966. Pp. 114–67.

————. "The 'Wife' Who 'Goes Out' Like a Man: Reinterpretation of a Clackamas Chinook Myth." *Social Science Information,* 7, no. 3 (1968): 173–99. Reprinted in *Structural Analysis of Oral Tradition,* ed. Pierre and Eli Köngas Maranda. Philadelphia: American Folklore Society, 1971.

————, ed. *Re-inventing Anthropology.* New York: Pantheon Books, 1972.

Jacobs, Elizabeth D. *Nehalem Tillamook Tales,* ed. Melville Jacobs. Eugene: University of Oregon Books, 1959.

Jacobs, Melville. "Areal Spread of Indian Oral Genre Features in the Northwest States." *Journal of the Folklore Institute,* 9, no. 1 (June 1972): 10–17.

————. *Clackamas Chinook Texts.* Bloomington: University of Indiana Research Center in Anthropology, Folklore, and Linguistics. Vol. 1, 1958; vol. 2, 1959.

————. *The Content and Style of an Oral Literature.* New York: Wenner-Gren Foundation, 1959.

————. *Coos Ethnologic and Narrative Texts.* University of Washington Publications in Anthropology, vol. 8, no. 1, 1939.

————. *Coos Myth Texts.* University of Washington Publications in Anthropology, vol. 8, no. 2, 1940.

————. "The Fate of Indian Oral Literatures in Oregon." *Northwest Review,* 3 (Summer 1962): 90–99.

————. *Kalapuya Texts.* University of Washington Publications in Anthropology, vol. 11, 1945.

————. *Northwest Sahaptin Texts.* Vol. 1, in Columbia University Contributions to Anthropology, 19 (1934): 206 ff.; vol. 2, in University of Washington Publications in Anthropology, 2, no. 6 (June 1929): 175–244.

——. "Our Knowledge of Pacific Northwest Indian Folktales." *Northwest Folklore*, 2, no. 2 (1967): 7 ff.

——. *Patterns in Cultural Anthropology*. Homewood, Ill.: Dorsey Press, 1964.

——. *The People Are Coming Soon*. Seattle: University of Washington Press, 1960.

——. *Texts in Chinook Jargon*. University of Washington Publications in Anthropology, vol. 7, no. 1, 1936.

Joseph, Chief. "An Indian's View of Indian Affairs." *North American Review*, 118 (April 1879): 419 ff.

Josephy, Alvin. *The Indian Heritage of America*. New York: Knopf, 1968.

——. *The Nez Perce Indians and the Opening of the Northwest*. New Haven, Conn.: Yale University Press, 1965.

Judson, Katherine Berry. *Myths and Legends of the Pacific Northwest*. Chicago: A. C. McClurg, 1910.

Kelly, Isabel. "Ethnography of the Surprise Valley Paiutes." *University of California Publications in American Archaeology and Ethnology*, 31 (1932): 67–209.

——. "Northern Paiute Tales." *Journal of American Folklore*, 51 (1938): 363–437.

Kinietz, W. Vernon. *John Mix Stanley and His Indian Paintings*. Ann Arbor: University of Michigan Press, 1942.

Kroeber, Theodora. *The Inland Whale*. Berkeley and Los Angeles: University of California Press, 1971.

Lévi-Strauss, Claude. *Structural Anthropology*. Trans. C. Jacobson and B. G. Schoepf. Garden City: Doubleday and Co., 1967.

Lewis, Lucien N. "Sunlight Legends of the Warm Springs Indians." *Southern Workman* 38 (Dec. 1909): 685 ff.

Lewis, Meriwether, and William Clark. *Original Journals of the Lewis and Clark Expedition*. Ed. Reuben Gold Thwaites. New York: Dodd, Mead, and Co., 1904–5.

Lowie, Robert. "The Northern Shoshone." *Anthropological Papers of the American Museum of Natural History*, 2 (1909): 220–303.

Lyman, H. S. "The Indian Arabian Nights." *Pacific Monthly*, March 1900, pp. 200–1.

——. "Items from the Nez Perce." *Oregon Historical Quarterly*, 2 (1901): 289 ff.

——. "Reminiscences of Louis Labonte." *Oregon Historical Quarterly*, 1 (1900): 167–88.

Lyman, William D. "Myths and Superstitions of the Oregon Indians." *Proceedings of the American Antiquarian Society*, 16 (1903–4): 221 ff.

McArthur, Lewis A. *Oregon Geographic Names*, Third Edition. Portland: Binfords and Mort, 1965.

Mackey, Harold. *The Kalapuyans*. Salem: Mission Mill Museum Association, 1974.

————, and Thomas Brundage. "A Molale Indian Myth of Coyote." *Northwest Folklore*, 3, no. 2 (Winter 1968): 10–11.

Marsden, W. L. "The Northern Paiute Language of Oregon." *University of California Publications in American Archaeology and Ethnology*, 20 (1923): 180–91.

Massignon, Genevieve. *Folktales of France*. Chicago: University of Chicago Press, 1968.

Meacham, A. B. *Wigwam and Warpath, or, The Royal Chief in Chains*. Boston: John P. Dale, 1875.

Mooney, James. *The Ghost Dance Religion and the Sioux Outbreak of 1890*. Fourteenth Annual Report of the Bureau of Ethnology, 1892–93.

Nash, Wallis. *Oregon: There and Back in 1877*. London: Macmillan, 1878.

Nelson, A. W. *Those Who Came First*. LaGrande, Oregon, 1934.

Notices and Voyages of the Famed Quebec Mission to the Pacific Northwest. Trans. Carl Landerholm. Portland: Oregon Historical Society, 1956.

Parker, Rev. Samuel. *Journal of an Exploring Tour beyond the Rocky Mountains*. Ithaca, N.Y., 1838.

Phinney, Archie. MS letter to Franz Boas, Nov. 20, 1929, in collection of American Philosophical Society Library, Philadelphia.

————. *Nez Perce Texts*. Columbia University Contributions to Anthropology, vol. 25, 1934.

Radin, Paul. *The Trickster*. New York: Philosophical Library, 1956.

Ramsey, Jarold. "Fish-Hawk's Raid against the Sioux: A Cayuse Hero-Story." *Alcheringa*. Forthcoming.

————. *Love in an Earthquake*. Seattle: University of Washington Press, 1973.

————. "Three Wasco–Warm Springs Stories." *Western Folklore*, 31 (April 1972): 116–19.

————. "What the Rocks Say." Northwest Magazine," *Sunday Oregonian*, April 20, 1969, pp. 18–23.

————. "The Wife Who Goes Out like a Man Comes Back as a Hero: The Art of Two Oregon Indian Narratives." *Publications of the Modern Languages Association*, 92, no. 1 (January 1977): 9–18.

Ray, Verne. *Lower Chinook Ethnographic Notes*. University of Washington Publications in Anthropology, vol. 7, no. 2 (May 1938).

————. *Primitive Pragmatists: The Modoc Indians of Northern California*. Seattle: University of Washington Press, 1963.

————, et al. "Tribal Distribution in Eastern Oregon and Adjacent Regions." *American Anthropologist*, 40 (1939): 384–415.

Reports of Explorations and Surveys to Ascertain the Most Practicable and Economic Route for a Railroad from the Mississippi River to the Pacific Ocean. Vol. 6. 1855.

Rothenberg, Jerome, ed. *Shaking the Pumpkin: Traditional Poetry of the Indian North Americas*. New York: Doubleday, 1972.

Ruby, Robert, and John A. Brown. *The Cayuse Indians: Imperial*

Tribesmen of Old Oregon. Norman: University of Oklahoma Press, 1972.

———. *The Chinook Indians: Traders of the Lower Columbia River.* Norman: University of Oklahoma Press, 1976.

St. Clair, Harry. "Traditions of the Coos Indians of Oregon." Ed. Leo J. Frachtenberg. *Journal of American Folklore,* 22 (1909): 25–41.

Sapir, Edward. "Religious Ideas of the Takelma Indians of Southwest Oregon." *Journal of American Folklore,* 20 (1907): 33–49.

———. *Takelma Texts.* Anthropological Publications of the University of Pennsylvania Museum, vol. 2, 1909.

———. *Wishram Texts.* Publications of the American Ethnological Society, vol. 2, 1909. Includes Jeremiah Curtin, "Wasco Tales and Myths."

Sauter, John, and Bruce Johnson. *Tillamook Indians of the Oregon Coast.* Portland: Binfords and Mort, 1974.

Scharbach, A. "Aspects of Existentialism in Clackamas Chinook Texts." *Journal of American Folklore,* 75 (1962): 15–22.

Seaman, N. G. *Indian Relics of the Pacific Northwest.* Portland: Binfords and Mort, 1967.

Slickpoo, Allen P., Sr. *Nu Mee Poom Tit Wah Tit: Nez Perce Tales.* Lapwai: Nez Perce Tribes of Idaho, 1972.

Smith, Silas. "Customs of the Northwest Coast Indians." *Oregon Historical Quarterly,* 2 (1901): 255–65.

Snyder, Gary. *Earth House Hold.* New York: New Directions, 1969.

Spier, Leslie. *Klamath Ethnography.* University of California Publications in American Archaeology and Ethnology, vol. 30, 1930.

———. "Tribal Distribution in Southwest Oregon." *Oregon Historical Quarterly,* 27 (1927): 358–65.

———, and Edward Sapir. *Wishram Ethnography.* University of Washington Publications in Anthropology, vol. 3, no. 3 (May 1930).

Spinden, Herbert. "Myths of the Nez Perce Indians." *Journal of American Folklore,* 21 (1908): 156 ff.

———. "Nez Perce Tales." In *Folk Tales of Salish and Sahaptin Tribes,* ed. Franz Boas. Memoirs of the American Folklore Association, 1917. Pp. 180 ff.

Stafford, William. *The Rescued Year.* New York: Harper and Row, 1966.

Stern, Theodore. *The Klamath Tribe.* Seattle: University of Washington Press, 1965.

———. "Some Sources of Variability in Klamath Mythology." *Journal of American Folklore,* 69 (1956): 1–9, 135–46, 377–86.

———. "The Trickster in Klamath Mythology." *Western Folklore,* 12, no. 3 (July 1953): 158–74.

Steward, Julian. "The Foundation of Basin-Plateau Shoshonean Society." *Languages and Cultures of Western North America,* ed. Earl H. Swanson Jr. Pocatello: Idaho State University Press, 1970.

Stewart, Omer C. "Culture Element Distribution XIV: Northern Paiute." *Anthropological Records,* 4, no. 3 (1941): 361–446.

Strong, W. D., W. E. Schenck, and J. H. Steward. "Archaeology of the Dalles-Deschutes Region." *University of California Publications in American Archaeology and Ethnology*, vol. 29, no. 1 (1930).

Swadesh, Morris. "Cayuse Interlinear Texts." MS notebooks in American Philosophical Society Library, Philadelphia.

Swanton, John. *The Indian Tribes of North America*. U.S. Bureau of American Ethnology Bulletin 195, 1952.

Tedlock, Dennis. *Finding the Center*. New York: Dial Press, 1972.

Thompson, Stith. *European Tales among the North American Indians*. Colorado Springs: Colorado College Publications in Language, 1919.

———. *Motif-Index to Folk-Literature*. 6 vols. Bloomington: University of Indiana Press, 1929, 1968.

———. *Tales of the North American Indians*. Bloomington: University of Indiana Press, 1929, 1968.

Underhill, Ruth, ed. *The Autobiography of a Papago Woman*. Memoirs of the American Anthropological Association, vol. 46, 1936.

Venn, George. "The Search for Sacred Space in Western American Literature." *Portland Review*, Spring 1976, pp. 6–19.

Wheat, Margaret M. *Survival Arts of the Primitive Paiutes*. Reno: University of Nevada Press, 1967.

Wheeler-Voegelin, Erminie. "The Northern Paiutes of Central Oregon." *Ethnohistory*, 2, no. 2 (Spring 1955): 95–132; 2, no. 4 (Fall 1955): 241–72; 3, no. 1 (Winter 1956): 1–10.

Whiting, Beatrice Blyth. *Paiute Sorcery:* New York: Viking Fund Publications, 1950.

Wilkes, Charles. *Narrative of the United States Exploring Expedition*. Vol. 2. 1852.

Wood, C. E. S. *A Book of Indian Tales*. New York: Vanguard, 1929.

Wood, Erskine. *Days with Chief Joseph*. Portland: Oregon Historical Society, 1970.